Contents

"For those who are willing to dream,
anything is possible."

— Stephen Hawking

1. The Intersection of Quantum Puzzles and Space Mysteries

In the expanse of the cosmos, where time and space intertwine in a dance of particles and waves, humankind stands on the brink of a monumental shift. Quantum computing, with its esoteric principles and vast potential, promises to unravel secrets formerly cloistered in the stars. As we explore deep space, the questions transform from mere whispers of curiosity to roars of scientific breakthroughs. Yet, the realm of quantum mechanisms still feels like a formidable puzzle to many. In this inaugural chapter, let's embark on a grounded journey, understanding how the realms of quantum mechanics and the vastness of space interconnect in revolutionary waves. From oscillating qubits embodying both ones and zeros, to the dark and cold expanse of space awaiting our inquiry, this book sets out to unveil new dimensions. Get ready to unlock phenomena that, until now, belonged solely to the realm of science fiction. Whether you are a starry-eyed novice or a seasoned physicist, prepare for a voyage beyond the ordinary into the extraordinary.

2. Foundations of Quantum Mechanics

2.1. The Double-Slit Experiment: Perceptions vs. Reality

The double-slit experiment stands as one of the most profound demonstrations of quantum mechanics and has significant implications for understanding the nature of reality—what we perceive versus what scientifically exists. First conducted by Thomas Young in 1801, its implications reach far beyond simple interference patterns. In the realm of quantum computing, especially in the context of deep space exploration, the experiment brings forth questions that challenge our very understanding of observation and the nature of existence.

In its classical form, the double-slit experiment involves shining light through two closely spaced slits onto a screen. When both slits are open, a pattern of alternating bands of light and dark appears, reminiscent of waves interfering with one another. However, when particles such as electrons or photons are observed as they travel through the slits, they behave differently. Instead of producing a wave-like pattern, they display particle-like behavior, causing the interference pattern to collapse. This leads to a fundamental question: does the act of observation influence the outcome? Quantum mechanics states that these particles exist in a probability wave until they are measured, suggesting that reality is, in part, contingent upon our observations.

This dependency on observation emphasizes a significant philosophical premise: is the universe independent of our observations, or is our consciousness entwined with the reality we perceive? In the context of quantum computing and deep space exploration, this interrogation manifests into practical quandaries. For example, when we consider data gathering instruments designed to capture phenomena in the cosmic expanse, the function of these devices is contingent upon our attempts to measure vast and often invisible forces in the universe. Questions arise about what is truly 'there' in the depths of space versus what our instruments present to us based on the limits of our observation capabilities.

The duality of nature represented in the double-slit experiment compels us to think in terms of probabilities rather than certainties. For instance, quantum bits—qubits—used in quantum computing exist in superpositions, embodying multiple possibilities until such a time as they are measured. This mirrors the double-slit findings where prior to observation, particles exhibit wave behavior, suggesting multiple paths or outcomes simultaneously. Such principles, when applied to the vast distances of space, create a nuanced dimension of uncertainty, where every measurement could potentially alter the 'truth' of what we perceive.

Reflecting on our journey into deep space, the implications of this interplay between perception and reality extend to the very design of our quantum sensors. These sensors must navigate the conundrum of measuring cosmic phenomena which might not exist in any real sense until we observe them. As astronauts and scientists think of exploring uncharted territories, they must grapple with the idea that much of what they uncover may not be concrete until they observe it, breaking the barriers of time and distance that traditional tools may impose. The question becomes less about what is truly there and more about how we design our explorative tools to interpret the indistinct dances of particles and waves in the universe.

Moreover, the implications of the double-slit experiment resonate deeply in the discourse of quantum communications within interstellar networks. In organizing a quantum internet, the fundamental properties of entanglement and superposition derived from the double-slit experiment must be taken into account. Essentially, the way in which qubits may collide or interfere during transmission between cosmic endpoints hinges on quantum states that may not be fully understood until we further examine the nature of measurement and observation.

As we delve deeper into the technological ramifications of quantum mechanics—a field long considered abstract and philosophical—integrating the principles illuminated by the double-slit experiment into our operational paradigms becomes essential. This will require not only a re-evaluation of our computational tools but our approach to knowledge itself. In a universe where observation may constitute reality, we must remain vigilant in our interpretations and expectations.

The bridge between perception and reality laid out by the double-slit experiment can inspire a shift in perspective as we harness quantum mechanics for cosmic exploration. Each photon, qubit, and measurement will carry with it the weight of uncertainty, affirming that within the dance of quantum mechanics, what we perceive may vary vastly from the underlying truth of existence in the cosmos. Thus, as we continue to unveil the dimensions of quantum computing and its pivotal role in exploring deep space, we also acknowledge the essential narrative that quantum mechanics presents—a story of inquiry, observation, and the unfolding realities that our instruments and consciousness will encounter.

In this light, the double-slit experiment reminds us that our pursuit of understanding is not merely about uncovering facts; it is about perpetually questioning what we understand of existence itself as we extend our gaze into the abyss of space. This journey will undoubtedly reshape our scientific paradigms and philosophical discussions alike as we navigate the uncharted waters of quantum exploration and discovery.

2.2. The Quantum World: Particles, Waves, and Entanglement

The essence of the quantum world is founded upon the intricate relationship between particles and waves and the surprising phenomena that arise from their dual existence. In this unique landscape, physicists grapple with concepts that defy classical understanding, propelling humanity into an era replete with remarkable discoveries and complex advancements.

At the heart of quantum mechanics lies the dual nature of matter and energy characterized by the principle that all particles, including photons, electrons, and even larger atoms, can behave both as particles and as waves. This phenomenon is not mere abstraction; it forms the basis for technologies that push the boundaries of computation and space exploration. When we delve into the implications of this wave-particle duality, we begin to see how it informs the very fabric of the universe and lays the groundwork for understanding how quantum computing can revolutionize our approach to deep space exploration.

The concept of wave-particle duality fundamentally instructs us to embrace a new perspective. For example, consider an electron floating in the vastness of space. Under conventional physics, we would conceptualize it either as a point-like particle or, at least in theory, as a wave, with measured properties such as frequency and wavelength. However, quantum mechanics reveals that electrons exist in a state of superposition, meaning they occupy many potential positions simultaneously until observed. This behavior challenges our classical intuition and invites us to think about spatial dimensions differently —suggesting connectivity and correlation that transcend simple location.

Entanglement—a hallmark of quantum mechanics—further complicates our understanding of distance and separation in the cosmos. When two particles become entangled, their states become irrevocably linked, such that a change in one will instantaneously affect the other, irrespective of the distance separating them. This enigmatic aspect of entanglement emerges from the quantum world's foundational principles, giving rise to what Einstein famously derided as "spooky action at a distance." In the vast, emptiness of space, where communication via traditional means grows increasingly challenging, entanglement presents a tantalizing possibility for instantaneous connectivity.

The potential of entangled states could redefine our communications strategies in interstellar networks. Imagine a future where quantum devices, bolstered by entanglement, could share information moments apart, enabling real-time updates on data gathered from far-off worlds or celestial bodies. This leap into the quantum realm offers a pathway toward a quantum internet, a universe spanning network linking our explorations, providing secure communication that remains invulnerable to the intervention of classical eavesdroppers.

As we explore the quantum properties of space, we must also confront the implications of this understanding on our technological capabilities. Quantum algorithms capitalizing on the duality of particles and waves allow quantum computers to outperform their classical counterparts. These systems excel in domains like optimization problems and information retrieval, enabling computations that are crucial for navigating the uncharted territories of space. Notably, tasks such as simulating complex cosmic phenomena—ranging from the formation of galaxies to interactions occurring in black holes—can harness the computational power that resides within quantum systems, representing an avant-garde method to unveil the mysterious dynamics of the universe.

The application of wave-particle duality and entanglement does not merely reside within theoretical constructs; they manifest in real-world technology. Quantum sensors, emerging from these principles, could revolutionize our ability to detect and measure cosmic signals previously considered undetectable. Utilizing the sensitivity afforded by quantum states, sensors could explore gravitational waves, cosmic microwave background radiation, or even the elusive signatures of dark matter. This leap in sensitivity represents a paradigm shift, one that amplifies our capacity to explore the cosmos with unprecedented precision.

However, in embracing these revolutionary concepts, we must also remain vigilant of the pitfalls inherent in quantum mechanics. The very nature of measurement introduces complexity; observing a quantum state unavoidably alters it, encapsulated in Heisenberg's Uncertainty Principle. Thus, navigation through the quantum landscape necessitates innovative techniques for quantum error correction and decoherence management, ensuring that our advances do not become mere theoretical discussions but generate practical, reliable technology.

As we embark upon this quantum journey in deep space, we are constantly reminded that our understanding is just the beginning. As qubits oscillate between possibilities, exhibiting the duality of existence, the cosmos invites us to perceive a more complex reality where particles and waves intermingle and entangle in fundamentally rich and multidimensional ways. Indeed, as we breathe life into quantum computing amidst the vacuum of the universe, we prepare to unlock entirely new dimensions—one where every leap informs our march toward discovery, fundamentally transforming how we perceive existence itself.

The intersections of particles, waves, and entanglement invite us to contemplate deeper questions of our universe. Are we merely observers of a reality outside ourselves, or do our actions in measurement influence the very nature of existence? These musings encourage scientists and philosophers alike to reassess the parameters of inquiry as we throw open the doors of quantum mechanics to understand not only the universe at large, but our place within it. As we navigate the vast seas of space with these new guiding principles, we find ourselves at the fulcrum of scientific and existential exploration, heralding a new era of quantum enlightenment that transcends the boundaries of what we once thought possible.

2.3. Heisenberg's Uncertainty Principle

Heisenberg's Uncertainty Principle stands as one of the cornerstones of quantum mechanics, illustrating foundational concepts that challenge our intuitive perceptions of the universe. Formulated by German physicist Werner Heisenberg in 1927, this principle articulates a profound limitation in our ability to simultaneously know both the position and momentum of a particle with absolute precision. In essence, the more accurately we measure one of these variables, the less accurately we can measure the other. This principle is not merely a statement about limitations in measurement technologies; it is a fundamental property of the quantum world itself, revealing deep insights about the nature of existence.

To comprehend the implications of the Uncertainty Principle, we must first understand the underlying mathematics and physics at play. Quantum mechanics posits that particles do not exist in fixed states or locations but rather in a haze of probabilities. Mathematically, this principle is often represented as $\Delta x \, \Delta p \geq \hbar/2$, where Δx is the uncertainty in position, Δp is the uncertainty in momentum, and $\hbar$ (h-bar) is the reduced Planck constant. This relationship asserts that the product of the uncertainties in position and momentum must always be greater than or equal to a specific constant. Thus, attempting to pinpoint a particle's location with extreme accuracy results in an inevitable broadening of the uncertainty in its momentum—and vice versa.

This principle carries vast implications for quantum computing and deep space exploration, illuminating how we gather, interpret, and manage data in both experimental and practical scenarios. Picture our approach to typical measurements in space, such as tracking the momentum of a distant spacecraft. To acquire precise information about its position alternatively limits our ability to determine its speed with the same degree of accuracy. When operating at vast distances, such limitations become pronounced, enforcing an awareness that our navigation systems and computational models must account for these inherent uncertainties.

The uncertainty principle also implores a reassessment of determinism within the cosmos. Classical physics operates under the assumption that if enough information is available about a system, its future can be predicted with accuracy. However, in the quantum realm, this predictability is challenged. Instead of deterministic trajectories, particles appear to behave more like waves of probability, existing in multiple states until an observation is made. This probabilistic nature of particles underscores the unpredictable behavior of matter at subatomic levels and heralds a new way of thinking about information and measurement in quantum computing.

In the landscape of quantum computing, Heisenberg's uncertainty applies directly to qubits, the elemental units of quantum information. Unlike classical bits, which reside distinctly in states of 0 or 1, qubits can exist in superpositions of these states. When observed or measured, however, this superposition collapses into one specific outcome. This collapse is not merely statistical but is influenced by the uncertainty principle's tenets. In essence, effective quantum computing involves navigating this realm of probabilities and uncertainties, designing algorithms that can optimize outcomes while acknowledging that precision in one parameter might inherently reduce predictability in another.

Moreover, Heisenberg's insights resonate throughout advancements in quantum sensors, especially those destined for the vastness of space. High-precision measurements, such as gravitational wave detection or analysis of cosmic signals, are fundamentally rooted in minimizing the uncertainties involved. As we deploy sensors designed to harness the properties of quantum states, we must comprehend the limitations imposed by uncertainty. Understanding how to balance precision in measuring cosmic phenomena without losing significant data fidelity becomes paramount in significant discoveries, potentially revealing fundamental insights into cosmic events such as black holes or the early stages of the universe.

Furthermore, the Uncertainty Principle leads us to reflect philosophically on our place in the universe. If certainty is elusive at the quantum level, what does that imply for our understanding of reality itself? This question extends into considerations for ethics and responsibilities in quantum computing. As we learn to navigate uncertainties with emerging technology, there are vital implications in terms of transparency and accuracy. The design of interstellar systems and their navigation protocols must respect these limitations, prompting discussions not just on technological capabilities but also on the larger implications of our moonshot goals and the scientific aesthetic of exploration.

In the framework of cosmic exploration, the Uncertainty Principle becomes the backdrop against which we design our approaches to probing the universe. Just as particles oscillate between probabilities, so too do we find ourselves at the crossroads of chance and choice in our exploratory endeavors. As we venture into deep space, armed with quantum computing capabilities, we must remember that the embrace of uncertainty will be foundational, heralding an exploration that is as much about learning from ambiguities as it is about attaining absolute truths.

In summary, Heisenberg's Uncertainty Principle is not just a theoretical assertion but a lived reality in the quantum domain, with intricate ramifications for quantum computing and space exploration. It encourages us to adapt our strategies and technologies, fostering a new awareness of the delicate balance between precision and uncertainty as we venture further into the cosmic unknown. Accepting these challenges and opportunities will enable us to unlock innovative pathways for discovery, reflecting an intentional and thoughtful approach in our quest to unveil the dimensions of our universe through the lens of quantum mechanics. In navigating the interplay of particles, waves, and uncertainties, we will gather not only data but wisdom as we embark on our infinite journey through the stars.

2.4. Understanding Qubits: Beyond Ones and Zeros

Qubits, or quantum bits, are the fundamental building blocks of quantum computing, representing a paradigm shift from classical binary computation, which relies strictly on bits that exist in one of two states—0 or 1. The underlying nature of qubits, however, extends far beyond this binary limit, encapsulating the profound intricacies of quantum mechanics itself. To understand qubits, one must traverse the landscape of superposition, entanglement, and quantum states, all of which create a multidimensional framework that exists outside the conventional logic of mere ones and zeros.

At the heart of a qubit's uniqueness is its ability to exist in a state of superposition, permitting it to be in multiple states at once. In a classical bit, information is either on (1) or off (0), resulting in a straightforward representation. In stark contrast, a qubit can embody a combination of states, represented as a linear superposition of both 0 and 1. This mathematical construct can be visualized with respect to a unit sphere, known as the Bloch sphere, where any point on this sphere represents a unique quantum state. A measurement of a qubit in superposition collapses its state to either 0 or 1, and the specific outcome follows particular probabilistic rules defined by quantum mechanics.

This capability extends the computational power of quantum systems exponentially. For instance, a system comprising n qubits can represent 2^n simultaneous states, allowing quantum computers to process enormous data sets and execute complex computations in parallel. This is a notable departure from classical computers, where a similar number of bits would correlate to each representing a specific state, thus operating sequentially. This parallel processing capability is particularly advantageous in applications such as simulating quantum systems, cryptographic algorithms, and optimizing complex logistical problems, all of which are vital considerations for deep space exploration.

Entanglement, another fundamental characteristic of quantum mechanics, complements the nature of qubits by forging deep correlations between the states of qubits regardless of the spatial distance between them. When two qubits are entangled, the measurement of one qubit instantaneously determines the state of the other, an effect that Einstein famously dubbed "spooky action at a distance." This phenomenon poses intriguing implications for quantum communication and information processing, where entangled qubits can enhance the efficiency and security of transmitting data across considerable distances—a critical factor in interstellar communications.

Understanding qubits also necessitates acknowledging the decoherence phenomenon, which represents the interaction of quantum systems with their environments and often leads to the loss of their quantum properties. Decoherence occurs when qubits establish interactions with external forces or particles, disrupting their superposition and entangled states. In the expansive universe filled with cosmic radiation and gravitational fluctuations, maintaining the coherence of qubits becomes a significant challenge for quantum computing technologies designed for deep space missions. This necessitates robust error correction methods for mitigating decoherence, ensuring the fidelity and longevity of quantum computations amidst the unpredictable conditions of space.

The exploration of qubits extends not only to theoretical discussions but also to practical applications in the burgeoning field of quantum computing. Research laboratories and tech industries are actively pursuing the development of qubit technologies utilizing various physical systems, including trapped ions, superconducting circuits, and topological qubits. Each approach presents unique advantages and challenges, shaping the future of quantum computation capabilities and their eventual deployment in space exploration tasks.

In deep space, the harnessing of qubits can unlock countless innovations. Imagine quantum sensors equipped with qubits capable of detecting gravitational waves from cosmic events, or quantum communication systems employing entangled qubits to exchange information across vast distances, from Earth to the outer reaches of our solar system. The formidable processing power of quantum computers, fueled by the unique properties of qubits, stands to enhance our ability to solve complex mathematical models that govern cosmic physics, universe models, and the behavior of dark matter—offering unprecedented insights into the fabric of the cosmos.

An important philosophical reflection accompanies our exploration of qubits: what does it mean to compute with quantum states fundamentally different from our classical experience? Our reliance on classical logic structures and definitive states puts forth intriguing questions regarding determinism, randomness, and the nature of reality itself. As we delve deeper into quantum mechanics and its computational ramifications, we are constantly reminded that qubits transcend mere calculations; they embody the uncertainties and probabilities that shape the universe.

As we propel toward a future driven by quantum computing, our understanding of qubits will continue evolving, manifesting as a vital asset in unraveling the mysteries of space and time. The expansion of humanity's capabilities hinges upon our ability to adapt and embrace these concepts, ultimately redefining our computational boundaries and revealing layers of knowledge previously deemed inaccessible. By exploring the nuanced nature of qubits, we open a pathway toward unprecedented advancements, encouraging a symbiotic relationship between quantum mechanics and our insatiable curiosity about the cosmos around us.

The exploration of qubits, thus, is far more than a technical endeavor; it is an invitation into the realm of possibilities, where every qubit carries the potential of its concurrent existence, entangled relationships, and the specter of uncertainty, reverberating throughout the vast expanses of space. It is within this intricate dance of existence and exploration that we find ourselves poised to redefine the boundaries of not only technology but also our understanding of the universe itself, ultimately preparing to unveil new dimensions awaiting discovery amidst the stars.

2.5. Quantum Superposition: The Realm of Possibilities

Quantum superposition stands at the very heart of quantum mechanics, representing one of the most fascinating and counterintuitive concepts that has captivated the imagination of scientists, philosophers, and enthusiasts alike. In classical physics, objects exist in definite states; a coin, for instance, is either heads or tails when observed. However, quantum superposition challenges this rigid binary perception, offering a realm where particles can exist in multiple states simultaneously, creating a vast landscape of possibilities that underlie the mechanisms of quantum computing and its applications in deep space exploration.

At its core, superposition asserts that a quantum system can be in a combination of states until it is measured or observed. This principle is often illustrated through the concept of a qubit, which is the basic unit of quantum information. Unlike classical bits that must be either 0 or 1, a qubit can embody a state that is a blend of both, expressed mathematically as a linear combination of its basis states: $|0\rangle$ and $|1\rangle$. The mathematical formulation allows for the representation of a qubit as a point on the Bloch sphere, where any point on the surface corresponds to a valid quantum state, symbolizing the inherent flexibility and richness of quantum information. This unique property enables quantum computers to perform operations on many different states at once, vastly enhancing their computational capabilities compared to classical computers.

To appreciate the implications of superposition, one must also consider the role of measurement. When a qubit in superposition is measured, it does not simply yield both outcomes; instead, the act of measurement collapses the superposition into one of its basis states, introducing an element of randomness dictated by the probabilities defined by its quantum state. This interplay between superposition and measurement forms the bedrock of quantum algorithms, allowing for insights and computations that were previously unattainable.

In the context of deep space exploration, the principle of quantum superposition opens up a multitude of possibilities for tackling complex problems related to navigation, optimization, and data processing. As we journey to the outer reaches of our solar system and beyond, we encounter a host of challenges that demand innovative computational solutions. The capacity to harness quantum superposition allows us to model and analyze these complexities more efficiently than ever before.

For example, consider the task of optimizing a spacecraft's trajectory. Traditional methods may involve brute-force calculations across vast parameter spaces, often yielding only approximate solutions efficiently. In contrast, quantum algorithms, such as those based on Grover's search or the Quantum Approximate Optimization Algorithm (QAOA), leverage superposition to explore multiple potential paths simultaneously, providing accelerated solutions to optimization problems that are crucial for mission planning. When traversing the swirling gravitational fields of planets or circumventing obstacles in the dynamically changing environment of space, the ability to calculate optimal routes—and adapt to real-time data—is a game-changer.

Moreover, quantum superposition amplifies the power of quantum sensors designed to detect faint cosmic signals. In situations such as gravitational wave detection or the measurement of minute vibrations in space, sensors utilizing qubit technology can maintain superpositions that enhance their sensitivity and accuracy. The presence of superposition allows these sensors to superimpose multiple measurements, providing an enriched understanding of cosmic events while improving the signal-to-noise ratio. This capability will empower future explorations, giving scientists a more profound insight into phenomena such as black holes, cosmic inflation, and the interactions of distant galaxies.

Entangled states offer yet another layer of complexity intertwined with superposition. When qubits are entangled, the state of one qubit becomes intrinsically linked to the state of another, creating a web of correlations that defy classical spatial separations. In deep space applications, entangled qubits afford unique possibilities for communication. If two qubits are entangled, measuring one instantaneously determines the state of the other, regardless of the distance separating them. This phenomenon can play an essential role in developing quantum communication networks that span vast interstellar distances, enabling secure, reliable information exchanges that are resistant to traditional eavesdropping techniques.

However, as we embrace the vast possibilities presented by quantum superposition, we must also remain aware of the challenges that arise. The very act of observing and measuring quantum states leads to decoherence, whereby the system interacts with its environment, compromising the superpositions essential for quantum computing. In the extreme conditions of deep space, where cosmic radiation and gravitational fluctuations abound, maintaining qubit coherence becomes a significant hurdle that engineers and scientists must address.

The development of error correction codes and other methods for protecting quantum states from decoherence is essential as we work toward realizing the full potential of quantum technologies in space.

At a fundamental level, the concept of superposition also invites philosophical inquiry about the nature of existence and reality itself. If particles can exist in multiple states at once, what does that imply for our understanding of the fabric of the universe? Can we envision a reality governed by probabilities rather than certainties? Does the phenomenon of superposition reflect a deeper truth about the interconnectedness of all things?

As we delve deeper into quantum mechanics and its implications for space exploration, we find ourselves standing on the precipice of a new frontier—one filled with intriguing possibilities yet tinged with uncertainties. Each advancement in our understanding of quantum superposition brings us closer to unlocking the secrets of the universe, allowing us to probe its depths with cutting-edge technologies that blend quantum physics with human ingenuity.

In summary, quantum superposition serves as a powerful reminder of the vast and enigmatic world hidden within the fabric of reality. As we stand at the convergence of quantum computing and deep space exploration, we find ourselves uniquely poised to harness its potential in ways that could redefine our relationship with the cosmos. Through continued exploration and understanding of superposition, we can unlock new dimensions of knowledge, paving the way for extraordinary discoveries that await us amidst the stars. Thus, we prepare not only to navigate the cosmic expanse but also to revel in the profound mysteries that quantum mechanics presents, transforming our journey into a boundless adventure filled with infinite possibilities.

2.6. Decoherence: When Quantum Meets Classic

As we venture into the intriguing domain where quantum mechanics meets classical mechanics, we encounter a fundamental challenge that epitomizes the complexity of quantum computing—decoherence.

This phenomenon serves as a crucial juncture in understanding how delicate quantum states interact with the macroscopic world, driving home the distinction between the seemingly seamless realm of quantum phenomena and the robust, classical realities we experience. Herein lies a pivotal narrative that grades the ambition of quantum technologies against the steadfastness of classical physics.

Decoherence occurs when quantum systems interact with their surrounding environment, leading to a loss of coherence, or the delicate superpositions that characterize their quantum states. This happens because the environment introduces interactions that force the quantum system to "choose" a classically defined state. Imagine a quantum superposition of a qubit that exists in both states of 0 and 1. If it remains undisturbed, its potential remains uncollapsed, allowing computations that harness this superposition to yield high computational efficiency. Yet, the moment this qubit interacts with the surrounding environment—whether through stray electromagnetic fields, temperature fluctuations, or even cosmic rays—its unity is compromised, pushing it toward classical states and consequently diminishing the advantages of quantum processing.

The implications of decoherence are particularly pronounced in the context of deep space exploration, where the quantum apparatus required to facilitate quantum computing is subjected to a host of environmental perturbations that could lead to rapid decoherence. An understanding of the remote conditions in outer space must inform any operational designs for quantum computers tasked with missions beyond Earth's protective atmosphere. Such environmental interactions pose a challenge not only to coherence but also to the practicality of retrieving quantum states after interaction, with loss of information becoming a critical barrier to effective computational processes in the cosmic expanse.

In navigating this boundary between quantum and classical, scientists and engineers have devised various strategies to mitigate the effects of decoherence. One prominent approach is the use of error correction codes specifically tailored for quantum systems. Unlike classical error correction schemes that may operate with redundancy, quantum error correction must contend with the unique characteristics of quantum information, such as the no-cloning theorem, which states that it is impossible to create an exact copy of an arbitrary unknown quantum state. Innovative methods like surface codes or topological quantum computing are being developed to enable fault-tolerant quantum computing by protecting qubits from decoherence through constant monitoring and correction of errors as they occur.

Additionally, researchers are exploring fault-tolerant quantum algorithms and protocols that account for decoherence by aligning computational strategies with the inevitable loss of quantum states. This involves designing algorithms that maintain a reliable performance even when decoherence affects the integrity of qubits. For instance, certain quantum algorithms may be developed that yield valid outcomes based on partial information, acknowledging that the system's coherent state may not be fully preserved throughout the computation.

The influence of decoherence extends to the strategic design of quantum sensors deployed in deep space. As quantum sensors leverage superposition and entanglement to enhance measurement capabilities, they remain susceptible to environmental interactions that threaten their sensitivity. Developing systems that can operate reliably amidst this decoherence becomes essential to capitalize on the quantum advantages inherent in these sensors. Practical innovations, such as high-fidelity qubit technology and isolated quantum systems operating in ultra-cold environments, aim to enhance robustness against decoherence. Such attempts directly impact our ability to gather information about cosmic phenomena, from probing gravitational waves to understanding the distribution of dark matter in our universe.

Philosophically, the understanding of decoherence draws attention to the fundamental question of reality. The loss of coherence leads to the emergence of classical behavior, highlighting how our observation instruments shape the nature of measurements we obtain from the universe. As we delve deeper into the charters of quantum computing and its applications for space exploration, we must grapple with the philosophical implications of observation and measurement, especially how these effects could reframe our understanding of existence.

Furthermore, while classically defined states provide a certain comfort, they also limit our exploration of the quantum realm. The interaction of quantum systems with their environment serves to remind us that reality is not isolated but interconnected; hence, the very questions we pose, the instruments we construct, and the observations we make influence the states of the systems we seek to understand.

Ultimately, the phenomenon of decoherence marks a significant milestone in the quest for harnessing quantum technologies for practical applications—especially as we extend our ambitions into deep space. Understanding decoherence will allow us to advance our strategies for developing stable quantum computers capable of performing complex computations despite environmental challenges. It acts as both a challenge and a catalyst, driving forward the need for innovative solutions that will enable humanity's interstellar ambitions to become a tangible reality.

As we navigate this complex interplay between quantum mechanics and classical environments, we find ourselves poised at a critical junction—where quantum computing promises to revolutionize space exploration, yet also forces us to confront and reconcile the influences of decoherence. Each step closer to overcoming these barriers propels us further into uncharted territories, revealing new dimensions waiting to be understood as we venture into the expansive cosmos. Thus, the journey into quantum computing is not just a pursuit of technology but an exploration of the fundamental nature of reality and our dynamic relationship with the universe at large.

3. The Origins of Quantum Computing

3.1. Birth of a New Discipline

The origin of quantum computing emerges from a transformative convergence of physics and computer science, a synthesis that reshapes our understanding of computation itself. Rooted in the enigmatic principles of quantum mechanics, this new discipline signals a radical departure from classical computational frameworks, integrating a host of complex phenomena that challenge traditional paradigms. Tracing the evolution of quantum computing involves an exploration of theoretical foundations, technological advancements, and the visionary pioneers who dared to imagine a revolution in computation.

At the heart of quantum computing lies the notion that information can exist not only in discrete states but also in superpositions, where a quantum bit, or qubit, can embody multiple states simultaneously. This potential allows quantum computers to process information in parallel, granting them substantial advantages over classical computers in solving certain types of problems. The journey begins with early theoretical discussions in the 1980s, when physicists such as Richard Feynman proposed the idea of a quantum computer as a means to simulate quantum systems inherent in nature, a task that classical computers struggle to address effectively due to their binary limitations.

Feynman, in his landmark presentation in 1981, underscored the challenges posed by traditional computational methods when attempting to model quantum phenomena. Classical computers, bounded by bits, could not efficiently perform simulations of quantum systems—a revelation that spurred the exploration of quantum principles for computation. This vision was further refined by David Deutsch, who introduced the concept of a universal quantum computer, positing that such a device could replicate any physical process, solidifying the theoretical framework for quantum computation.

As the newly birthed discipline began to flourish, significant milestones emerged in its development. The 1990s heralded an era of quantum algorithms, where key breakthroughs attracted considerable attention. Peter Shor's algorithm for factoring large integers stood as a watershed moment, illustrating the capability of quantum computers to outperform classical counterparts in specific tasks, particularly in cryptography. This discovery ignited urgency in the realm of secure communications, prompting inquiry into the implications of quantum computing on information security while simultaneously attracting interest from governmental and corporate sectors.

Another pivotal figure in the birth of quantum computing is Lov Grover, who developed a quantum search algorithm that exponentially accelerates search queries in unsorted databases. These early breakthroughs laid the groundwork for understanding how quantum properties could yield efficient solutions to complicated computational problems, spawning a burgeoning field that entwined physics, computer science, and information theory.

As researchers further examined the nuances of quantum properties such as superposition and entanglement, the understanding of qubits evolved in tandem. The nature of qubits—as combinations of 0s and 1s—transcended classical limitations, introducing new paradigms in processing, which fueled the desire to explore practical implementations in real-world computing environments. The engineering challenges associated with constructing viable quantum systems broadened the field, compelling collaborations across disciplines and industries to advance the quest for functional quantum devices.

Over the past two decades, technological advancements have accelerated the transition from theory to practice. Companies such as IBM, Google, and startups in the quantum space race have engaged in a heightened competition to build scalable quantum computers that can solve real-world problems. Progress in quantum error correction, decoherence management, and the physical realization of qubits using materials such as superconducting circuits and trapped ions have all integrated into the rapid evolution of the discipline.

Yet, as quantum computing enters the early stages of practical application, the crossroads of technical achievements and scientific exploration lay fertile ground for innovation. The pace of discovery and the urgency to establish quantum capabilities within deep space missions has prompted interdisciplinary research efforts aimed at integrating quantum computing with space exploration methodologies. The very principles that underpin quantum mechanics enable unprecedented advantages for navigating cosmic complexities, from optimization and navigation tasks to enhanced data processing for the interpretations of signal retrival in an expansive universe.

As we usher in the next chapter of this discipline, we also confront inevitable obstacles. The complexities of programming quantum computers, clearer definitions of quantum algorithms, and addressing the ethical implications of transformative technologies framing future explorations present avenues of critical examination. The ramifications of quantum computing not only alter the disciplines of computer science and physics but also evoke broader societal discussions about national security, privacy, and equitable access to groundbreaking technologies.

The birth of quantum computing represents not merely a technological breakthrough but also a profound reevaluation of how we conceive computation within the framework of our universe. It invites society to grapple with the implications of harnessing quantum phenomena for practical uses, urging questions regarding the moral dimensions of deploying such capabilities in humanity's quest for understanding and exploration of the cosmos.

In essence, quantum computing emerges as a new discipline—a mélange of theoretical inquiry and experimental endeavor—that points toward extraordinary possibilities. Each facet of this evolution reflects the agility of human ingenuity as we endeavor to crystallize our understanding of quantum phenomena, signaling the dawn of a transformative era dedicated to unraveling the mysteries that intertwine computation with the cosmos. In the vast expanse awaiting our exploration, quantum computing stands not just as a tool for manipulation but as an open gateway to the enigmas of existence itself, perpetually inviting us to unlock new dimensions of inquiry as we push beyond the known into the infinite unknown.

3.2. Turing's Machine and Quantum Evolution

In the exploration of computing paradigms, the evolution from classical computing to quantum computing represents a seismic shift in our understanding of information processing, pushing the boundaries of what machines can achieve. One of the seminal influences in this transition is Alan Turing's theoretical vision of computing, encapsulated in what is known as the Turing Machine—a foundational concept in computer science that lays out the principles of algorithms, computation, and ultimately the broader implications of machine intelligence. As we weave Turing's insights into the quantum context, it opens a dialogue on how quantum evolution can redefine computation as an operational paradigm, especially within the frontier of deep space exploration.

The Turing Machine is an abstract theoretical model capable of simulating any algorithmic process. It consists of an infinite tape—representing memory—divided into discrete cells that can be read or written, with a head that moves across this tape, manipulating data according to a set of defined rules or states. This construct became the bedrock of computability theory, demonstrating that any computable function can be executed by such a machine. Turing's illumination came not just from the ability to compute but from a profound understanding of what it means for machines to 'think,' conjuring visions of mechanical beings that could process information similarly to human intelligence.

However, when we pivot to the realm of quantum mechanics, a new layer of complexity arises, heralding a period of transformation in computing. Quantum computing diverges from Turing's classical framework, introducing principles like superposition and entanglement that defy the traditional linear processing of information. Qubits, the fundamental units of quantum information, can exist in multiple states simultaneously, enabling quantum computers to explore a vast computational landscape concurrently. While a Turing Machine processes one input at a time, a quantum computer can simultaneously evaluate numerous possibilities, drastically increasing computational efficiency. This capability can be likened to Turing's vision; however, it transcends it into dimensions previously thought impossible.

The implications of quantum evolution on computation extend significantly into the realm of deep space exploration. As we design missions to traverse interstellar distances and unravel cosmic mysteries, the complexity of calculations grows exponentially—encountering diverse challenges such as trajectory optimization, resource management, and data analysis. Classical methods, bound by Turing's models, may stall when faced with the sheer enormity of data and uncertainty in deep space environments. Conversely, quantum computing's inherent capacity to engage in parallelism offers a potent tool to tackle these challenges. By drawing upon the principles of Turing's concepts while integrating quantum mechanics, we find ourselves equipped with machines that can navigate these complexities more dynamically and efficiently.

Consider the task of simulating the dynamics of gravitational interactions among celestial bodies; classical approaches may struggle as the number of variables increases, resulting in computational bottlenecks. In contrast, quantum algorithms, leveraging superposition, could simultaneously evaluate various configurations, leading to precise simulations and predictive modeling of cosmic systems. This paradigm shift is akin to reinventing Turing's original vision—where computation does not merely track linear algorithms but expands into a multidimensional assessment of possibilities and outcomes.

Furthermore, quantum computing enables the enhancement of Turing's concepts in the realm of artificial intelligence and machine learning, elevating the prospect of creating advanced intelligent systems capable of autonomous decision-making in deep space missions. Traditional AI systems, rooted in deterministic algorithms, may find themselves at a disadvantage when processing the chaos inherent in cosmic data streams. Quantum machines, in contrast, allow AI to harness the probabilistic nature of quantum states, better accommodating the indecision and complexity evident in vast interstellar environments. This synthesis of Turing's foundations with quantum principles may yield breakthroughs in navigational strategies, optimizing pathways among celestial objects, and ensuring robust responses to unforeseen challenges.

The evolution toward quantum systems does not come without its challenges, primarily regarding the practicality of constructing stable quantum computers capable of functioning in extreme conditions, such as those found in space. Issues related to decoherence, noise, and maintaining coherent quantum states loom large, necessitating innovative technological strategies to overcome them. However, these challenges echo the early skepticism surrounding Turing's ideas, when the feasibility of practical computation was often questioned. Just as Turing's disruption reshaped the landscape of traditional computing, so too does quantum evolution stand poised to redefine the limits of computational capabilities.

Moreover, the philosophical implications of merging Turing's theories with quantum mechanics resonate deeply within the broader discourse of intelligence and existence. What does it mean for machines capable of processing information through the non-intuitive framework of quantum mechanics? As quantum computers emerge, they carry an essence of intelligence that may mirror complex cognitive processes, challenging us to reconsider definitions of 'thought' and 'computation.' Understanding Turing's legacy within this quantum context encourages us to grapple with profound questions about the potential of machines to surpass mere calculation—venturing into realms of creativity, intuition, and understanding.

In conclusion, the interplay between Turing's Turing Machine and the evolution of quantum computing casts a transformative light across the horizon of space exploration. It represents not merely a technological advancement, but a reimagining of computation itself—intertwining theoretical underpinnings of algorithms with the enigmatic principles of quantum mechanics that expand the vistas of discovery. As we navigate the frontiers of the cosmos, combining Turing's foundational insights with quantum dimensions may not only propel our scientific inquiries but also reshape our philosophical understanding of intelligence and existence within the vast, unfathomable universe. Together, we stand on the cusp of a bold new chapter—one that transcends boundaries and invites us to unlock new dimensions of knowledge waiting just beyond the stars.

3.3. The Pioneers: From Feynman to Shor

The journey into the realm of quantum computing is indelibly linked to a remarkable cast of pioneers whose intellectual endeavors catalyzed the development of this transformative field. From theoretical underpinnings to practical implementations, their collective contributions weave a narrative that showcases the evolution of ideas and technologies shaping the future of computation, especially in the context of space exploration. In this exploration of pioneers like Richard Feynman and Peter Shor, we witness how visionary ideas rooted in quantum mechanics have led to the inception and growth of quantum computing as we know it today.

In the early 1980s, Richard Feynman, an iconic theoretical physicist renowned for his work in quantum electrodynamics, posed a question that would reverberate through the halls of scientific inquiry. Recognizing the limitations of classical computers in simulating quantum systems—an endeavor essential for understanding the complexities of nature—Feynman proposed the conceptual framework for a quantum computer. He pointed out that classical models constricted the processing of quantum states, leading to inefficiencies and inaccuracies in simulations of physical systems. In a seminal paper, Feynman articulated how a quantum mechanical model of computation could mirror the operations of the systems it seeks to simulate, inviting a paradigm shift in computing itself.

This groundbreaking thinking crystallized the idea that a quantum computer could operate using the principles of superposition and entanglement, allowing it to process vast amounts of information simultaneously. The very idea that qubits could exist in multiple states at once laid the groundwork for a new realm of computation, where the limits of classical binary logic could be transcended. Feynman's insights fueled excitement in the exploration of quantum mechanics as a valid framework for not just understanding the universe but also for building a new generation of computational machines.

Following closely in Feynman's footsteps, David Deutsch emerged as a significant figure in the establishment of quantum computing theory. Deutsch's vision of a universal quantum computer, which could emulate any physical process, showcased the profound potential of qubit-based computation. His work built upon Feynman's initial sketches, elaborating further on principles and laying the foundation for developing quantum algorithms that leverage the unique properties of qubits. Deutsch's contributions ignited further exploration into the capabilities of quantum computers, establishing a theoretical basis that would inspire future researchers to consider what computational tasks could potentially be solved exponentially faster with quantum systems.

As the 1990s rolled in, the burgeoning field of quantum computing began to witness concrete breakthroughs, thanks to the revolutionary contributions of scholars like Peter Shor. In 1994, Shor introduced an algorithm that would change the landscape of cryptography forever: the quantum factoring algorithm. By demonstrating that a quantum computer could efficiently factor large integers—a problem that underpins the security of classical cryptographic protocols—Shor's work unveiled a harrowing prospect for traditional information security methods. With the potential rise of quantum computers, the implications for data privacy and cybersecurity loomed large, revealing vulnerabilities in a system that had been relied upon for decades.

This pivotal algorithm captured the imagination of both the scientific community and the technosphere, generating a sense of urgency around the exploration of quantum capabilities. Shor's work served as a clarion call that spurred research into building practical quantum devices capable of executing his algorithm, thus transforming the theoretical aspirations of quantum computation into actionable, tangible goals.

Concurrently, Lov Grover introduced another watershed moment with his groundbreaking quantum search algorithm, which showcased how a quantum computer could drastically speed up the process of searching unsorted databases. Grover's algorithm demonstrated that, whereas classical search methods would necessitate checking every entry one at a time, a quantum computer could achieve results with quadratically fewer operations. This significant advancement reinforced the notion that quantum computational capabilities could fundamentally transform areas such as database management, logistics, and beyond.

As the theoretical boundaries of quantum computing expanded, so too did collaborative efforts across academia and industry to materialize the concepts introduced by these pioneers. From rudimentary prototypes to sophisticated quantum processors, each advance brought the community closer to realizing the dream of functional quantum computers. Organizations like IBM, Google, and a myriad of startups began to invest heavily in quantum research, creating teams dedicated to overcoming the engineering challenges that would enable practical applications of these technologies.

As quantum computing evolved, so too did its relation to deep space exploration. The unique computational advantages offered by quantum mechanics resonate deeply with the complexities of navigating and understanding our universe. Tasks such as trajectory optimization, resource management, and data analysis for cosmic phenomena benefit from the extraordinary capabilities fostered by superposition and entanglement—principles embedded in the very fabric of quantum computing.

Inspired by the groundwork laid by Feynman, Deutsch, Shor, and Grover, a new generation of scientists and researchers continues to push the bounds of what is conceivable. Their contributions serve as a guiding beacon for understanding how quantum principles do not merely represent a novel means of computation but offer a new lens through which we can investigate and explore the universe itself.

In reflecting on the journey from Feynman to Shor, we celebrate the spirit of collaboration and inquiry that characterizes quantum computation's evolution. The pursuit of knowledge by these pioneers embodies a commitment to unlocking the mysteries of existence and recognizing the interconnectedness of their ideas in addressing future challenges. Today, as humanity prepares to journey through deep space equipped with the power of quantum computing, it is the foundational principles and breakthroughs established by these visionaries that serve as the cornerstone of our aspirations—illuminating the path toward a future ripe with possibilities waiting to be discovered across the cosmos.

3.4. Classical vs. Quantum: A Computational Rethink

In the realm of computational platforms, the advent of quantum computing represents not merely an enhancement of existing technologies but a revolution that redefines the very concept of computation itself. Classical computing, which adheres to the principles laid out by Turing and others, operates on a binary system of ones and zeroes, using bits as the fundamental units of information. Each classical algorithm is executed on linear pathways, evaluating options step-by-step, thereby limiting the speed and efficiency at which tasks can be processed. By contrast, quantum computing capitalizes on the principles of quantum mechanics, embracing a world governed by probabilities and superposition that challenges our traditional notions of information and computation.

The primary tenants of quantum mechanics introduce complexities and potentials that extend far beyond the simplistic binary processing of classical computers. Quantum bits, or qubits, serve as the cornerstone of quantum systems. Unlike classical bits that are strictly defined as either a 0 or a 1, qubits exhibit the capability of being in a state of superposition—where they can simultaneously represent both values. This means that a quantum computer can explore multiple solutions to a problem concurrently, exponentially increasing its processing capabilities. For instance, a quantum computer with n qubits can analyze 2^n states simultaneously, a drastic improvement over classical computers which process information linearly.

Entanglement adds yet another layer of complexity to the computational landscape. When qubits become entangled, the state of one qubit is closely correlated with the state of another, no matter the distance separating them. This allows quantum computers to perform complex computations involving qubits that are interconnected in ways classical systems cannot replicate. As a result, entangled qubits serve as conduits of information, facilitating operations across vast computations with efficiencies unattainable through classical means. It heralds a new era of interconnectedness in computing, where information is not simply transferred but shared across dimensions governed by quantum mechanics.

Yet, the transition to quantum frameworks necessitates not only the development of new algorithms but also a rethinking of how we structure problems and systems of computation. Classical algorithms must be reshaped or entirely reimagined to exploit the potential offered by quantum systems. Quantum algorithms such as Shor's Algorithm for integer factorization and Grover's Algorithm for database searching are pioneers in this new domain, showcasing the vast speed advantages that these new technologies can harness to address complex problems that have long posed challenges with conventional methods.

One of the more insightful aspects of embracing quantum computation involves recognizing the inherent uncertainties and probabilistic nature that quantum mechanics embodies. This introduces a fundamental question: how do we manage and interpret the outputs from a system rooted in randomness? Whereas classical computers yield deterministic results based on precise operations, quantum systems deliver results that reflect the probabilities of various outcomes influenced by quantum states and behaviors.

As we traverse the landscapes of deep space exploration, the implications of these principles extend profoundly. The complexities of navigating vast and dynamic cosmic territories, the challenges of interstellar communication, and the need for advanced computational power to analyze astronomical data become starkly evident. Each of these challenges requires novel, innovative solutions that can only arise from the unique computational characteristics offered by quantum mechanics. For example, trajectory optimizations of spacecraft traveling to distant celestial bodies may be solved with quantum algorithms that appreciate the simultaneous paths available—unfolding solutions in a tapestry of possibilities as opposed to a linear call and response pattern traditionally embraced in classical approaches.

Equally, the applications for quantum technologies can reshape our understanding of communications in space. With the potential for quantum entanglement to enable instantaneous data transfer across seemingly impossible distances, interstellar networks could fundamentally transform the way we share information. Such developments not only promise advancements in interstellar communication but could also provide enhanced security protocols based on the principles of quantum cryptography, shielding our communications from potential interception with unyielding assurance.

Nonetheless, while the prospects brought forth by quantum technologies appear limitless, accompanying these paradigms shift are significant challenges. Decoherence—what happens to quantum states when they interact with their environment—remains a primary hurdle in translating quantum theoretical constructs into practical, operable systems. The fragility of qubits and the sensitivity required in their operational designs must be addressed to ensure the reliability of quantum computations, especially in the variable conditions of outer space.

Moreover, as we stand upon the cusp of this computational renaissance, the readiness to embrace ethics, governance, and frameworks surrounding the use of these technologies takes precedence. Navigating the moral implications, societal impact, and potential regulations needed to govern new developments underscores the consequential nature of quantum advancements.

Ultimately, the distinction between classical and quantum computing is more than a simple technical alteration; it encapsulates an ongoing dialogue about our approach to understanding and interacting with the fabric of the universe. As we continue to further investigate the quantum properties within the limitless reaches of space, we find ourselves not merely adapting existing paradigms but reenvisioning the entire landscape of computation, carving pathways into the heavens where new potentials lie waiting to be harnessed. The subtle weave of these quantum threads into our approaches, frameworks, and conversations signifies not only a technological evolution but a profound awakening to the possibilities of our existence within the cosmos—a rethinking that may, perhaps, open new dimensions yet unknown.

3.5. Qubits in Practice: The Silicon Race

In the rapidly evolving landscape of quantum computing, the so-called "silicon race" has captured the attention of researchers, tech companies, and astute observers alike. This subchapter delves into how qubits—the fundamental units of quantum information—are being harnessed using silicon-based technologies, leading to significant advances in computational capabilities, particularly in the context of deep space exploration.

Historically, silicon has served as the backbone of classical computing. Its semiconductor properties have revolutionized the electronics industry, enabling the miniaturization and performance enhancement of classical bits. However, as the shift toward quantum computing began taking shape, the properties of silicon attracted renewed interest. The primary question arising was whether silicon could be leveraged as a hosting medium for qubits, thus expanding the vast potential of quantum systems while capitalizing on existing semiconductor infrastructure.

One of the foremost advantages of silicon as a material for quantum computing is its compatibility with established semiconductor manufacturing techniques. This compatibility allows researchers to utilize existing fabrication plants and supply chains, significantly reducing the resources and time required for development. Companies such as Intel, IBM, and various startups are undertaking pioneering work to enhance the stability and scalability of silicon-based qubits.

The rise of qubits in silicon mostly revolves around two types: spin qubits and superconducting qubits. Spin qubits harness the intrinsic angular momentum of electrons, allowing information to be stored in the "spin" states of an electron confined in a silicon lattice. These spin states offer exceptional potential for coherence times, an essential factor in the performance of quantum devices. The ability to maintain coherence for extended periods increases the fidelity of quantum operations, allowing for more complex algorithms.

Superconducting qubits, enabled partially through advancements in silicon designs, represent another method for creating qubits utilizing the principles of superconductivity. These qubits function at very low temperatures, relying on the behavior of electrons within a superconducting circuit. By using silicon-based materials, researchers have innovatively addressed challenges related to decoherence stability and quantum gate fidelity, achieving notable success in developing reliable quantum gate operations.

The implications of silicon qubits extend beyond the laboratory and into real-world applications, particularly in the context of deep space exploration. The potential for deploying quantum computing systems in space is both enticing and complex. Traditional classical computers face immense challenges due to the vast distances, delays in communication, and the unpredictable nature of the cosmic environment. Here, silicon-based quantum computers can radically transform the capabilities of space operations, enhancing our ability to process data from distant sources, optimize trajectories, and model complex cosmic phenomena.

Consider a mission tasked with navigating a spacecraft through the intricate gravitational fields of multiple celestial bodies. A silicon-based quantum computer could utilize algorithms designed specifically to operate under quantum superposition, allowing it to evaluate numerous pathways simultaneously. This computational brilliance contrasts with classical systems, which would methodically analyze one trajectory at a time, ultimately leading to longer calculations and potential inefficiencies.

Additionally, quantum sensors built using silicon qubits can elevate our ability to detect and analyze cosmic events with unprecedented precision. From measuring gravitational waves to identifying minute fluctuations in cosmic background radiation, such sensors will provide insights previously unattainable under classical measurement methods. Expanding the understanding of dark matter and energy, or mapping the distribution of cosmic phenomena, relies upon the precision that quantum sensors can deliver.

As the silicon race heats up, competition among private companies, research universities, and governmental agencies intensifies. Investment in quantum technology is booming, fueled by the recognition that advancements in silicon-based quantum computing could yield both economic benefits and transformative scientific discoveries. For instance, much attention is being directed toward developing quantum networking capabilities that could enable secure communications between deep space probes and Earth. Effectively transmitting vast amounts of data from the cosmos will be critical as explorations extend beyond our solar system.

Moreover, with quantum cryptography emerging as a vital field, the integration of silicon-based quantum systems could offer unprecedented security for interstellar data transmission. By harnessing the properties of entanglement and superposition, these systems may lead to the establishment of secure communication links that protect sensitive information across light-years, ensuring that the insights gleaned from deep space remain shielded from potential interception.

However, despite the promising narrative surrounding silicon quantum computing, challenges remain to translate theoretical advancements into practical applications. Issues such as managing decoherence, improving qubit connectivity, and ensuring scalability are integral to the success of these technologies. Additionally, as research progresses, ethical considerations regarding the implications of quantum advancements persist, reflecting the pivotal need for responsible innovation as we strive to navigate the unknowns of space with cutting-edge tools.

In summary, the silicon race encapsulates a pivotal turning point in the arena of quantum computing, positioning silicon as a foundational element in facilitating qubits that could redefine our exploration of deep space. The engagement of qubits, fashioned using established semiconductor techniques, may not only propel advancements in computation but also transform the very fabric of space exploration across the cosmos. As we harness the potential of silicon-based quantum technologies, we prepare to embody the spirit of discovery that extends beyond mere computation—a journey into the infinite possibilities of the universe awash with curiosity, unanswered questions, and the desire to unveil new dimensions through the lens of quantum advancements.

4. The Mechanics of Quantum Computers

4.1. Quantum Gates and Circuits

In the intricate world of quantum computing, quantum gates and circuits represent the fundamental building blocks that govern how quantum information is processed. Unlike classical digital circuits that manipulate bits using logical gates, quantum circuits operate on the principle of quantum mechanics, leveraging phenomena such as superposition and entanglement to achieve computational efficiency that far exceeds that of classical counterparts. This subchapter will explore the mechanics of quantum gates and circuits, their design and operation, and the revolutionary implications for space exploration.

At the core of quantum circuits lie quantum gates, which are analogous to classical logic gates but operate under entirely different principles. Quantum gates manipulate qubits—quantum bits that can exist in a state of superposition of both 0 and 1. When a qubit is subjected to a quantum gate, its state is transformed according to defined quantum mechanical rules. Each gate corresponds to a specific operation that alters the probabilities associated with the qubit's state.

The most common quantum gate is the Hadamard gate, which is instrumental in creating superposition. When a qubit in the state $|0\rangle$ is passed through a Hadamard gate, it is transformed into $(|0\rangle + |1\rangle) / \sqrt{2}$, creating a state that holds equal probability of being measured as 0 or 1. This fundamental transformation is crucial for quantum algorithms that rely on parallel processing, allowing a quantum computer to explore multiple outcomes simultaneously.

Another critical component of quantum gates is the Pauli gates, which consist of the Pauli-X, Pauli-Y, and Pauli-Z gates. Each of these gates rotates the qubit's state around different axes on the Bloch sphere, allowing for precise control over its values. For instance, the Pauli-X gate acts similarly to a classical NOT gate, flipping the state of a qubit from $|0\rangle$ to $|1\rangle$ and vice versa. By combining different gates, complex quantum operations can be constructed, enabling the realization of intricate computations.

Quantum circuits are built by connecting these gates together in a specified sequence to perform specific algorithms. Just as classical circuits can perform a series of arithmetic operations or logical deductions, quantum circuits can execute quantum algorithms that may exploit parallelism to solve problems more efficiently than their classical counterparts. The arrangement and interconnection of quantum gates—known as quantum circuit design—are vital, as the fidelity of computations is heavily influenced by how closely the execution of the circuit adheres to theoretical models.

The fidelity of quantum circuits is particularly significant in the domain of deep space exploration, where quantum computing's potential hinges on stable and reliable operations. Space missions often require complex calculations over vast distances, where the traditional computational models may collapse under the astronomical demands of real-time data processing. Quantum circuits, constructed with careful consideration of gate design and error resilience, can provide the necessary computational power to navigate trajectory planning and optimize deep space operations. For example, a quantum circuit can model the gravitational influences of various celestial bodies while simultaneously analyzing potential trajectories for spacecraft, facilitating navigation through complex gravitational fields.

Moreover, implementing quantum gates and circuits in the unique conditions of space offers extraordinary possibilities for innovations in quantum sensors. Quantum circuits can be designed to enhance measurement capabilities, enabling scientists to capture elusive cosmic signals with unparalleled accuracy. For instance, quantum sensors utilizing entangled states can amplify the sensitivity of measurements, allowing for the detection of gravitational waves or fluctuations in the cosmic microwave background radiation—phenomena that classical sensors may struggle to unveil.

The practicality of quantum circuits in space missions also extends to the implications of error correction, a challenge that emerges from the delicate states of qubits. Quantum circuits must be crafted with an inherent robustness to decoherence and noise—two significant obstacles that compromise calculations' accuracy. The field of quantum error correction has emerged as a vital pillar for ensuring fault-tolerant quantum operations, employing techniques that include encoding qubits into larger logical qubits, thereby safeguarding essential information during computations. Developing effective algorithms for quantum error correction and incorporating them into quantum circuit designs are paramount to achieving success in space applications.

Additionally, quantum gates and circuits create exciting avenues for advancing secure communications in space. Quantum cryptography, which uses the principles of quantum mechanics to ensure secure information transfer, relies heavily on the foundational operations afforded by quantum gates. Through entangled states, quantum circuits can facilitate secure transmission protocols that encircle classical eavesdropping attempts, thereby safeguarding communication links between space missions and their Earth counterparts. Such encryption methods directly impact the feasibility of operating an interstellar quantum internet, where instruments deployed in deep space can communicate securely with base stations on Earth.

As we endeavor to explore the cosmos, the architecture and functionality of quantum gates and circuits will play a pivotal role in shaping our computational strategies. The versatility afforded by quantum circuits fosters the potential to unlock solutions to challenges that lie beyond the reach of classical computing, from optimizing spacecraft trajectories to analyzing complex cosmic phenomena. This advancement enhances our overall capacity for exploration, rendering quantum computing a cornerstone for future missions.

In summary, the mechanics of quantum gates and circuits represent a paradigm shift in how we approach computation. By harnessing the potential of qubits through intricate gate operations, we can develop circuits capable of performing astounding computations that extend well beyond traditional limits. As we venture into deep space with aspirations of exploration and discovery, the role of quantized information processing will serve as a beacon guiding humanity's quest to unveil the unknown dimensions of the cosmos. It reminds us that beneath the surface of what we perceive, complex interactions govern reality—waiting for us to explore, understand, and ultimately embrace the extraordinary realms that lie ahead in our quantum journey through the stars.

4.2. Entanglement and Teleportation

Entanglement, a phenomenon arising from quantum mechanics, represents one of the most profound and counterintuitive principles underpinning quantum computing. It refers to the condition where two or more particles become interconnected in such a way that the state of one particle cannot be adequately described without the state of the other(s), even when they are separated by vast distances. This interconnectedness paves the way for potential applications that could radically transform our approach to space exploration and communication in deep space.

At its core, entanglement is often illustrated through the paradigm of quantum superposition, where particles can exist in multiple states simultaneously. When measured, entangled particles display correlated behavior; a change in the state of one particle will instantaneously influence the state of its entangled counterpart, regardless of the distance separating them. This "spooky action at a distance," as Einstein famously referred to it, defies classical intuitions about locality and causality, challenging our understanding of how information transmits across spacetime.

In the landscape of quantum computing, entanglement serves as a vital resource for performing quantum operations that leverage the intertwined nature of qubits. Quantum gates acting on entangled qubits create circuits that far exceed classical capabilities, dramatically enhancing computational power through parallel processing. This characteristic becomes especially pertinent in deep space missions, where vast data interpretations, modeling complex celestial dynamics, and optimizations of trajectories can be achieved far more efficiently than classical algorithms would allow.

One of the most exciting implications of entanglement in this context is the potential for teleportation. Quantum teleportation is a method for transferring quantum information from one location to another without the physical transmission of the particle itself. It relies on the presence of entangled qubits; while the original information cannot be transferred fully, a qubit's state can be reconstructed at a distant location through the entanglement process. As a result, teleportation showcases a possibility for ultrafast communication systems that could help navigate the challenges of deep space exploration.

Imagining the scenario of space communication, quantum teleportation raises enticing prospects for sending information between distant spacecraft or relay stations scattered across the solar system and beyond. Traditional data transmission methods are limited by the speed of light, imposing constraints on communication speeds across interplanetary distances. Quantum entanglement offers a radical alternative: the potential for instantaneous state determination across vast space, dramatically revolutionizing the way we transmit data.

However, this application would be contingent upon the infrastructure capable of maintaining entangled states over significant distances. Engineers and physicists are already exploring and developing strategies for creating stable quantum networks, capable of generating and sustaining entangled qubits. Future space missions could leverage these networks to ensure secure information exchange, aiding both exploratory initiatives and operational communications. By establishing entangled communication links, mission control could receive real-time data, improving decision-making, and bolstering collaboration with distant spacecraft.

Moreover, the implications of entanglement extend beyond communication and processing; its applications also encompass quantum cryptography, where it provides heightened security for transmitted data. Quantum cryptographic protocols utilize the entangled states of qubits to safeguard information against interception, ensuring secure channels for data exchange across vast distances in the cosmos. This aspect becomes critical as humanity embarks further into deep space, where protecting sensitive information is paramount.

Yet, while entanglement and teleportation present possibilities, there are challenges that must be addressed before these ideas can be fully realized in deep space applications. The crucial issue of maintaining entangled states over long distances—a consequence of decoherence —must be tackled. Quantum systems are inherently sensitive to environmental disturbances, which can disrupt the delicate correlations between entangled particles. Consequently, researchers are exploring error-correcting codes and sophisticated techniques to safeguard entangled states and map out communication networks that could withstand the unforgiving conditions of space.

In conclusion, entanglement and teleportation will arguably serve as cornerstones in the future of quantum computing and its applications in deep space exploration. As we continue to unlock the secrets of quantum mechanics, embracing the interconnectedness of particles might open novel pathways for communication, data processing, and security. The exploration of entangled states is not merely an academic pursuit but a crucial step toward redefining how we approach space as an interconnected domain, where barriers of distance may dissipate in the face of quantum phenomena, heralding new dimensions of inquiry, interaction, and understanding in the cosmos.

As humanity prepares to take the next giant leap into the deep unknown, the integration of quantum principles into actual technological applications is set to reshape our understanding of the universe, tapping into realms of exploration that were once relegated to the domains of science fiction. The shift promises to redirect our trajectory as a species—transforming how we harness technology, engage with one another, and interact with the universe surrounding us in ways that echo the infinite possibilities inherent within the nature of existence itself.

4.3. Quantum Algorithms: Beyond Classical Limits

Quantum algorithms represent a revolutionary step in the evolution of computational methodologies, transcending the limitations of classical computing by harnessing the intrinsic properties of quantum mechanics. In the realm of deep space exploration, these algorithms don't just offer alternative solutions but present an entirely new framework for tackling complex problems inherent in navigating the cosmos, processing vast amounts of data, and optimizing mission parameters. The advantages of quantum algorithms arise from their ability to manipulate qubits—quantum bits that can exist in superposition and become entangled—capitalizing on phenomena that have no classical counterparts.

To understand quantum algorithms and their promise beyond classical limits, we first need to address their foundational principles. Classical algorithms operate on bits that are either in a state of 0 or 1. This binary system constrains operations to sequential processing. In contrast, quantum algorithms exploit superposition, which allows qubits to exist in multiple states simultaneously, and entanglement, which creates correlations between qubits in a manner that enables complex interactions and computations to occur in parallel. This parallelism underlies the unique processing capabilities of quantum systems, making them potentially exponential in their ability to solve certain problems.

One of the most profound examples is Shor's algorithm, which addresses the problem of integer factorization. In classical computing, factoring large integers—a task essential for encryption—becomes increasingly difficult as numbers grow larger, leading to impractical computation times. Shor's algorithm revolutionizes this landscape by enabling quantum computers to factor these integers efficiently through a series of quantum operations that leverage superposition and periodicity. The implications are staggering, fundamentally threatening classical cryptographic systems that depend on the difficulty of this very problem for security. In the context of deep space exploration, the ability to quickly and securely send and receive data is paramount. Shor's algorithm could ensure that communications from distant space missions remain safeguarded against potential threats, allowing us to exchange sensitive information without fear of interception.

Another significant quantum algorithm is Grover's algorithm, which provides a quadratic speedup for unstructured search problems. In classical terms, if you wanted to find a specific item in an unsorted database of N items, you would need to check an average of N/2 items, leading to a complexity of $O(N)$. Grover's algorithm reduces this to $O(\sqrt{N})$, representing a substantial leap that can dramatically enhance our capabilities in data retrieval and analysis—critical for processing the immense datasets generated in cosmic explorations. Whether it is identifying relevant astrophysical data from vast archives or navigating the vast quantities of information generated from interstellar missions, Grover's algorithm enables more efficient sorting and detection, allowing scientists to extract meaningful insights in a fraction of the time compared to classical searches.

In addition to Shor's and Grover's algorithms, various other quantum algorithms play critical roles in computational tasks such as quantum simulation, optimization, and machine learning, each offering distinct advantages that propel our capabilities in space exploration. Quantum simulation allows researchers to explore complex quantum systems that cannot be efficiently modeled by classical computers. This capability opens vast potential for simulating physical phenomena, such as the interactions of particles in extreme environments—fundamentally important for understanding cosmic events like black holes or neutron stars.

When integrated into deep space missions, these algorithms hold transformative power. For instance, mission planning for interstellar probes demands extensive calculations of spacecraft trajectories, including gravitational assists from celestial bodies and navigation through unpredictable cosmic debris fields. Quantum algorithms can process and optimize these paths in real-time, adjusting course instantaneously based on incoming data. The accelerated processing power afforded by quantum systems facilitates dynamic route recalibrations that are crucial for successful deep space missions.

Moreover, machine learning, when enhanced with quantum principles, holds significant promise for identifying and predicting patterns in complex astronomical data. Quantum-enhanced machine learning algorithms, capitalizing on entangled states to process multidimensional datasets, could unlock new insights into universe formation and evolution—sensing anomalies and correlations within data streams that classical systems may overlook. This synergy between quantum algorithms and machine learning heralds a new age of discovery, potentially elucidating the secrets of dark matter or the elusive nature of cosmic inflation.

However, realizing the theoretical advantages of quantum algorithms in practical applications is not without challenges. The coherence times of qubits—the duration they can maintain their quantum state without collapsing—pose significant hurdles. Quantum error correction must be woven into the fabric of quantum algorithms to ensure that calculations remain accurate over time, counteracting the effects of decoherence and minimizing errors during operations. Addressing these obstacles requires not just advancements in algorithm development but also committed efforts towards robust quantum hardware engineering capable of sustaining qubit coherence amidst complex cosmic environments. Lessons learned from attempts to build and refine quantum computers here on Earth may aid in creating resilient systems for use in the unforgiving conditions of space.

Aside from technological challenges, there are also fundamental questions regarding the integration of quantum algorithms into current computational frameworks. As quantum computing continues to develop, the intersection with classical systems demands careful consideration of methodologies. Hybrid systems balancing classical and quantum processing will likely emerge as a viable path forward, optimizing resources while facilitating various tasks fitted to each system's strengths.

In summary, quantum algorithms stand poised to break classical bounds, rewriting the narrative of computation, especially in the context of deep space exploration. By harnessing the unique properties of qubits—superposition, entanglement, and the transformative capabilities afforded by quantum mechanics—scientists and researchers can fundamentally change how we navigate, analyze, and understand the universe. As we embark on this monumental exploration, quantum algorithms signify not merely a computational tool but a key that unlocks unexplored dimensions of cognitive possibility, inviting humanity into a vast realm where the mere act of computation propels us deeper into the mysteries of existence itself within the cosmos. The future of space exploration may very well be defined by those who dare to journey beyond classical limits, leveraging the extraordinary power of quantum algorithms to unveil the secrets waiting to be uncovered among the stars.

4.4. Error Correction in a Quantum World

In the quest to harness the extraordinary potential of quantum computing, error correction stands as an essential and intricate challenge. Within the framework of classical computing, error detection and correction are well-established practices utilized to maintain data integrity; however, the world of quantum mechanics introduces unique complexities that demand wholly new approaches. The delicate nuances of quantum states make error correction a formidable endeavor, especially in the context of deep space explorations, where the risks of interference and decoherence are magnified.

At the heart of quantum error correction lies the understanding that qubits—the building blocks of quantum information—are inherently sensitive to their environments. Their quantum states can be disrupted by external factors such as thermal noise, cosmic radiation, and even light itself. This interaction can cause qubits to lose their entangled states and superpositions, leading to errors that could obliterate the output of quantum computations. Moreover, once a qubit's state is measured, it collapses into a definite state of either 0 or 1, making it impossible to retrieve the original quantum information after measurement. This property challenges the traditional methods of error correction that rely on redundant copies of information.

To effectively preserve quantum information, researchers have developed various quantum error correction codes, which rigorously encode logical qubits into multiple physical qubits. One iconic example is the Shor code, which was developed by Peter Shor, the same pioneering mind behind the eponymous factoring algorithm. The Shor code uses nine physical qubits to encode a single logical qubit, allowing for the correction of a single qubit error in the encoding process. The innovative design of these codes arises from the fundamental principles of quantum mechanics, which ensure that by manipulating a quantum state using carefully orchestrated gates, we can protect against errors while still allowing for valuable operations to be performed.

The robustness provided by these quantum error correction codes serves vital functions, particularly for potential applications in deep space exploration. As missions venture farther from Earth, the risk of decoherence intensifies due to increased exposure to cosmic radiation and environmental fluctuations. Quantum error correction protocols play a critical role in safeguarding the integrity of quantum computations during these missions. For instance, envision a spacecraft equipped with quantum sensors designed to analyze gravitational waves. The data collected needs to be processed with extreme precision; therefore, implementing quantum error correction can mitigate potential errors from environmental variables, enhancing the reliability of results.

Moreover, the development of fault-tolerant quantum computation hinges on the ability to execute error correction seamlessly and efficiently. Fault-tolerant architectures allow quantum operations to continue despite the presence of noise or defects in the qubits. These architectures are essential for constructing scalable quantum computing systems that can perform calculations without significant performance degradation—a requirement that becomes increasingly essential during extended space missions characterized by harsh and unpredictable conditions.

A noteworthy approach to error correction also encompasses the utilization of topological qubits, which promise increased stability and resilience against decoherence. Topological qubits leverage braiding of particle-like excitations called anyons, changing the state of the qubit in a manner that is inherently protected from local disturbances. These systems operate according to the principles of topology, thereby enhancing their resistance to errors caused by environmental factors prevalent in space. While research into topological qubits is still in nascent stages, their potential implications for fault-tolerant quantum computing in the unforgiving domains of deep space exploration are profound.

As we integrate these advanced error correction techniques, we encounter additional considerations regarding the algorithms employed for optimizing quantum computations. Many quantum algorithms, such as those used for trajectory optimization and complex simulations of cosmic phenomena, require repeated operations. The demands for maintaining coherence during these operations reinforce the necessity for implementing robust error correction mechanisms. Researchers are continually testing and refining algorithms that not only optimize the execution of quantum gates but also incorporate error-correcting codes as integral components of the computational workflow.

The future of quantum error correction in space exploration is not without its challenges. Ensuring the stability of qubits in sensitive quantum systems requires innovative designs and strategies for shielding qubits from environmental disturbances. Furthermore, the scalability of quantum error correction must be addressed to facilitate large-scale quantum computers capable of undertaking extensive computations over long durations.

The intersection of quantum error correction and potential applications in deep space denotes a future filled with promise—a promise hinged on the ability to maintain the integrity of quantum systems amidst the chaotic cacophony of cosmic phenomena. As humanity prepares to unlock the secrets of the universe and venture into the cosmic unknown, the success of quantum technologies will rely heavily on the implementation of advanced error correction. The duality of innovation and robustness provides a pathway forward, expanding our computational capabilities and unlocking new dimensions of understanding.

In conclusion, error correction in a quantum world embodies an intricate tapestry woven from the delicate fibers of quantum mechanics and engineering ingenuity. By embracing error correction techniques, we move beyond the purely theoretical realms of quantum computing, setting the stage for tangible advancements applicable to deep space exploration and beyond. The meticulous pursuit of precision in quantum computations is not merely about preserving information; it symbolizes humanity's relentless quest to traverse the cosmic expanse—a journey illuminated by the endless possibilities contained within the quantum realm. As we unravel the complexities of error correction, we open pathways to new dimensions of inquiry, unveiling the universe one qubit at a time.

4.5. Quantum Annealing and Optimization

Quantum annealing is a specialized form of quantum computing that employs quantum mechanics principles to address optimization problems. Unlike traditional computers, which tackle these problems through sequential calculations, quantum annealers utilize quantum superposition and tunneling to traverse the solution space, enabling them to find optimal or near-optimal solutions more efficiently. This principle is particularly relevant in deep space applications, where complex optimization tasks arise, such as trajectory planning for spacecraft or resource allocation in interstellar missions.

At the core of quantum annealing lies the process of finding the ground state of a given optimization problem, represented by a cost function that needs to be minimized. In essence, ordinary optimization involves navigating a landscape with various peaks and valleys, where the lowest point is the optimal solution. Classical algorithms often struggle with such landscapes, particularly when they contain numerous local minima—suboptimal solutions that can mislead standard optimization methods and trap them in less desirable outcomes.

Quantum annealing addresses this challenge through the principle of quantum superposition, allowing a system to exist in multiple states simultaneously. When a quantum annealer is initialized, it starts in a superposition of all possible configurations of a problem. Over time, the system is gradually evolved towards its ground state—essentially "annealing" the system. This evolution exploits quantum tunneling, allowing the system to pass through energy barriers that might obstruct a classical algorithm, which could get stuck on a local minimum. As the system cools down, it ideally settles into the lowest energy configuration, revealing the optimal solution.

D-Wave Systems is a prominent player in the quantum annealing space. Their machines are designed to tackle specific types of optimization problems using quantum annealing techniques. Deep space missions often require swift and efficient decision-making, making these quantum systems potential game-changers. For instance, quantum annealers could optimize flight paths, adapting to gravitational interactions from multiple celestial bodies or adjusting to new data collected en route. This capacity could minimize travel time and resource expenditure, providing significant advantages for long-duration space missions.

The implications of quantum annealing extend beyond trajectory optimizations. In the realm of resource allocation, deep space missions depend on effective management of limited resources, whether it be power management in spacecraft or organizing communication bandwidth between multiple devices. Quantum annealing algorithms provide a unique mechanism to model and solve these problems efficiently, transforming decision-making processes.

Moreover, the unique nature of quantum annealers lends itself well to certain types of machine learning tasks, where they can uncover patterns in vast datasets that classical systems might miss. Given that data analysis is vital in space exploration—whether for studying planetary atmospheres, geological compositions, or cosmic phenomena—quantum annealers could significantly enhance our capability to extract actionable intelligence from previously intractable problems.

However, deploying quantum annealing in practical space missions is not without its challenges. Decoherence—the loss of quantum information due to interactions with the environment—remains a critical issue. As quantum systems are sensitive to external influences, ensuring the stability of qubit states over extended periods and distances in the harsh conditions of space presents a significant technical challenge. Additionally, the need for error correction within the quantum processing framework adds complexity to the system design.

Furthermore, there is a pressing need for continued research into the types of problems that quantum annealers can solve effectively. Not all optimization problems may benefit from quantum annealing, and distinguishing between instances that can be solved classically versus those that truly leverage quantum capabilities is ongoing.

The use of quantum annealing in deep space presents both phenomenal opportunities and challenges. By providing a framework that embraces the complexities of quantum mechanics, researchers are carving a path toward advanced solutions that could revolutionize our approach to interstellar exploration. The efficiencies gained from quantum mechanics promise to enhance humanity's ability to navigate the challenges of space, pushing the boundaries of what is possible in our quest to explore the cosmos.

In summary, quantum annealing represents a novel approach to optimization problems, closely aligning with the unique demands of deep space exploration. By harnessing the principles of superposition and tunneling, quantum annealers could redefine how spacecraft navigate their trajectories, allocate resources, and analyze vast datasets. As advancements continue to unfold in quantum technology, the collaborative efforts of scientists and engineers will help propel humanity further into the quantum frontier, revealing new horizons both in the realm of computing and the vast expanse of space itself. Through these endeavors, we are set to unveil dimensions of understanding and discovery previously deemed unreachable.

5. Exploring Deep Space: A Quantum Perspective

5.1. A New Era for Space Exploration

In recent years, we have entered what can only be described as a revolutionary new epoch for space exploration, driven by the synergy of quantum computing and novel technologies. This transformative era is characterized by the convergence of quantum mechanics and space science, enabling previously unimaginable capabilities in data processing, communication, and navigation. The advances in quantum computing have the potential to unlock mysteries of the universe, enhance our exploration strategies, and fundamentally alter our understanding of cosmic phenomena.

One of the key enablers of this new era is the development of quantum sensors, which utilize the principles of quantum mechanics to achieve unprecedented levels of sensitivity and accuracy in measurements. These sensors are poised to transform traditional methods of mapping the universe, tracking distant celestial objects, and detecting faint signals that were once thought to be beyond our grasp. Equipped with quantum sensors, space missions will be able to collect data with such precision that we can unravel the complexities of gravitational waves, dark matter, and other enigmatic aspects of the cosmos.

The marriage of quantum communication and satellite technology is another prominent chapter in the narrative of this new age. Entangled communication systems, powered by quantum entanglement, can enable secure data transmission over vast interstellar distances. As we send spacecraft deeper into space, these systems offer the potential to maintain communication links that are resistant to interception, ensuring that sensitive information remains protected even in the exposed depths of the universe.

Moreover, quantum telescopes hold the promise of revolutionizing our observational capabilities. By leveraging the principles of quantum optics, these advanced instruments will allow us to detect and visualize phenomena that have remained hidden in the darkness of space. They could potentially uncover new aspects of stellar evolution, gas clouds, and the formation of galaxies, leading to breakthroughs in our understanding of the universe's formation and evolution.

As we look toward the future of space exploration, our reliance on quantum technologies will require an interdisciplinary approach —melding physics, engineering, computer science, and ethics. The development of quantum-enabled spacecraft will not only require advancements in propulsion technologies but also a careful consideration of how these innovations impact our exploration strategies and the ethical dimensions of utilizing quantum capabilities responsibly in the pursuit of knowledge.

Navigational capabilities will similarly benefit from embracing quantum mechanics. The innate precision of quantum clocks, combined with the processing power provided by quantum computing, will lead to advancements in GPS systems that extend beyond Earth's atmosphere. Spacecraft navigating through complex gravitational fields can leverage optimized trajectories calculated through quantum algorithms, enabling quicker and more efficient journeys far from home.

Yet, as with any revolutionary technology, opportunities are accompanied by significant challenges. The road to unlocking these advancements in quantum space exploration will necessitate overcoming obstacles such as maintaining coherence and managing the effects of decoherence from cosmic radiation and environmental interactions. Researchers will need to develop robust error correction methods and ingenious designs to protect qubits from disturbances, all while advancing our understanding of quantum phenomena.

The unfathomable depths of space call for a commitment to ethical practices as we push the frontiers of technology. With the advent of quantum computing, we must carefully consider the ramifications of our explorations and harness these technologies in a manner that reflects a deep respect for the cosmos. As we progress into an era characterized by the convergence of quantum innovation and space exploration, the ethical considerations must guide our planning, ensuring we navigate not only toward scientific advancement but also toward fostering a responsible relationship with the universe.

Ultimately, we stand at the precipice of a new frontier in space exploration that is rich with possibilities. The integration of quantum mechanics into our exploratory endeavors can elevate our capabilities and enhance our understanding of the universe in ways that extend far beyond our current realizations. Embracing this quantum era invites us to rethink our approach to exploration—enabling us to delve deeper into the cosmos, uncovering the secrets that lie in the vast, uncharted territories that lie beyond our reach. As we embark on this transformative journey, we not only unlock phenomena that were once relegated to fiction but set forth on a path that promises profound discoveries and insights into the very nature of existence within the boundless cosmos.

5.2. Mapping the Universe with Quantum Sensors

In the quest to map the universe, quantum sensors are emerging as vital instruments, driven by the principles of quantum mechanics that offer unparalleled precision and sensitivity. Unlike classical sensors, which operate on well-established physical principles, quantum sensors leverage quantum superposition and entanglement to transcend the limitations of classical measurement techniques. This innovative approach can enhance our understanding of cosmic phenomena, enabling us to probe the depths of the universe in ways previously deemed unattainable.

Quantum sensors capitalize on the fundamental properties of quantum mechanics to achieve extraordinary levels of sensitivity. For example, one of the key types of quantum sensors is based on atomic interferometry, wherein cold atoms are manipulated to create interference patterns that are sensitive to external fields such as gravity, magnetic fields, and gravitational waves. The capabilities of these sensors to detect minuscule variations make them invaluable assets for exploring the universe.

Mapping the universe with quantum sensors can fundamentally alter the way we gather data about celestial objects, phenomena, and events. Take for instance gravitational waves—ripples in spacetime caused by massive accelerated objects like colliding black holes. Traditional detectors, such as LIGO, have recorded these waves through highly sensitive laser interferometry. However, quantum sensors can potentially enhance this capability. By using squeezed light techniques, quantum-enhanced gravitational wave detectors may achieve higher sensitivity, allowing us to detect fainter signals from more distant cosmic events. This could lead to a renaissance in our understanding of astrophysics, unveiling previously hidden cosmic interactions.

Moreover, quantum sensors can enrich our ability to map cosmic structures. Quantum magnetometers are capable of detecting weak magnetic fields from celestial bodies. By employing cold-atom technologies, these sensors can measure magnetic fields with high accuracy. This capability allows for detailed mapping of planetary magnetic fields, potentially revealing insights into their internal structures, atmospheric dynamics, and geological histories. Armed with such knowledge, scientists can formulate theories about the evolution of planets and their atmospheres, yielding greater understanding of planetary habitability.

The potential for quantum sensors extends to the study of dark matter and dark energy, which comprise a significant fraction of the universe yet remain elusive in terms of direct detection. Quantum technologies can be employed to design sophisticated detectors that capitalize on the interactions between dark matter particles and normal matter, aiming to unveil the properties of these mysterious components of the universe. Utilizing quantum-enhanced techniques, we may enhance our experimental sensitivity to capture and analyze dark matter interactions, paving the way for groundbreaking advancements in cosmology.

In addition to magnetic and gravitational measurements, other applications of quantum sensors include interferometric imaging techniques, such as those used in the observation of far-off celestial bodies. Current imaging technologies often face limitations based on noise and resolution constraints. By integrating quantum algorithms and sensors, astronomers may be capable of significantly improving spatial resolution and clarity of images from cosmos, leading to clearer observations of distant stars, galaxies, and celestial phenomena.

Nonetheless, the practical implementation of quantum sensors in space exploration poses several challenges. First and foremost, the deployment of quantum sensors must address the issues of decoherence—the loss of quantum information caused by interactions with the environment. The harsh conditions of outer space, including radiation and extreme temperatures, necessitate innovative engineering approaches to shield quantum systems and maintain their coherence over long durations.

Moreover, ensuring the right communication protocols and data processing capabilities to handle the high volume of data generated by quantum sensors is essential. Advanced algorithms capable of interpreting the output from these sensors will significantly enhance our ability to extract meaningful information from complex datasets. The design of efficient data pipelines, integrated with quantum algorithms, will ensure that insights gathered from cosmic measurements translate into actionable scientific knowledge.

As we look to the future of deep space exploration, the mapping of the universe through quantum sensors illuminates an exciting frontier. The potential to capture dark matter interactions, improve imaging of celestial bodies, enhance gravitational wave detection, and unravel magnetic fields of planets opens myriad pathways to discover the universe's secrets that have thus far remained obscured.

In summary, the convergence of quantum mechanics and sensor technology offers a transformative capability to map the universe with unparalleled precision. Quantum sensors, driven by the principles of superposition and entanglement, hold the transformative potential to enhance our observational prowess across numerous domains—gravitational physics, planetary science, cosmology, and astrophysics. As technology progresses and our understanding of quantum systems deepens, we embark on a new cosmic quest, paving the way toward profound discoveries that await among the stars. This journey will illuminate not just the universe around us, but also the very nature of existence itself as we endeavor to unveil new dimensions of understanding.

5.3. Harnessing Quantum Satellites

In the vastness of space, where the dimensions of time and distance stretch beyond human comprehension, quantum satellites represent a groundbreaking integration of technology and fundamental physics. These satellites harness the principles of quantum mechanics to revolutionize space exploration, communication, and data gathering in ways that classical technology cannot achieve. By employing quantum properties such as superposition, entanglement, and quantum states, these satellites promise to enhance our capabilities in understanding and navigating the cosmos.

At the heart of the quantum satellite revolution lies the concept of quantum entanglement. This phenomenon allows qubits to become interconnected, creating a system where the state of one qubit is intrinsically linked to another, regardless of the distance that separates them. By leveraging entangled states, quantum satellites could facilitate instantaneous communication across vast distances—a remarkable advancement over the current transmission methods limited by the speed of light. Imagine a network of quantum satellites orbiting distant celestial bodies, each communicating secure data streams in real time, effectively creating a cosmic internet that transcends the limitations of classical data transmission.

The involvement of quantum satellites in enhancing communication systems reaches beyond mere speed; it promises to improve security through quantum key distribution (QKD). By employing the principles of quantum mechanics, QKD ensures that any attempt by an eavesdropper to intercept information will alter the quantum states being transmitted—a property that classical encryption schemes cannot match. This degree of communication security is critical as humanity embarks on deeper explorations of space, where sensitive data about missions, scientific discoveries, and interstellar coordination will need protection from potential threats.

Consequently, quantum satellites hold the potential to transform navigational techniques in space exploration. Equipped with advanced quantum sensors, these satellites can detect minute fluctuations in gravitational fields, magnetic variations, and other cosmic phenomena. This capability facilitates more accurate mapping of celestial objects and enables enhanced maneuvering of spacecraft navigating through complex gravitational fields. Quantum sensors can provide precise positioning data essential for trajectory adjustments, ultimately improving the efficiency of deep space missions.

Additionally, quantum satellites can enhance our detection capabilities for cosmic events. By deploying a network of quantum sensors that leverage entangled states, we can drastically improve our sensitivity to gravitational waves, dark matter interactions, and other subtle cosmic signals that escape traditional detection methods. The ability to map these faint signals with unparalleled accuracy can yield insights into the formation of the universe, the behavior of black holes, and other phenomena that remain shrouded in mystery.

The practical deployment of quantum satellites, however, presents significant challenges. Encounters with cosmic radiation, extreme temperatures, and other environmental factors pose threats to the coherence of quantum states. To enable these satellites to function effectively in the harsh conditions of space, robust engineering solutions must focus on protecting qubits from decoherence and noise. This may include isolating quantum components from destructive external influences and developing new materials that can maintain qubit states and facilitate quantum gate operations.

Moreover, establishing a fleet of quantum satellites necessitates advancements in manufacturing and technology. As researchers aim to build reliable and scalable quantum systems, collaboration across industries and disciplines will be essential. National and international partnerships could expedite this journey, merging expertise from academia, aerospace, and quantum technology sectors. Additionally, the exploration of ground-based quantum optics could lead to leaps in satellite technology certification, enhancing reliability and robustness before launching into space.

As we proceed into an era where quantum technologies begin to underpin our space endeavors, ethical considerations must also be brought to the forefront. The implications of interstellar communications, data privacy concerns, and equitable access to quantum-enhanced systems will shape discussions surrounding the responsible integration of quantum satellites. Navigating the consequences of these advancements will require careful deliberation among scientific communities, policymakers, and society at large.

In summary, harnessing quantum satellites heralds a new epoch of discovery and exploration in the cosmos. Their ability to utilize quantum entanglement for secure communication, enhanced navigational precision, and the detection of cosmic phenomena marks a transformative shift in how we perceive and interact with space. As we foster technological innovations and embrace the ethical considerations alongside these advances, quantum satellites will undoubtedly redefine our trajectory in the exploration of the universe, leading us to unveil new dimensions and experience the unfathomable depths of the cosmic frontier. In this boundless expanse, we prepare to unlock secrets that deepen our understanding of existence itself while equipping us to traverse the stars and embrace the infinite possibilities of the cosmos.

5.4. Entangled Communication Beyond Earth

In our quest to unlock the secrets of the cosmos, entangled communication beyond Earth is emerging as a transformative avenue that could redefine how we connect and share information across the vast expanses of space. At the crux of this endeavor lies the phenomenon of quantum entanglement, a cornerstone of quantum mechanics that enables particles to be instantaneously connected regardless of the distance separating them. This unique property holds profound implications for establishing communication systems that are not only faster but also fundamentally more secure than anything currently available.

Entangled communication relies on quantum bits, or qubits, that exist in states that are interdependent. When two particles become entangled, a state change in one particle will instantaneously affect the state of the other, no matter how far apart they are. This phenomenon challenges classical notions of locality, where information transfer is constrained by the speed of light. In essence, entanglement enables the possibility of instantaneous communication, making it an alluring idea for future communication networks stretching beyond our solar system.

The potential applications of such entangled communication systems are vast and varied. For instance, in interstellar missions where spacecraft are exploring distant celestial realms, secure communication channels are paramount. Traditional communication methods, which are based on radio waves that take time to traverse space, often face delays and potential interception. Quantum communication, facilitated by entangled particles, could create a form of instantaneous signal transmission that may safeguard sensitive scientific data, ensuring that any findings from the depths of space remain secure from outside interference.

Establishing quantum communication links also implies enhanced resilience against eavesdropping. The quantum state of entangled particles is inherently linked to the principles of quantum measurement—any attempt to observe or measure the system collapses its state, alerting the communicating parties of any potential interference. This characteristic allows for a level of security unattainable through classical encryption methods that could potentially be compromised as computational power increases.

However, implementing entangled communication systems is not without its challenges. The maintenance of entanglement over long distances remains a significant hurdle due to decoherence—the process through which quantum states lose their quantum properties due to interactions with the surrounding environment. Researchers are diligently investigating methods to preserve entanglement, including the development of quantum repeaters that can amplify entangled states over vast distances.

The design of satellite-based quantum communication networks also necessitates advanced engineering solutions. Satellites equipped with quantum communication capabilities could serve as relay stations, forming a constellation that links Earth with distant missions. These satellites would need to be equipped with technology capable of producing, distributing, and maintaining the entangled pairs of particles. Innovative approaches to scaling these systems are crucial for developing a viable framework capable of interstellar communication.

Moreover, as we venture further into the cosmos, the function of entangled communication extends beyond data exchange; it prompts a reconsideration of our relationship with the universe and the ethical dimensions surrounding technological advancements. As humanity delves deeper into the phenomena of quantum mechanics, we must grapple with the implications of harnessing such powerful capabilities for interstellar communication. Will this technology widen the gaps between those who have access and those who do not? How do we ensure that our explorative innovations are deployed responsibly?

In addition, the entangled communication landscape will necessitate collaboration across different fields, including physics, engineering, computer science, and ethics. Creating a multi-disciplinary framework for deploying these networks guarantees that technological advancements are leveraged for the benefit of society as a whole. As we contemplate the future of entangled communication, interdisciplinary partnerships can expedite breakthroughs in achieving successful satellite-based quantum communication networks capable of enabling swift informational exchanges across the cosmos.

As we prepare for a future that harnesses the power of quantum entanglement for communication beyond Earth, the prospects for discovery and understanding are exhilarating. The realization of instantaneous and secure communication could revolutionize our approach to space exploration, enabling seamless data exchange between spacecraft navigating the cosmos and mission control on Earth. This could facilitate agile decision-making during missions, enhance collaborative efforts within the global scientific community, and unlock transformative insights from the uncharted territories of the universe.

In conclusion, entangled communication represents a bold frontier in our pursuit of the cosmos. By leveraging the principles of quantum mechanics, we can build networks that allow instant, secure, and resilient exchanges of information across vast distances. As we embark on this journey, we must remain vigilant in ensuring that our advancements are guided by ethical considerations, collaboration across disciplines, and an unwavering commitment to exploration and understanding. As we prepare to reach for the stars, let us also strive to unlock the mysteries of the universe, bringing us closer to understanding our place within the grand tapestry of existence.

5.5. Quantum Telescopes: Seeing the Invisible

In the age of modern astronomy, the limitations of classical telescopes become increasingly apparent as scientists seek to explore realms that lie beyond the observable spectrum. Enter quantum telescopes—a revolutionary concept that fuses the principles of quantum mechanics with astronomical observation, allowing us to 'see' the invisible dynamics of the universe. By utilizing unique quantum properties such as superposition and entanglement, these advanced instruments promise to unlock unparalleled insights into cosmic phenomena, fundamentally altering our understanding of the universe.

The core advantage of quantum telescopes lies in their ability to manipulate and enhance light at unprecedented sensitivity levels. Traditional telescopes capture light in its classical wave form, encountering challenges in imaging distant objects due to atmospheric distortions and the limits of photon capture. However, quantum telescopes employ quantum-enhanced techniques that allow for the utilization of entangled photons. By generating pairs of entangled photons, researchers can leverage correlations between the pairs to improve measurement accuracy, effectively enhancing the resolution of observations made on distant astronomical bodies.

One promising approach involves quantum interference patterns that arise from using squeezed light in telescopic systems. Squeezed light is a state of light where uncertainties in certain quadratures are reduced below the standard quantum limit, thereby amplifying the precision of measurements. This enhanced sensitivity allows for the detection of weaker signals that classical telescopes might fail to identify. In practical terms, this means that quantum telescopes could discern fainter stars or identify minute details on planets that are millions of light-years away, revealing tectonic activity, atmospheric compositions, and potentially even signs of life.

The implications of quantum telescopes extend beyond mere observational prowess; they also reshape our understanding of the fundamental processes driving the universe. For example, by leveraging the properties of quantum sensors, quantum telescopes could detect gravitational waves with heightened sensitivity. The ability to observe the ripples in spacetime caused by massive cosmic events, such as black hole collisions or neutron star mergers, would provide invaluable data, contributing to our understanding of phenomena that shape the cosmos and validate paradigms in astrophysics.

Moreover, quantum telescopes raise intriguing questions about the nature of the universe itself. The phenomenon of quantum entanglement invites consideration of how interconnected the cosmos truly is. If we can manipulate and coordinate measurements across vast distances through entangled photon streams, does that imply a deeper level of connectivity throughout space? Such questions prompt philosophical inquiries into the nature of existence and our relationship with the universe, encouraging us to think beyond our classical perceptions of separateness.

As we explore the potential for quantum telescopes, it becomes evident that their deployment in space exploration is not without technical challenges. Much like quantum computing, quantum sensing faces hurdles such as decoherence—the loss of quantum correlations due to environmental interactions. In the harsh conditions of outer space, shields must be engineered to protect these delicate quantum states, ensuring that the telescopes can maintain their functionality long enough to capture crucial astronomical data.

In addition, the interplay between quantum mechanics and observation raises fundamental questions about measurement in astronomy. The act of observing distant cosmic objects changes our understanding of them, echoing themes established by the double-slit experiment and Heisenberg's Uncertainty Principle. As we deploy quantum telescopes into the universe, researchers must remain vigilant regarding the interpretations of the data and how they correlate with the intrinsic nature of the objects being observed. These considerations will be paramount as we strive to marry quantum mechanics with observational astronomy in meaningful ways.

Nonetheless, the integration of quantum telescopes into the field of astronomy heralds a new era of exploration. As they capture data and unveil cosmic mysteries, we will gain a richer, more nuanced understanding of the cosmic tapestry that surrounds us. Quantum telescopes will not merely be instruments for star-gazing; they will be gateways to new dimensions of inquiry, allowing humankind to probe deeper into the heart of creation itself.

In conclusion, the advent of quantum telescopes signals a transformative leap in our capacity to observe the universe. By harnessing the principles of quantum mechanics, these instruments empower astronomers to "see" in ways that transcend traditional limits. The capability to dissect the subtle nuances of cosmic phenomena paves the way for extraordinary advancements in our understanding of the universe and ultimately invites us to rethink our place within it. As we look to the stars with the lens of quantum mechanics, we prepare to uncover the secrets of existence, redefining what we know about the cosmos and challenging the very nature of reality itself. This journey toward the invisible holds the potential for groundbreaking discoveries that shall illuminate the paths of future explorations among the stars.

6. Quantum Propulsion and Spacecraft

6.1. Theoretical Models of Quantum Drives

In the exploration of advanced propulsion systems, theoretical models of quantum drives represent a groundbreaking avenue that melds the complexities of quantum mechanics with the imperative of interstellar travel. By grasping the intrinsic behaviors of quantum particles, researchers are envisioning propulsion technologies that could fundamentally transform how we navigate the cosmos. This discussion includes a deep dive into the principles underpinning quantum drives, theoretical frameworks, potential implementation pathways, and the implications for deep space exploration.

The Quantum Vacuum: A Source of Power? At the frontier of quantum propulsion theory lies the concept of harnessing the vacuum of space itself as a potential source of energy. The idea stems from the quantum field theory, which postulates that even in a vacuum —where no particles exist—there are fluctuations of energy that can be exploited for propulsion. Researchers have theorized that manipulating these fluctuations, sometimes referred to as "vacuum energy," could lead to propulsion systems that do not rely on conventional fuels but instead utilize the latent energy present in the cosmic void.

This form of propulsion could operate on principles similar to those proposed by the concept of the Casimir effect, where two closely spaced, uncharged conductive plates experience an attractive force due to quantum vacuum fluctuations. By developing a device capable of altering the space around it to take advantage of these vacuum fluctuations, it might be possible to create thrust without expending fuel in the traditional sense, thereby revolutionizing our approach to long-distance space travel.

Building the First Quantum-Enabled Craft Designing and constructing the first quantum-enabled craft involves addressing numerous challenges and hurdles. The fundamental architecture of such a spacecraft must integrate advanced materials and technologies capable of operating at quantum levels. This includes developing highly

sophisticated quantum systems that can function while maintaining coherent quantum states amidst external interferences such as cosmic radiation and extreme environmental conditions.

One vision for a quantum spacecraft could involve a series of quantum engines powered by controlled vacuum energy or utilizing quantum tunneling to facilitate propulsion. Quantum tunneling, a phenomenon where particles can traverse potential barriers, could allow a spacecraft to shift between different dimensions or states, enabling it to navigate vast distances in short periods. Imagine a spacecraft capable of entering a quantum state that folds space-time locally, allowing it to effectively bypass the limitations imposed by the speed of light—an idea that, while speculative, highlights the potential transformative power of quantum mechanics.

Overcoming the Technological Constraints To bring quantum propulsion systems to fruition, it is vital to overcome several technological constraints inherent in quantum theory. The delicate stability of qubits, as well as the coherent functioning of quantum systems, is challenged by environmental noise and decoherence—factors that can disrupt the quantum state and thereby derail propulsion mechanisms.

Developing robust engineering solutions to maintain coherence in quantum systems will be paramount. Strategies may include isolating quantum components from external disturbances through advanced shielding and employing error correction mechanisms that ensure stability during operation, especially in the dynamic conditions of space travel.

Additionally, crafting algorithms that can optimize the use of quantum systems for navigation and propulsion will be essential. Such algorithms would need to account for the complexities of trajectory planning under the influence of gravitational bodies and cosmic forces, maximizing the effectiveness of the quantum propulsion driving system. Researchers in quantum computing and aerospace engineering will need to collaborate closely to cultivate a framework for integrating these technologies seamlessly.

The Role of Quantum AI in Navigation In concert with quantum propulsion systems, quantum artificial intelligence (AI) will play a vital role in navigation and operational efficiency. Quantum AI can process vast datasets generated by spacecraft sensors with exceptional speed and efficacy, allowing real-time decision-making that adapts to dynamic space environments.

AI systems utilizing quantum algorithms could facilitate optimal trajectory adjustments during interstellar missions, dynamically responding to gravitational influences and adapting flight paths based on incoming data. Furthermore, by analyzing complex patterns in cosmic phenomena, quantum AI could make informed predictions that enhance mission outcomes, thereby transforming our ability to explore the far reaches of space.

As we strive toward realizing the potential of quantum drives, the convergence of quantum mechanics, advanced propulsion, and artificial intelligence marks a new frontier in space exploration—one where the sophistication of quantum technologies enables humanity to navigate the cosmic expanse with unprecedented efficacy.

In conclusion, theoretical models of quantum drives represent not merely a novel propulsion system but a revolutionary paradigm shift that embodies the intersection of physics, engineering, and exploratory ambition. As research progresses and breakthroughs emerge, the vision of quantum-powered spacecraft becomes a tantalizing prospect, echoing humankind's relentless pursuit of knowledge and discovery amid the stars. Complex quantum principles beckon us to explore new dimensions, prompting reflections on how we could, one day, traverse the cosmos not just as observers but as active participants in the unfolding narrative of the universe.

6.2. The Quantum Vacuum: A Source of Power?

In the quest for a sustainable and efficient energy source for the future of space exploration, the notion of harnessing the quantum vacuum emerges as a fascinating frontier. The quantum vacuum, often perceived as a mere void, is inherently rich with fluctuations that challenge our classical understanding of empty space. This sub-chapter delves into the theoretical underpinnings of this quantum phenomenon and its potential to serve as a profound source of power, revolutionizing propulsion systems for spacecraft venturing into the deep cosmos.

The quantum vacuum is a realm where virtual particles continually pop in and out of existence due to quantum fluctuations. These fleeting particles exist for extremely brief moments, yet during their ephemeral lifetime, they demonstrate energy characteristics that can be harvested under specific conditions. The foundational concept here is that even the most seemingly empty space is teeming with energy, which can be manipulated to create propulsion systems un-tethered from conventional fuel sources.

Theoretical Framework

One pivotal framework that illustrates this concept is rooted in the Casimir effect, which posits that two parallel uncharged conductive plates, placed in close proximity within a vacuum, will experience an attractive force due to the suppression of virtual particle pairs between them. As these plates constrain the quantum fluctuations of the vacuum, they create a differential pressure that effectively pulls them together. The implications of this effect suggest that if harnessed appropriately, the energy from the vacuum could be converted into usable propulsion.

If a spacecraft could manipulate the vacuum energy through innov-ative designs that utilize similar principles to the Casimir effect, a propulsion system could be developed that generates thrust without the need for conventional fuels. This technology would not only minimize costs associated with transporting fuel from Earth but could also provide an essentially unlimited source of energy for long-duration missions to distant celestial bodies.

Quantum Drives: Conceptual Models

The notion of a quantum drive emerges from the potential of utilizing vacuum energy as a propulsion method. Conceptual models envision a spacecraft equipped with devices capable of manipulating the fabric of spacetime around it, generating thrust by altering the local vacuum energy density. This model relies on creating specific resonances that excite vacuum fluctuations, resulting in a net directional thrust.

One such proposal aligns with the concept of "warp drives," which are often discussed in the context of science fiction but rely heavily on theoretical physics. The warp drive model theorizes creating a bubble of spacetime around a spacecraft, contracting spacetime in front while expanding it behind, effectively allowing faster-than-light travel. Although purely theoretical at this stage, such concepts highlight the promising intersection between quantum mechanics and space travel optimization, inviting further inquiry into practical applications in propulsion systems.

Building a Quantum-Enabled Craft

Initiating the construction of quantum-enabled spacecraft involves addressing a cascade of technical challenges and innovative engineering solutions. A crucial aspect is developing advanced materials that can withstand the potentially extreme environmental conditions encountered in space while enabling the manipulation of quantum states effectively. The proposed aerospace materials must exhibit extraordinary properties to facilitate stability and coherence in a vacuum-driven propulsion system through precise quantum control.

Moreover, the experimental realization of such engines demands rigorous quantum mechanics understanding to effectively manipulate vacuum fluctuations for propulsion. Researchers will need to devise practical experimental models that can test these intricate concepts within terrestrial laboratories akin to the environments of deep space. These groundbreaking investigations can lay the foundation for the operational frameworks required for interstellar travel.

Overcoming Challenges and Hubris

Despite the promising prospect of utilizing the quantum vacuum, numerous challenges lay on the horizon. Continually grappling with the phenomenon of decoherence—a situation where quantum systems lose their fragile states due to interactions with their environment —remains the primary hurdle. Effective shielding techniques, which isolate quantum components from environmental disturbances, will be critical to maintaining the necessary coherence times.

Furthermore, addressing the energy requirements for generating sufficient thrust poses additional complexity. The machinery needed to tap into vacuum energy effectively must be finely tuned, necessitating breakthroughs in engineering to convert vacuum energy into usable propulsion force reliably. Additionally, there is an openness to interdisciplinary collaboration, unifying quantum physicists, aerospace engineers, and material scientists to explore and experiment with innovative methodologies.

The Role of Quantum Artificial Intelligence

Finally, the successful implementation of quantum propulsion systems would significantly benefit from incorporating quantum artificial intelligence (AI) into navigation and operational planning. Quantum AI can process vast amounts of data from onboard sensors, enhancing decision-making and optimizing trajectory management based on real-time data analysis. By harnessing the increased computational power and pattern recognition capabilities of quantum AI, navigating the complexities of gravitational interactions, optimally utilizing vacuum energy, and adjusting dynamically to unforeseen conditions becomes feasible.

Conclusion

In conclusion, the quantum vacuum presents not only a profound theoretical source of energy but also a potential turning point in the evolution of space travel. While the journey to harness this source for propulsion is fraught with challenges, the applications of manipulated vacuum energy could redefine interstellar exploration, ushering in a new era of cosmic discovery unencumbered by traditional limitations. As research progresses, continued inquiry into the nature of the quantum vacuum will not only expand our understanding of the universe but may also equip humanity with the tools necessary for traversing the infinite realms of space in ways we have yet to fully conceive. With the ambitions of humanity and the wonders of the cosmos converging, the possibilities awaiting reveal dimensions of exploration beyond our wildest dreams.

6.3. Building the First Quantum-Enabled Craft

In the era of advanced exploration, the ambition to build the first quantum-enabled craft encompasses a transformative endeavor that promises to redefine our capabilities in deep space travel. This revolutionary leap into the realm of quantum mechanics not only offers unprecedented computational power and efficiency but also poses unique challenges that will require innovative solutions to bring the vision to fruition.

To embark on this venture, we first need to comprehend the foundational principles and technologies that underpin quantum-enabled crafts. The purpose of such crafts is to leverage the powerful mechanisms of quantum mechanics—superposition, entanglement, and tunneling—to achieve propulsion, navigation, and communication in ways inconceivable with classical technology.

At the core of any quantum-enabled craft is the design of quantum propulsion systems, which harness energy fluctuations inherent in the quantum vacuum. The theoretical frameworks pointing to the utilization of vacuum energy as a propulsion method suggest a future where spacecraft can generate thrust without the burdens of conventional fuel consumption. By creating engines capable of manipulating the quantum vacuum to produce thrust, we could navigate the deep cosmos with efficiency previously deemed unattainable.

However, crafting a quantum-enabled craft culminates in more than just propulsion. The successful integration of quantum systems requires a paradigm shift in material science, engineering, and systems design. Materials capable of maintaining quantum states under the harsh conditions of space are essential, as they must withstand cosmic radiation, extreme temperatures, and other environmental pressures without allowing decoherence to compromise their operation.

To support this journey, researchers must develop sophisticated quantum circuits and computations that function effectively in the vacuum of space. Moreover, collaborations between physicists and aerospace engineers will necessitate dedicated programs and facilities to explore and fabricate the innovations capable of making quantum propulsion viable.

The ideal craft will not only possess quantum propulsion but will also integrate quantum AI for navigation and real-time decision-making. Quantum AI, informed by extensive datasets from onboard sensors, will enable the craft to adapt to dynamic environments, optimize routes with precision, and make autonomous decisions when communication delays with Earth hinder immediate responses necessary for mission success. This technological integration could fundamentally change how humanity approaches deep space exploration, allowing for responsive and intelligent systems capable of maneuvering through complex gravitational fields and adapting to unforeseen challenges.

As we envision the first quantum-enabled craft, we also encounter a series of technological constraints that must be overcome. Key challenges include enhancing qubit coherence, creating fault-tolerant quantum systems, and ensuring effective error correction algorithms that can operate under the extreme conditions of space travel. Continuous research into mitigating decoherence—the loss of quantum state coherence due to environmental interactions—folds prominently into this equation, necessitating innovative shielding techniques and robust materials.

Additionally, the specifics of power management become critical when building a quantum spacecraft. Effective energy management systems will need to be responsive to fluctuations in energy demands during propulsion and navigation phases, while also taking into account the need for stability in powering quantum computational elements and other onboard instruments.

Beyond the engineering challenges, the ethical implications of utilizing advanced quantum technologies in space exploration must be addressed. As we push the boundaries of what is possible, considerations surrounding the responsible use of quantum advancements, the potential impact on international regulations regarding space travel, and the ethical dilemmas posed by interstellar exploration warrant diligent attention.

In this new chapter of human exploration, the construction of the first quantum-enabled craft symbolizes not merely a technological breakthrough but a profound commitment to embracing the future. It calls for collaborative efforts among scientists, engineers, ethicists, and policymakers to chart a course that ensures our ambitions align harmoniously with our responsibilities as stewards of the universe.

Ultimately, as we navigate the complexities of building quantum-enabled crafts, we stand on the precipice of a bold new journey into the unknown. The fusion of quantum mechanics with aerospace engineering possesses the potential to turn our aspirations into reality, granting us the capabilities to traverse the cosmos in ways that will inspire generations to come. With every step taken, we inch closer to unlocking new dimensions of existence—perpetually reaching for the stars and unveiling the mysteries that await us in the vast expanse of the universe.

6.4. Overcoming the Technological Constraints
Overcoming the Technological Constraints

As the ambition of integrating quantum computing into deep space exploration advances, the technological constraints that emerge must be systematically addressed. The quantum realm, while holding profound promise for transforming our understanding of the universe, presents numerous challenges that complicate its practical application in harsh and unpredictable environments. Harnessing the power of quantum mechanics, particularly in space, requires a multifaceted approach to developing resilient, efficient, and reliable systems.

One of the primary challenges confronting the endeavor to establish quantum computing in space is the phenomenon of decoherence. Quantum states, which are fundamentally delicate, can easily lose their integrity when exposed to environmental noise and disturbances. In the depths of space—where radiation levels are high, temperatures fluctuate drastically, and vacuum conditions prevail—maintaining coherent quantum states becomes a formidable task. To counteract these effects, researchers must innovate in the realm of materials science, developing advanced quantum devices that can effectively isolate qubits from the influences of their surroundings.

Shielding quantum systems from cosmic radiation becomes a pressing priority, as particles from solar flares and other cosmic events can induce unwanted interactions with qubits. Engineers may explore the use of advanced materials that absorb or deflect radiation, or new shielding techniques that could enhance the resilience of quantum systems. Additionally, operational strategies, such as employing redundancy in quantum circuit designs, can help fortify systems against the inevitable uncertainties that arise in the space environment.

The second significant constraint arises from the challenges associated with long-distance communication in quantum networks. While the allure of instantaneous communication via entangled particles tantalizes scientists and engineers alike, practical implementations often face limitations due to the loss of entanglement over distance. The development of robust quantum repeaters that can maintain entanglement and amplify signals is essential to establishing interstellar quantum communication networks. Such repeaters would enable the creation of a quantum internet across the cosmos, allowing for continuous and secure communications between Earth and distant spacecraft.

Creating an interstellar communication framework also entails addressing bandwidth limitations and ensuring that the data transmitted can be processed effectively. Quantum sensors and systems onboard spacecraft must be capable of handling high throughputs while maintaining the integrity of quantum information. Innovations in data compression techniques, coupled with advancements in quantum data retrieval and processing, will be pivotal to improving the efficiency of quantum communications within space exploration protocols.

Furthermore, the intricacies of system calibration must also be navigated when deploying quantum computing in space. Ensuring that quantum systems retain their functionality at extreme distances poses considerable challenges. Regular calibration routines, especially for onboard quantum sensors and devices, are essential for maintaining accuracy and reliability throughout missions. The use of autonomous calibration algorithms could facilitate real-time adjustments during operation, ensuring that the quantum systems adapt dynamically to changing environmental conditions.

Temperature extremes in space additionally complicate the deployment of quantum technologies, particularly those reliant on superconducting qubits, which operate at cryogenic temperatures. The implementation of advanced thermal insulation and control strategies becomes crucial to preserving the quantum state over the timeline of deep space missions. Researchers might further explore alternative qubit technologies capable of functioning at higher temperatures to mitigate the challenges associated with maintaining cooling systems in space.

Collaboration across disciplines is fundamental to overcoming these technological constraints. Within the academic, governmental, and industrial sectors, aligning expertise on quantum mechanics, materials science, and aerospace engineering will facilitate breakthroughs that can enhance our capacity for quantum applications in space. The engagement of global initiatives and partnerships can foster knowledge exchange, drive innovation, and collectively tackle the challenges faced in interstellar exploration.

As we strive to integrate quantum computing into our space missions, there lies an imperative to develop ethical frameworks that guide the use of these technologies. The responsible deployment of quantum-driven systems necessitates addressing concerns surrounding privacy, data security, and the potential impacts of quantum advancements on society. A candid dialogue among researchers, policymakers, and the public must occur to navigate the long-term implications of quantum technologies in our quest to understand the cosmos.

In sum, while the path to overcoming the technological constraints intertwined with quantum computing in space exploration is multifaceted and riddled with challenges, it simultaneously offers a vibrant landscape for innovation and discovery. The interplay between ingenuity and adversity sets the stage for transformative advancements that can redefine humanity's role in the cosmos. By championing interdisciplinary collaboration and addressing the intricacies of quantum technologies head-on, we stand on the brink of an extraordinary journey—one that not only propels us deeper into the universe but also impels us to rethink our understanding of existence itself. As we endeavor to unleash the full potential of quantum computing and its myriad applications in deep space, we embody not only the scientific spirit of inquiry but the innate human desire to explore the unknown and transcend the boundaries of possibility.

6.5. The Role of Quantum AI in Navigation

In the rapidly evolving field of space exploration, the integration of quantum artificial intelligence (AI) into navigation systems encapsulates a transformative potential that could reshape humanity's journey into the cosmos. Quantum AI stands at the intersection of quantum computing and machine learning, leveraging the principles of quantum mechanics to process vast datasets and enhance decision-making processes. This technology promises to augment navigation capabilities in a way that classical systems cannot achieve, granting spacecraft the ability to respond dynamically to unpredictable conditions and effectively chart their courses through the complexities of deep space.

At its core, quantum AI relies on qubits—quantum bits that can exist in multiple states simultaneously thanks to superposition. This property allows quantum algorithms to simultaneously evaluate numerous potential trajectories, optimizing navigational pathways during a mission. Traditional AI systems, confined to classical bits, process information sequentially; conversely, quantum AI can analyze multiple outcomes instantaneously, drastically reducing computational time and maximizing efficiency in navigation protocols.

For example, when planning the trajectory of a spacecraft, quantum AI can utilize the principles of quantum optimization algorithms to evaluate the gravitational influences of celestial bodies and calculate the most efficient routes in real-time. By processing data about gravitational fields, fuel consumption, and potential hazards, quantum navigation systems can develop adaptive flight paths that respond to changing environmental conditions, ensuring that missions remain on course even as circumstances evolve.

Furthermore, the integration of quantum AI extends beyond mere route calculation. Autonomous navigation systems powered by quantum algorithms can facilitate more robust decision-making processes during critical phases of a mission, such as takeoff, in-flight adjustments, and landing procedures. In scenarios where communication with Earth might encounter delays—due to vast distances or various interferences—quantum AI enables spacecraft to make instantaneous decisions based on pre-processed simulations and real-time data collected from onboard sensors. This capability is invaluable for missions venturing into uncharted territories, where human oversight may be impractical or insufficient.

Moreover, the advent of quantum AI in navigation enhances safety protocols by enabling proactive hazard detection. Quantum sensors, utilized in conjunction with quantum AI, can detect potential threats such as gravitational anomalies or unexpected debris fields with heightened sensitivity. The data generated through these advanced sensors can be analyzed promptly, allowing for calibrated responses that can prevent accidents and critical failures during missions.

As we consider the potential of quantum AI in navigation, it is vital to acknowledge the challenges that lie ahead. The successful deployment of quantum navigation systems necessitates navigating complexities such as ensuring qubit coherence amidst environmental disturbances, developing scalable systems that can operate reliably in the harsh conditions of space, and addressing the intricate calibration of quantum sensors trained on diverse cosmic phenomena.

Additionally, the ethical implications surrounding the utilization of quantum AI in space operations must not be overlooked. There is a pressing need to consider the interactions between autonomous systems and human oversight, ensuring that ethical standards guide the development and deployment of AI technologies in deep space. Awareness of biases in AI algorithms, accountability for decisions made by autonomous systems, and the transparency in how data is collected, processed, and utilized will be paramount as we venture further into the unknown.

Looking ahead, the role of quantum AI in navigation promises to be pivotal not just for individual missions but for the broader exploration of our solar system and beyond. As humanity continues to push the boundaries of discovery, the integration of quantum technologies into navigational protocols will enhance our capability to traverse the cosmos effectively, enabling missions that unlock the mysteries of the universe.

In summary, the fusion of quantum AI with navigation systems represents a novel evolution in space exploration, one characterized by enhanced decision-making, autonomous capabilities, and real-time adaptability. As we embark on this remarkable journey, the challenges will be matched by extraordinary opportunities. Embracing these technologies will propel us to new frontiers, allowing humanity to navigate the vast expanse of space with unprecedented precision and insight—a truly quantum leap into the future of cosmic exploration.

7. Quantum Networking Across the Cosmos

7.1. Interstellar Quantum Networks

In the realm of deep space exploration, the emergence of interstellar quantum networks presents a paradigm shift in how we envision communication and data transmission across vast cosmic distances. These pioneering systems leverage the principles of quantum mechanics, particularly entanglement, to enable instantaneous, high-fidelity data exchange that transcends the limitations imposed by classical communication methods. This subchapter delves into the intricacies of interstellar quantum networks, exploring their design, implementation, and transformative implications for our capacity to interact with and explore the cosmos.

The foundation of an interstellar quantum network lies in quantum entanglement—an enigmatic phenomenon where qubits become interconnected in such a way that the state of one instantly correlates with the state of another, regardless of the distance separating them. This extraordinary property enables the potential for instantaneous communication across vast distances, challenging our classical understanding of information transmission, which is constrained by the speed of light. By utilizing entangled particles, we can establish a form of communication that appears to occur outside the normal temporal and spatial limitations.

Designing an interstellar quantum network requires meticulous planning and innovative engineering. The network would be constructed around distributed quantum nodes—satellites equipped with advanced quantum communication capabilities that generate, maintain, and distribute entangled states. These nodes would serve as relay stations, enabling secure and reliable data exchange between distant points in space, including spacecraft exploring other celestial bodies and mission control centers on Earth. Each node would need to be equipped with sophisticated quantum sensors capable of preparing, manipulating, and measuring quantum states, ensuring that entanglement remains intact even amidst the challenges posed by the cosmic environment.

One critical component of developing an interstellar quantum network is the creation of quantum repeaters. These devices are essential for amplifying entangled states over long distances and mitigating the loss of entanglement that occurs due to noise and decoherence. Quantum repeaters utilize entanglement swapping, a method that allows pairs of entangled particles to be linked indirectly through intermediary particles, effectively extending the distance over which entanglement can be maintained. As teams work to construct these repeaters, they must consider the operational parameters required to maintain coherence while integrating efficient error correction mechanisms.

Moreover, the development of interstellar quantum networks is not purely a technical undertaking; it also raises significant ethical considerations. As we forge ahead into a future where quantum communication underpins our deep space explorations, we must grapple with implications surrounding data security, privacy, and access. The entangled nature of quantum data necessitates robust encryption protocols to protect sensitive information transmitted through these networks. Quantum key distribution (QKD), built on the principles of quantum mechanics, offers a method for generating secure encryption keys, ensuring that data remains safeguarded from potential eavesdroppers who might attempt to intercept communications across light-years.

While the prospect of interstellar quantum networks is tantalizing, several challenges loom large. The realities of deploying such a network in the harsh conditions of space—where temperature extremes, cosmic radiation, and gravitational forces can disrupt delicate quantum states—underscore the need for robust engineering solutions. Advanced materials capable of protecting quantum components from external influences must be explored, alongside techniques for managing decoherence. Developing efficient cooling systems and shielding mechanisms will be essential as we aim to maintain the delicate conditions necessary for successful quantum communication.

Furthermore, achieving functioning interstellar quantum networks necessitates interdisciplinary collaboration among physicists, engineers, computer scientists, and ethicists. The complexity of deploying quantum communication systems across vast distances creates a need for integrated approaches that draw upon the strengths of each discipline. Global cooperation will be instrumental in navigating the obstacles posed by integrating quantum technologies into existing communication infrastructures—ultimately fostering a new era of interconnectedness within our cosmic aspirations.

As we embark on this ambitious quest to build interstellar quantum networks, we must also envision the future applications these systems might enable. With secure, rapid communication links, mission control could collate real-time data from distant spacecraft, enhancing scientific understanding and decision-making. Interstellar probes gathering insights from remote celestial bodies could transmit findings instantaneously, leading to collaborative analysis and exploration efforts between astronauts, scientists, and researchers worldwide.

In summary, interstellar quantum networks embody a remarkable confluence of quantum mechanics and space exploration. By harnessing the principles of entanglement and leveraging cutting-edge technologies, these networks promise to revolutionize communication across the cosmos, ushering in an era defined by rapid, secure, and reliable data exchange. The journey toward establishing interstellar quantum networks will undoubtedly pose significant challenges, but the potential rewards—transforming our understanding of the universe and enhancing our exploratory ambitions—make it an endeavor worthy of our most profound scientific and engineering efforts. Through this endeavor, we not only seek to unveil the mysteries of the cosmos but also to redefine the very fabric of communication in our quest to explore the infinite dimensions of space.

7.2. The Power of Entanglement in Communications

In the vast arena of communication technologies, quantum entanglement emerges as an unprecedented phenomenon, opening the doorway to a realm where distance and time intermingle in ways that challenge our conventional understanding. While classical communication relies on electromagnetic signals that traverse space at the finite speed of light, quantum entanglement presents the tantalizing possibility of instantaneous information transfer, effectively allowing us to rethink the fundamental limits of communication. Within this framework, entangled communication not only redefines how we share data across expansive distances but also holds the potential to revolutionize exploration endeavors in deep space.

At the heart of quantum entanglement is the idea that once two particles become entangled, their properties are interlinked regardless of the distance that separates them. This intrigue stems from the fact that a measurement performed on one particle instantaneously affects the state of the other particle, creating correlations that classical mechanics deems impossible. In practical terms, this supernatural connectivity implies that a signal transmitted via entangled particles could be instantly observed by a recipient on the opposite side of the cosmos, ushering in a paradigm shift in interstellar communication. Unlike classical methods that encounter delays due to the finite speed of light, the instantaneous nature of entanglement raises questions about the coherence of data transmission across vast interstellar distances.

Establishing an entangled communication network in deep space requires the construction of sophisticated quantum nodes—satellites or relay stations endowed with quantum mechanics capabilities that generate, maintain, and distribute entangled states. These nodes could operate collaboratively, forming a highly interconnected communication system capable of relaying information between spacecraft exploring distant celestial realms and mission control on Earth. The challenge lies in maintaining the integrity of entangled states while ensuring scalability across immense distances.

The implementation of quantum repeaters is a critical component in deploying entangled communication systems. Quantum repeaters work to extend the distance over which entanglement can be preserved, compensating for the decoherence that diminishes entangled states. Utilizing a process known as entanglement swapping, repeaters can create pairs of entangled qubits that are distant from one another through intermediary particles, amplifying the entanglement across long stretches of space. Developing efficient quantum repeaters will be fundamental in facilitating real-time communications that amplify the speed at which data is shared between deep space assets.

Moreover, the security advantages presented by entangled communication cannot be understated. The unique characteristics of quantum states allow for the establishment of ultra-secure transmission protocols, as any interception or measurement of the quantum state would irreversibly alter it, thereby revealing the presence of an eavesdropper. Quantum key distribution (QKD)—a technique grounded in the principles of quantum mechanics—provides a means of securely transmitting encryption keys between parties, ensuring that information exchanged across deep space communications remains shielded from potential threats.

As we gaze toward the horizon of deep space exploration, the prospect of entangled communication systems unfolds the promise of enhanced data transfer, rapid response capabilities, and improved decision-making processes in missions. However, practical challenges remain that must be surmounted. The establishment of stable and scalable entangled states necessitates significant advancements in materials science, engineering innovations, and a thorough understanding of quantum mechanics. Protecting quantum systems from decoherence—heightened by the radiation and unpredictable environments found in space—is an ongoing priority that requires deploying advanced shielding technologies and exploring robust techniques for maintaining coherence.

Additionally, while technical hurdles are prevalent, ethical dilemmas surrounding the implementation of such technology must also be considered. As entangled communication resources become essential for human endeavors in the cosmos, questions concerning access, equity, and the societal implications of employing such advanced technologies must be integrated into policy discussions and regulations guiding space activities.

In conclusion, the integration of entanglement in communications marks a transformative moment that heralds potential breakthroughs in our approach to deep space exploration. By harnessing the concept of entangled states, we can reshape the boundaries of information sharing, enabling secure and instantaneous communication that defies classical limitations. As researchers innovate to create sustainable quantum communication frameworks, we stand poised to fundamentally alter humanity's relationship with the cosmos. Embracing this extraordinary opportunity will pave the way for unprecedented discoveries and a deeper understanding of the universe we inhabit—one where connections extend far beyond spatial confines, celebrating the uncharted territories waiting to be explored.

Entangled communication within this evolving paradigm not only propels us toward a future enriched with insight and knowledge but also challenges us to think critically about the responsibilities we hold as explorers, innovators, and stewards of the boundless expanse that lies before us. The journey into deep space is not merely a quest for knowledge, but an opportunity to engage with the very essence of quantum reality, where every breakthrough reaffirms our commitment to unraveling the mysteries that connect us to the universe.

7.3. Challenges of Cosmic Data Transmission

The vastness of space presents unique challenges for data transmission, particularly in the context of quantum communication and computing. As humanity aims to extend its reach into the cosmos, understanding and overcoming these challenges will be crucial for the success of deep space missions and the development of interstellar networks. The essence of these challenges lies in the intricate nature of quantum mechanics, the limitations of current technologies, and the unpredictable environment of outer space.

One of the most profound issues in cosmic data transmission is the fundamental principle of quantum mechanics itself—specifically, the phenomenon of decoherence. As quantum systems interact with their environment, they can lose their quantum properties, which are critical for maintaining the integrity of quantum states, such as super-position and entanglement. In the harsh conditions of space, cosmic radiation and extreme temperatures can exacerbate decoherence, potentially leading to the catastrophic failure of quantum communications. Engineers will need to develop robust shielding methods and advanced materials that can protect quantum chips and entangled states from these environmental challenges.

Furthermore, the distances involved in deep space exploration introduce additional obstacles. The speed of light, while a constant source of transmission for classical communications, imposes a delay in the transmission of data over interstellar distances. Quantum communication theoretically promises instantaneous data transfer through entangled states, yet creating a practical application of this principle at scale is still a goal on the horizon. Quantum repeaters will be essential in extending the reach of quantum networks, allowing the relay of entangled information across vast distances. Designing these repeaters will require innovative approaches to sustain entanglement over longer stretches, ensuring that cosmic data transmission can happen reliably and efficiently.

Another significant challenge is the synchronization of quantum states across potentially vast networks. Quantum systems rely on precise coordination for optimal performance, and maintaining syn-chronization among numerous interstellar quantum nodes poses complex logistical and engineering considerations. Researchers will need to explore efficient methodologies for timekeeping and state preparation, ensuring that entangled qubits can be accurately measured and that the systems can operate coherently across the network.

Additionally, the aspect of data integrity and security in quantum communication presents its own set of challenges. While quantum key distribution (QKD) offers enhanced security against eavesdropping, it necessitates the establishment of secure connections that are free from external interference during transmission. The potential for interruptions in quantum channels due to cosmic phenomena or environmental factors places added pressure on communication protocols, forcing developers to create resilient systems capable of maintaining data integrity even in less-than-ideal conditions.

Moreover, we must anticipate the complexities of data processing once the information is received on Earth. The vast amount of data that could be transmitted from distant cosmic events will require sophisticated algorithms and high-performance computing systems to analyze and interpret. The integration of quantum computing capabilities for processing this data will be vital, representing another layer of challenge in terms of coordinating and synchronizing quantum operations while ensuring the algorithms used can handle the scale and complexity of astronomical data.

As we look to the future of quantum data transmission in space, we should also embrace the myriad of opportunities that arise alongside these challenges. The promise of quantum networking systems enables not only the ability to communicate across light-years but also the potential to craft a coherent approach to data gathering and analysis that redefines our exploration of the cosmos. Realizing such systems may pave the way for an interconnected web of spacecraft and observatories that can share information seamlessly, drastically improving our collective understanding of celestial phenomena.

In cultivating these technologies, interdisciplinary collaboration between physicists, engineers, aerospace experts, and quantum computing specialists will be essential. As we confront the obstacles of cosmic data transmission and explore new pathways for communication, embracing a holistic, cooperative approach will lead to advancements that can elevate our ambitious explorations.

In conclusion, the challenges of cosmic data transmission embody the complexities inherent in merging quantum mechanics with space exploration. These challenges, ranging from decoherence to synchronization and security, serve as potent reminders of the intricacies of operating in the vast reaches of space. However, they also illuminate the immense potential that arises as we grapple with these issues, paving the way for innovative solutions that extend our capabilities for interstellar communication and scientific discovery. By diligently addressing these challenges, humanity stands poised to unlock the mysteries of the cosmos, forging connections across the infinite expanse of space.

7.4. Building a Quantum Internet in Space

In our pursuit of harnessing quantum technologies for space exploration, the construction of a quantum internet in space is an ambitious venture that holds transformative potential. This endeavor represents not just a leap in communication technology, but a fundamental shift in how we interact with the cosmos and a means to orchestrate complex operations across vast distances. Building a quantum internet involves interconnecting quantum devices through a network that utilizes the principles of quantum mechanics, particularly entanglement and superposition, to ensure secure and instantaneous data transmission.

To lay the groundwork for developing a quantum internet in space, several key components must be addressed. First, the creation of quantum communication nodes, akin to classical internet nodes, is essential. These nodes will serve as relay stations disseminating quantum signals across the network, connecting multiple spacecraft and ground stations on Earth. The nodes must be equipped with advanced quantum processors capable of producing, maintaining, and entangling qubits, thereby enabling reliable communication links.

The backbone of the quantum internet is built on entanglement—an extraordinary phenomenon wherein qubits become interconnected in such a way that the state of one qubit instantaneously impacts the state of another, regardless of distance. This property not only offers the potential for faster communication but also provides unprecedented security. Any attempt to eavesdrop or intercept quantum data would disturb the quantum state, alerting the communicating parties to the intrusion. Embedding this layer of security into interstellar communication will be crucial, as the exchange of scientific data and sensitive mission information from remote space missions is paramount.

Moreover, maintaining entanglement over astronomical distances poses significant challenges. Quantum repeaters will be necessary to extend the reach of entangled signals and mitigate the loss of entanglement over long distances. These devices will work by employing techniques such as entanglement swapping, effectively enabling an entangled link to traverse segments of the network while circumventing the constraints imposed by decoherence. Developing a robust network of quantum repeaters that can function reliably in the unpredictable environment of space is essential for the successful deployment of a quantum internet.

Once established, a quantum internet will provide revolutionary enhancements to deep space missions. For instance, quantum sensors equipped with entangled quantum communication capabilities can transmit data instantaneously back to mission control, allowing for real-time updates from distant space probes and enhancing our understanding of cosmic phenomena. The ability to communicate securely and quickly across vast distances will facilitate a framework for collaborative scientific exploration, enabling multiple teams across Earth and distant celestial bodies to coordinate efforts and share findings efficiently.

Further, the quantum internet will elevate monitoring capabilities essential for interstellar missions. Spacecraft equipped with quantum-assisted communication can relay complex data about gravitational fields, environmental conditions, and potential hazards, enabling autonomous adjustments to trajectories in response to real-time information. This responsiveness becomes crucial in unknown environments where safety and precision are paramount.

However, the journey to build a quantum internet in space is fraught with challenges, many of which hinge on overcoming technical limitations associated with quantum technology. Protecting qubits from decoherence while ensuring consistent operation of quantum systems in the dynamic conditions of space will require ongoing research and innovations. Novel materials and shielding strategies must be developed to encompass quantum devices, fortifying them against cosmic radiation and environmental fluctuations.

Furthermore, the ethical and regulatory considerations surrounding a quantum internet in space must be addressed. As we extend our capabilities into the cosmos, forming a shared understanding of the laws governing quantum communications—amidst broader discussions about privacy, security, and accessibility—will be crucial. Ensuring that the quantum infrastructure serves all aspects of humanity reflects a commitment to responsible exploration, emphasizing collaboration over competition.

In essence, the construction of a quantum internet in space embodies the spirit of exploration that drives humanity forward. It connects the complexities of quantum mechanics with our innate desire to discover and understand the universe. By seamlessly interlinking spacecraft, ground stations, and scientific communities, this quantum network can revolutionize communication, enhance our capacity for exploration, and ultimately deepen our connection with the cosmos. As we embark on this extraordinary journey, we open pathways toward new dimensions of inquiry, unraveling the mysteries of existence itself as we push boundaries in both technology and human understanding. The vision of a robust quantum internet extends beyond mere communication; it signifies our commitment to pioneering an interconnected future, inviting humanity to embrace the infinite possibilities awaiting us in the vast expanse of space.

7.5. Interplanetary Data Nodes

In the expansive framework of space exploration, interplanetary data nodes represent a pivotal innovation that merges quantum computing with advanced communication systems, establishing decentralized hubs for information processing and dissemination across vast cosmic distances. These nodes, operating on the principles of quantum mechanics, are designed to enhance our capabilities for data manipulation, storage, and transmission, laying the groundwork for a future where humanity can interact with the universe more efficiently and securely than ever before.

At the core of the concept of interplanetary data nodes is the deployment of quantum communication technology, which utilizes the phenomena of quantum entanglement and superposition to facilitate instantaneous data exchanges across light-years. Imagine a network of satellites or spaceborne relay stations strategically positioned throughout the solar system, each equipped with quantum communication capabilities that enable them to both generate and maintain entangled quantum states. These nodes will serve as critical data hubs, collecting and transmitting astronomical information from deep space missions back to Earth, while simultaneously communicating with one another to ensure seamless connectivity and data integrity.

The advantages of utilizing such quantum data nodes for interplanetary communications are immense. One of the fundamental benefits is the inherent security provided by quantum key distribution (QKD), a method that secures communication by making any attempt to eavesdrop on quantum states detectable. In a universe where sensitive data regarding exploratory missions and scientific discoveries must be protected, interplanetary data nodes will help safeguard this information against potentially malicious entities that seek to intercept or manipulate communications across space.

Moreover, these nodes will operate autonomously, leveraging quantum artificial intelligence (AI) to optimize data management and processing. Quantum AI will be instrumental in evaluating vast datasets generated by spacecraft and telescopes, diagnosing potential issues, and adapting to changing mission parameters in real-time. This degree of autonomy significantly reduces the need for constant communication with Earth, allowing interplanetary missions the flexibility and responsiveness necessary for navigating the uncertainties of space exploration.

However, building interplanetary data nodes mandates overcoming numerous technological challenges. First and foremost, the phenomena of decoherence—a situation in which quantum states lose their fidelity due to environmental interactions—poses a substantial risk to maintaining entangled states during data transmission. As these nodes operate in the alien environments of space, engineers and scientists must develop innovative materials and systems capable of protecting quantum states from cosmic radiation and extreme temperatures. A rigorous focus on the engineering aspects of quantum devices will be essential to ensure their reliability in the unforgiving conditions of deep space.

Additionally, scalability is a vital consideration when designing interplanetary data nodes. Establishing a robust network that can accommodate multiple spacecraft and observatories requires careful planning and coordination. Implementing quantum repeaters within the network architecture will amplify and maintain entangled states over long distances, ensuring that data can be effectively disseminated across vast expanses while countering the challenges of signal degradation.

Furthermore, the operational protocols must be developed to govern the interactions between nodes, managing how they share data, react to new information, and adapt to unexpected challenges. A coherent framework that facilitates seamless communication between the nodes will amplify their effectiveness, allowing for swift collaboration among scientists, engineers, and mission planners when interpreting astronomical data from distant sources.

Ethical considerations also play a critical role in the development of interplanetary data nodes, raising questions around privacy, equity of access, and the sustainability of quantum technologies. As quantum capabilities revolutionize our ability to collect and analyze cosmic data, it is vital to ensure that these advancements are deployed responsibly, allowing for broad access to the tools and insights generated within the quantum domain.

In summary, interplanetary data nodes signify an unprecedented development in the realm of space exploration, intertwining quantum communication with advanced data systems to enable robust and secure interactions across the cosmos. As humanity sets forth on this ambitious journey, the integration of these nodes into our missions will enhance our ability to explore the universe, providing the potential for rapid, reliable, and secure data transmission that transcends the limitations of classical communication technologies. By continuing to confront the technological challenges inherent in establishing interplanetary data nodes and fostering ethical discussions around their deployment, we will uncover new dimensions of understanding in our quest to explore the boundless reaches of space. These nodes embody not just a technological innovation but a glimpse into the future of how we engage with the cosmos, potentially revolutionizing our approach to scientific discovery and exploration.

8. Quantum Sensor Applications in Space Exploration

8.1. Detecting Remote Cosmic Events

In the modern scientific quest to understand and map the cosmos, the ability to detect remote cosmic events stands as a pinnacle challenge. The vastness of space is filled with extraordinary phenomena—some fleeting and others enduring—ranging from supernova explosions and gamma-ray bursts to gravitational waves from colliding black holes. Traditionally, our ability to observe and capture these events has relied on a variety of classical and terrestrial sensors, often limited by the astronomical distance and intervening cosmic obscuration. However, with the innovations in quantum computing and the advent of quantum sensors, we find ourselves on the cusp of a new era in our exploration and understanding of these remote cosmic occurrences.

Quantum sensors, leveraging the principles of quantum mechanics, offer enhanced sensitivity and accuracy that far surpasses classical measurement techniques. One striking feature of these sensors is their capability to exploit quantum entanglement, which enables them to detect and measure incredibly subtle variations in space without the interference that affects classical systems. For instance, when detecting gravitational waves—ripples in spacetime caused by massive astronomical events—quantum sensors can achieve a sensitivity level that dramatically improves our chances of observing these elusive signals amidst the noise of cosmic radiation.

To illustrate, consider the potential of using quantum-enhanced interferometers for gravitational wave detection. By employing entangled photon pairs in an interferometry setup, researchers could supersede the standard quantum limit of sensitivity, allowing them to register gravitational waves from events occurring billions of light-years away. This is not merely theoretical; experiments designed to test these capabilities are already underway, demonstrating the profound power of quantum sensors in capturing cosmic signals previously deemed too faint.

Additionally, quantum sensors equipped with atomic interferometry represent another promising avenue for detecting remote cosmic events. These sensors manipulate cold atoms to create interference patterns sensitive to minuscule changes in gravitational fields or electromagnetic forces. Such sensitivity can lead to a new understanding of the dynamics of celestial bodies and their interactions. When deployed in deep space, these sensors can effectively monitor the influence of gravitational fields on spacecraft, providing data critical for navigating amidst the complex gravitational interactions of planets, moons, and asteroids.

The capacity of quantum sensors to provide precise measurements extends beyond gravitational waves and cosmic structures; they also contribute to the investigation of dark matter and dark energy—the elusive substances that make up most of the universe's mass-energy content. By capturing and analyzing interactions between dark matter particles and standard matter, quantum sensors could unveil the fundamental underpinnings of these cosmic mysteries. Innovative designs could lead to detectors capable of measuring the faintest signatures of dark matter, illuminating new paths for cosmological research and deepening our understanding of the universe's composition.

Furthermore, the combination of quantum sensors with advanced machine learning algorithms paves the way for analyzing the vast magnitude of data generated from cosmic observations. By employing quantum-enhanced AI, data processing capabilities can expeditiously sift through enormous datasets to identify patterns and correlations, enabling a faster and more accurate interpretation of remote cosmic events. These neural networks, augmented by quantum computations, adaptively learn to recognize and categorize cosmic phenomena, ultimately translating raw data into actionable scientific insights.

However, integrating quantum sensors into space missions requires careful design and engineering. Addressing practical challenges such as shielding the sensors from cosmic radiation and temperature variations is essential. Quantum sensors must maintain coherence in their delicate quantum states, necessitating advanced materials and designs to ensure resilience in the unforgiving environments of space.

Further considerations revolve around the decision-making processes involved in missions that deploy these quantum sensors. Real-time data transmission back to Earth must be executed efficiently, utilizing the principles of quantum communication to relay time-sensitive information seamlessly. The phenomenon of quantum key distribution (QKD) could be harnessed to secure this data, protecting the integrity of the information transmitted from distant spaces.

In summary, the potential for quantum sensors to detect remote cosmic events marks a transformative leap in our ability to explore and understand the universe. By harnessing the profound intricacies of quantum mechanics, these advanced instruments can unlock new dimensions of investigation into gravitational waves, dark matter, and other cosmic phenomena that remain shrouded in mystery. As we delve deeper into the cosmos with quantum technology, we stand poised not only to witness distant events but to unravel the very laws governing the universe. This journey into quantum detection promises to reshape our scientific paradigms and inspire further inquiries into the unknown, illuminating the intricate dance of existence within the vast expanse of space.

8.2. Mapping Dark Matter and Energy

In our journey to unravel the mysteries of the cosmos, understanding dark matter and dark energy remains one of the most formidable challenges confronting modern astrophysics. Although they constitute approximately 95% of the universe's total mass-energy content, their elusive nature has defied direct detection, rendering them some of the greatest enigmas in cosmology. However, leveraging quantum computing techniques presents a groundbreaking opportunity to decode these cosmic phenomena and enhance our comprehension of the universe at large.

The first crucial step in mapping dark matter and energy lies in the inherent properties of dark matter itself. Predominated by its gravitational effects, dark matter does not interact with electromagnetic forces, making it invisible to conventional observational tools. Existing surveys of the cosmic microwave background radiation and the large-scale structure of the universe provide indirect evidence for its presence, yet much about its true nature remains elusive. Quantum simulations present a unique avenue to model the interactions of dark matter particles and their gravitational influences upon visible matter. These simulations can offer insights into the spatial distribution of dark matter, illuminating how it shapes the structure of galaxies and galactic clusters.

Furthermore, the advantages of quantum superposition and entanglement allow researchers to explore a multitude of scenarios in parallel. By harnessing the computational power of quantum systems, we can create complex models of dark matter dynamics that evolve over time, accounting for various interactions and behaviors that would be computationally prohibitive through classical means. Such modeling informs our understanding of galaxy formation and evolution, revealing how dark matter plays a pivotal role in shaping the observable universe.

Dark energy, which is thought to drive the accelerated expansion of the universe, poses another layer of complexity. Despite being classified as a constant in Einstein's cosmological model, its underlying mechanics remain poorly understood, leading to intense speculation about its true nature. Quantum mechanics provides tools to probe potential explanations, from modifications of general relativity to the existence of new fields or particles. Quantum simulations can help test these models while facilitating novel theoretical frameworks that could explain the nature of dark energy and its implications for the cosmos.

For instance, researchers can employ quantum simulations to explore the concept of "vacuum energy" within quantum field theory as a potential source of dark energy. Encoding models of spacetime dynamics and evaluating their outcomes in a quantum system allows physicists to ascertain whether such descriptions align with astronomical observations, lending insight into the cosmic landscape that dark energy resides within.

Moreover, utilizing quantum-enhanced sensors represents a contemporary strategy for mapping dark matter and dark energy. By deploying quantum sensors in space, we can hone our ability to detect gravitational waves and gravitational lensing events associated with dark matter distribution. Quantum sensors operate with exceptional sensitivity, enabling detection of minute changes in gravitational fields that may provide indirect but crucial evidence for dark matter.

The interplay between these advanced quantum technologies and our celestial observations creates a synergistic relationship, unlocking a deeper understanding of cosmic phenomena. As we gather increasingly detailed data regarding galaxy formation, structure, and expansion, quantum computing facilitates the formulation and testing of hypotheses, driving a cycle of inquiry that fuels scientific discovery.

While the theoretical and technological groundwork for mapping dark matter and energy is promising, challenges persist. These include securing funding for quantum research initiatives, developing robust algorithms for quantum data analysis, and managing the uncertainties associated with quantum decoherence in space environments.

In conclusion, the integration of quantum computing techniques into the cosmological investigation of dark matter and dark energy marks a pivotal advancement in contemporary astrophysics. By leveraging the strengths of quantum systems, we can refine our models, conduct simulations that embrace the intricacies of these cosmic enigmas, and meaningfully enhance our understanding of the universe. As we strive to unravel the mysteries embedded within the very fabric of existence, the confluence of quantum mechanics and cosmological inquiry will undoubtedly illuminate the path forward, suggesting new dimensions waiting to be unveiled amid the cosmos. This quantum exploration will not only enrich our scientific knowledge but may also redefine our place in the universe as we tread further into the depths of its mysteries.

8.3. Quantum Clocks and Precision Navigation

In the pursuit of understanding the vastness of space, quantum clocks —a manifestation of quantum mechanics—play an increasingly pivotal role, particularly in precision navigation. As we venture deeper into the universe, the limitations of traditional navigation methods become evident. The immense distances involved, combined with the need for accurate timing, prompt a fundamental shift toward quantum technology, offering extraordinary precision and enhancing our navigational capabilities.

At the heart of quantum clocks lies the unique behavior of atoms and subatomic particles governed by quantum mechanics. Traditional clocks often rely on the oscillation of mechanical components or the steady vibrations of atoms. In contrast, quantum clocks exploit the quantum states of atoms, particularly those of highly stable isotopes, which oscillate at frequencies determined by fundamental physical constants. These clocks utilize the transitions between energy levels in atoms—such as cesium or strontium—as their timekeeping mechanism, leading to remarkable levels of accuracy.

One of the most impressive features of quantum clocks is their stability. They can maintain extremely consistent frequency standards, deviating by mere fractions of seconds over extended periods. This remarkable precision is vital for navigating through the unpredictable expanses of space, where the gravitational influences of celestial bodies and the constraints of relativistic time dilation must be meticulously accounted for. Quantum clocks have the potential to redefine not just timekeeping on Earth but also the synchronization of multiple spacecraft, facilitating precise positioning and reliable data transmission during interstellar missions.

As we develop advanced quantum navigational systems, the implications for space travel become profound. Accurate timing is crucial for a range of navigational functions, from determining the position of a spacecraft relative to other bodies to synchronizing communication with mission control on Earth. Through quantum clocks, spacecraft can enhance their potential for autonomous navigation, dynamically adjusting routes based on real-time data while accounting for the intricate gravitational influences encountered or the potential hazards that may arise during travel.

Precision navigation through quantum mechanics also leads to innovative developments in quantum communication systems. By facilitating the instantaneous transfer of time signals across vast distances, quantum clocks can underpin a new era of secure communication networks. This interconnectivity stems from the principles of quantum entanglement, which ensure that any attempt to eavesdrop on the transmission alters the quantum state, alerting the parties involved to security breaches. As missions venture further into uncharted territories, this secure communication becomes essential, protecting sensitive data and maintaining robust links between spacecraft and Earth.

Integrating quantum clocks into a navigational framework transforms navigation protocols fundamentally. Imagine a future where spacecraft equipped with quantum clocks can operate autonomously while continually monitoring their precise location relative to each celestial body encountered. The inclusion of quantum sensors could detect gravitational anomalies and celestial bodies, providing invaluable data that quantum navigational systems can process and relay instantaneously. Coupled with AI capabilities, these systems can enhance route optimization, ensuring that spacecraft execute the most efficient trajectories during missions.

Nevertheless, implementing quantum clocks for precision navigation in space does not come without challenges. The technical intricacies of developing stable quantum clocks capable of enduring the conditions of space remain paramount. Tracking systems must be sophisticated enough to maintain coherence amidst cosmic radiation and temperature fluctuations while being lightweight and adaptable for spacecraft deployment. Moreover, calibration methods must be developed that allow these clocks to operate synchronously across vast distances, addressing the delays introduced by light-speed limitations in data transmission.

Moreover, as we advance toward the integration of quantum clocks into space navigation systems, ethical considerations surrounding quantum technologies must inform our endeavors. Ensuring that the benefits of such enhancements are equitable and accessible, as well as considering the broader implications of navigation advancements on our exploration strategies, remains essential in our quest for cosmic understanding.

In conclusion, quantum clocks represent a transformative leap in precision navigation as humanity ventures deeper into the cosmos. By harnessing the unparalleled accuracy and stability provided through quantum mechanics, these clocks enhance celestial navigation, secure communication, and foster autonomous space travel. As we continue down this path of discovery, navigating the quantum dimension deepens our understanding of time, space, and the intricate tapestry of the universe. The integration of quantum clocks into our navigational toolkit heralds a new dawn in space exploration—one where the quest for knowledge transcends boundaries and unveils the mysteries that await among the stars.

8.4. AstroQuantumometry: Measuring the Unmeasurable

In the context of deep space exploration, the concept of AstroQuantumometry emerges as a groundbreaking approach to measuring phenomena that have long evaded direct observation and quantification. This subchapter endeavors to delve deeply into the principles, methodologies, and potential applications of AstroQuantumometry, presenting a holistic view of how quantum mechanics can revolutionize our understanding of cosmic entities and their intricate behaviors.

AstroQuantumometry stands at the confluence of quantum mechanics and astrophysics, aiming to leverage the unique properties of quantum states to obtain precise measurements of celestial phenomena. Unlike traditional measurement techniques, which often depend on electromagnetic radiation to gather data, AstroQuantumometry capitalizes on quantum correlations that can enhance sensitivity and accuracy when probing the vast realms of space. This innovative method redefines the limits of what can be measured, providing new tools to unravel the mysteries of dark matter, gravitational waves, and elusive interstellar events.

At its core, AstroQuantumometry is rooted in the principles of quantum entanglement and superposition. By entangling quantum particles, researchers can create interconnected systems where measurements made on one particle instantaneously reflect the state of another, even over vast distances. Such entangled systems can serve as highly sensitive measuring instruments, enabling scientists to probe cosmic phenomena with unprecedented precision. For instance, measuring the minute fluctuations in gravitational waves—ripples in spacetime generated by colossal cosmic events—can be enhanced significantly through the use of entangled quantum systems, allowing us to detect signals that would otherwise blend into the noise of cosmic background radiation.

One of the critical advantages of AstroQuantumometry is its potential application in studying dark matter—a substance that comprises approximately 27% of the universe's total mass but remains largely invisible. By employing quantum sensors to detect the gravitational effects of dark matter on visible matter, researchers can map its distribution across cosmic structures. Quantum-enhanced gravitational measurements can elucidate the interactions between ordinary and dark matter, offering insights into galactic formations and evolution.

Moreover, the implications of AstroQuantumometry extend to the study of exotic astrophysical phenomena, such as pulsars and black holes. These entities produce strong gravitational fields that influence surrounding matter and light. By deploying quantum sensors designed to measure gravitational waves or detect high-energy particles emitted during events associated with black holes and neutron stars, we can gain a deeper understanding of their emissions and dynamics. The sensitive nature of quantum measurements means that subtler phenomena, previously considered undetectable, could now be within reach.

AstroQuantumometry also yields opportunities to enhance observational capabilities, particularly in deep-space explorations. Quantum-enhanced telescopes could leverage the principles of quantum optics to capture elusive signals from distant galaxies, nebulae, and other celestial phenomena. By operating with entangled photons and employing advanced quantum imaging techniques, scientists can achieve greater resolution and sensitivity—significantly improving our ability to map the cosmos and analyze the diverse structures and processes that govern it.

However, as we venture into the application of AstroQuantumometry, several technical and practical challenges must be navigated. The phenomenon of decoherence remains a critical obstacle, as quantum states can lose their coherence through interactions with environmental factors, particularly cosmic radiation. To mitigate these effects, protective measures must be developed to safeguard sensitive quantum instruments deployed in the unforgiving environments of space. Engineers and scientists will require robust designs and cutting-edge materials that ensure the reliability of quantum systems over extended periods amid the cosmic environment.

Conferring ethical considerations is equally important in the pursuit of AstroQuantumometry. As we develop sophisticated technologies for measuring cosmic phenomena, a responsible framework must guide our operations in space. Questions arise regarding data privacy and ownership, especially as interstellar measurements and discoveries will spur wider scientific collaboration, competition, and responsibility in sharing insights.

In conclusion, AstroQuantumometry represents a revolutionary shift in how we contemplate measurement in astrophysics and quantum mechanics. By harnessing quantum properties to measure the unobservable, we unlock a new frontier in cosmic understanding—one that facilitates exploration beyond our current boundaries. As we engage with this dynamic intersection of technology and inquiry, we prepare to unveil the mysteries that remain shrouded amongst the stars. The journey toward integrating AstroQuantumometry into our scientific practices not only serves to expand our understanding of the universe but encapsulates our relentless pursuit of knowledge—a pursuit that dances at the crossroads of the infinite possibilities that lie ahead in quantum exploration.

8.5. Quantum Geophysical Surveys of Cosmic Bodies

In the vast expanse of the cosmos, quantum geophysical surveys of cosmic bodies represent a significant leap forward in our ability to explore and understand the universe. These surveys, employing the principles of quantum mechanics, unlock new dimensions of investigation by enhancing our capabilities to gather and analyze data from celestial objects, providing insights that were previously unattainable with conventional methods.

At the heart of quantum geophysical surveys lies the integration of quantum sensors designed to probe the intrinsic properties of cosmic bodies. Unlike traditional sensors, which rely on classical measurements, quantum sensors exploit the unique behaviors of quantum states—such as superposition and entanglement—to achieve unparalleled precision and sensitivity. This heightened sensitivity enables scientists to detect subtle changes in gravitational fields, temperature variations, and electromagnetic signatures, revealing crucial information about the composition and structure of distant planets, moons, asteroids, and more.

For instance, when surveying planetary surfaces or atmospheres, quantum sensors leveraged on atomic interferometry can measure minute gravitational variations caused by the presence of mass. Such meticulous measurements offer insights into the internal structures of celestial bodies, unraveling mysteries around their geological history or potential for hosting life. Additionally, quantum sensors can detect specific elemental signatures in the atmospheres of exoplanets, informing us about their potential habitability and the presence of water or organic compounds critical for life.

One of the profound applications of quantum geophysical surveys is in the study of gravitational waves—ripples in spacetime caused by the motion of massive celestial bodies. By deploying networks of quantum sensors designed to detect these waves, scientists can analyze cosmic events such as black hole mergers or neutron star collisions with unprecedented accuracy. The data collected will redefine our understanding of astronomical phenomena, enriching our knowledge of the forces at play in the universe and the events that shape its evolution.

Furthermore, the potential for mapping celestial bodies in three dimensions offers compelling insights into their formation and evolution. Quantum geophysical surveys can create detailed models that depict the spatial distribution of mass across a body, revealing how geological processes have shaped its surface over time. Such surveys encourage interdisciplinary collaboration, merging expertise from astronomers, physicists, and geologists to construct comprehensive narratives about the evolution of planets and other cosmic entities.

As we engage in these pioneering efforts, the challenges posed by the cosmic environment cannot be overlooked. Quantum sensors must maintain coherence and stability amidst extreme temperatures, radiation, and other factors that could disrupt the delicate quantum states essential for accurate measurements. Research into robust material developments and innovative shielding techniques becomes paramount to ensure the reliability of quantum instruments in the unforgiving conditions of space.

Moreover, ensuring the efficient transmission of data collected by quantum sensors must become a priority. As interstellar communication networks evolve, integrating quantum key distribution and secure data transmission protocols into the infrastructure is crucial. The interconnectivity fostered by quantum technologies could facilitate real-time sharing of geophysical survey data with researchers on Earth, allowing for swift analysis and, consequently, more responsive exploration strategies.

In summary, quantum geophysical surveys of cosmic bodies represent a transformative frontier in our quest to uncover the mysteries of the universe. By employing advanced quantum technologies and sensors, we unlock enhanced observational capabilities that allow us to probe the depths of space with extraordinary precision. The application of these techniques holds great promise, redefining our understanding of celestial formations and behaviors while underpinning future exploration initiatives. As we venture further into the cosmos with quantum-driven methodologies, we not only expand our scientific horizons but also continue to deepen our connection with the universe, leading us to explore the intricate tapestry of existence that lies beyond our terrestrial realm.

The pursuit of quantum geophysical surveys heralds a new era in cosmic exploration, one that transcends the limits of our current technologies and aspirations. Through the steadfast commitment to innovation and collaboration, we stand poised to unveil new dimensions of knowledge, unlocking the secrets of the cosmos waiting to be discovered, and transforming humanity's place within the grand narrative of existence.

9. Simulating the Cosmos with Quantum Computers

9.1. Modeling Black Holes and Singularities

In the quest to understand the enigmatic phenomena that populate our universe, the modeling of black holes and singularities using quantum principles represents a cutting-edge intersection of quantum mechanics and relativistic astrophysics. As our explorations delve into the profound depths of spacetime, it becomes imperative to harmonize the intricate laws governing the quantum realm with the predictions of general relativity. This complex interplay challenges our understanding of some of the universe's most mysterious entities —black holes—and the singularities that lie within.

Black holes, as regions in spacetime where gravity is so immense that nothing—not even light—can escape, have long intrigued physicists and astronomers alike. These cosmic titans are typically formed when massive stars collapse under their own gravity, leading to the creation of a singularity at their core, where spacetime curvature becomes infinite and the laws of physics as we know them cease to function normally. Traditional models of black holes often rely on classical physics, but as we look to the future, the incorporation of quantum mechanics promises to reshape our understanding of these phenomena.

One of the forefront theories in unifying quantum mechanics and black hole physics is the idea of quantum gravity. A successful model of quantum gravity aims to reconcile the fundamentally different frameworks of quantum mechanics and general relativity, leading us closer to comprehending what happens at the core of a black hole's singularity. Various candidate theories, such as string theory and loop quantum gravity, provide alternative viewpoints on how spacetime behaves under extreme conditions. They suggest possible resolutions to the infinities encountered in classical theories, proposing that spacetime may have a discrete structure at very small scales.

Using quantum simulations enables scientists to model black holes and their singularities in ways that classical computational methods cannot achieve. Quantum computers harness the power of qubits, allowing them to explore complex scenarios involving multiple variables simultaneously. This parallelism makes them uniquely suited to tackle the intricate equations that describe the dance of particles and fields near black holes, revealing insights into their dynamics, thermodynamics, and the interplay between particles and gravitational fields.

One of the remarkable consequences of applying quantum principles to black holes is the concept of Hawking radiation—a theory proposed by physicist Stephen Hawking. According to this theory, black holes are not entirely black; they emit radiation due to quantum effects near the event horizon. Modeling this radiation using quantum simulations not only provides evidence for the black hole's gradual evaporation over time but also sheds light on the deeper implications regarding information preservation and the fate of information that falls into a black hole—a dilemma that has incited intense debate among physicists, often dubbed the "black hole information paradox."

Moreover, quantum simulations can incorporate thermodynamic principles, allowing researchers to probe the thermodynamic properties of black holes. By connecting thermodynamic laws to black hole mechanics, scientists can better understand the implications of entropy and temperature associated with black holes, linking them to foundational principles of quantum statistical mechanics.

The exploration of singularities is equally profound, posing questions about the structure of spacetime and the nature of reality itself. In quantum cosmology, quantum fluctuations are believed to play a pivotal role in the universe's infancy, potentially giving rise to concepts like the Big Bang singularity. Advanced quantum simulations could explore these early cosmic conditions, enabling us to model the behavior of matter and energy as spacetime begins to unfold—a task that classical simulations struggle to perform.

Additionally, as we seek to unravel the intricacies of black holes and singularities, we must address the technological constraints associated with simulating quantum systems. The development of suitable quantum algorithms for modeling black holes requires comprehensive understanding and expertise across domains, bridging quantum field theory, computational physics, and astrophysics. Researchers are continuously refining these algorithms and enhancing their capabilities to accurately portray the complex dynamics of spacetime.

Despite the challenges present in merging quantum mechanics with classical gravity, the promise that quantum principles hold for understanding black holes and singularities cannot be understated. It represents a colossal leap toward comprehending some of the universe's most profound enigmas—offering insights that may redefine our understanding of existence itself.

The modeling of black holes and singularities through quantum simulations invites us to gaze deeply into the heart of the cosmos, illuminating paths of inquiry previously left obscured. As scientists venture into these extraordinary realms, the answers we glean may hold keys not only to the fate of black holes but potentially illuminate the very nature of our universe and the cosmic fabric that binds us all. Embracing this quest will continue to inspire generations, reminding us that within the quest for knowledge lies the infinite possibility for discovery amid the stars.

9.2. Quantum Simulations of Cosmic Evolution

Within the realms of theoretical physics and astrophysics, the quest to understand cosmic evolution represents a formidable challenge marked by specific intricacies and profound implications. Quantum simulations have emerged as a pivotal means of exploring these complexities, providing us with innovative tools capable of decoding the myriad processes that have shaped the universe over its vast temporal span. Utilizing the principles of quantum mechanics, simulations can model the behavior of astronomical systems at unprecedented scales and resolutions, illuminating our understanding of the universe's origins, development, and potential futures.

At the core of quantum simulations of cosmic evolution lies the ability to examine vast swathes of data generated from cosmic observations, while simultaneously engaging with complex mathematical models that govern the interactions of matter and energy. Classical simulations, while useful, often encounter limitations when dealing with the multifaceted nature of the cosmos; they may struggle to incorporate the nuances of quantum effects that govern behavior at subatomic levels. Quantum simulations, on the other hand, afford researchers the opportunity to analyze multiple variables simultaneously through qubits—quantum bits that embody the principle of superposition.

One crucial application of quantum simulations is in modeling the formation and evolution of galaxies. By applying quantum algorithms to simulate the gravitational interactions among clusters of dark matter and baryonic matter, researchers can explore how galaxies coalesce and evolve over billions of years. Quantum simulations can elucidate how various physical processes—including star formation, accretion of materials, and dark matter influences—interact dynamically to create the structures we observe today. By delving into this modeling, scientists can gain insights into the historical context of galaxy formation and its accompanying phenomena, contributing to a more integrated understanding of our cosmic environment.

Additionally, the intriguing dynamics of cosmic inflation—an exponentially rapid expansion of the universe immediately following the Big Bang—also lends itself to quantum simulations. The challenges intrinsic to modeling the rapid inflationary phase, coupled with the role of primordial fluctuations, require advanced computational frameworks that quantum simulations can facilitate. Investigating these primordial fluctuations within the context of quantum field theories will provide insights into the seeds of structure formation that led to galaxies, stars, and ultimately planets—setting the stage for the emergence of life.

Quantum simulations extend their reach to other areas, such as studying the evolution of exotic states of matter in the early universe. The conditions prevalent shortly after the Big Bang were so extreme that matter existed in states that defy our classical intuitions. Quantum simulations allow us to model transitions between phases, such as from quark-gluon plasma to hadronic matter, revealing details about the interplay between fundamental forces. Gaining an understanding of these transitions enhances our grasp of the thermal history of the universe and connects seamlessly to nuclear physics and particle simulations.

The impact of quantum simulations on our understanding of dark matter and dark energy also deserves emphasis. These elusive components account for a substantial portion of the universe's mass-energy content, yet they remain shrouded in uncertainty. Quantum simulations can aid researchers in hypothesizing potential models for dark matter interactions that would elucidate its structure and distribution in the universe, while also engaging with quantum gravitational theories that could shed light on the nature of dark energy fueling the universe's accelerated expansion.

However, as we push the boundaries of cosmic evolution modeling, sunlight must be shone upon the profound challenges that lie ahead. The realization of robust quantum simulations is contingent upon the availability of technological advances in quantum computing capabilities. As we endeavor to build practical quantum computing systems, we must also address issues related to coherence, error correction, and scalability in quantum algorithms. Moreover, translating theoretical frameworks into operational simulations demands interdisciplinary collaborations that draw upon expertise from cosmology, particle physics, and quantum information science.

Through thoughtful engagement with these quantum simulations, future explorations of cosmic evolution can be further informed, allowing researchers to unlock not just the secrets of the universe, but perhaps the very nature of existence itself. As humanity ventures deeper into the cosmic narrative, the implications of quantum simulations will extend beyond theoretical constructs, illuminating a pathway to greater understandings of the intricate tapestry that weaves our universe together.

In conclusion, quantum simulations of cosmic evolution represent a transformative frontier, bridging the gap between quantum mechanics and astrophysics. This interdisciplinary approach stands to enhance our knowledge of galaxy formation, cosmic inflation, dark matter, and other intricate phenomena that shape the universe. Acknowledging the challenges inherent in developing these simulations propels us toward innovative solutions and deeper cooperation across scientific disciplines. As we continue to unlock the mysteries of our cosmic home, we position ourselves at the forefront of discovery, ready to explore the tightly woven fabric of existence that surrounds us, illuminating the universe's secrets one quantum state at a time.

9.3. Dark Energy Decoded Through Simulations

Dark Energy Decoded Through Simulations

In the vast landscape of cosmological inquiry, dark energy stands as one of the most perplexing and pivotal components shaping our universe. Comprising approximately 68% of the universe's energy density, dark energy is believed to be responsible for the accelerated expansion of space. Despite its prevalence, its nature remains shrouded in mystery, inviting scientific exploration through innovative methodologies, among which quantum simulations emerge as a critical tool for decoding this enigmatic force.

The foundations of understanding dark energy require a multifaceted approach, and the application of quantum simulations represents a promising pathway. Quantum mechanics provides a framework that allows researchers to investigate the behavior of cosmic systems at scales beyond the capabilities of classical simulations. By harnessing quantum computing principles, scientists can model complex interactions and phenomena related to dark energy, enhancing our understanding of its implications for cosmic expansion and structure formation.

One of the most significant challenges in studying dark energy is the need to reconcile its effects with the large-scale structure of the universe. Quantum simulations enable researchers to incorporate variables such as gravitational interactions, the presence of dark matter, and the dynamics of radiation to create comprehensive models that more accurately reflect the true state of cosmic evolution. Moreover, these simulations can explore various theoretical models of dark energy, including the cosmological constant (the simplest form of dark energy) and dynamic models that propose changing energy densities over time. Each model carries its unique implications for the universe's expansion and behavior, enabling a nuanced understanding of how dark energy influences cosmic phenomena.

By employing quantum algorithms capable of running parallel computations, researchers can conduct simulations that explore multiple scenarios and variables simultaneously. This parallelism excels in modeling cosmic events and structures, which involves complex calculations that would be computationally prohibitive on classical computers. Such capability permits scientists to simulate the expansion of the universe across different epochs, observing how variations in dark energy models affect cosmic evolution over billions of years.

Also central to quantum simulations is the capacity to investigate the finer details of cosmic expansion. As dark energy drives the acceleration of galaxies moving farther apart, quantum simulations can help analyze the interactions between dark energy and other forms of energy or matter present at various scales within the universe. By measuring the influence of dark energy on the formation of galaxies, galaxy clusters, and large-scale structures, these simulations enable insights into how dark energy interacts with the fabric of spacetime itself.

Moreover, the study of cosmic microwave background radiation (CMB)—the faint afterglow of the Big Bang—can benefit from quantum simulations that model its fluctuations influenced by dark energy. Researchers can explore how dark energy dynamics might impact the anisotropy of the CMB, revealing critical insights into the early universe and its expansion history. The information gleaned from CMB observations, when coupled with quantum simulations of dark energy effects, can lead to a comprehensive understanding of both the early and late-time universe.

However, executing quantum simulations of dark energy also presents educational and logistical challenges. Developing the hardware and software infrastructures necessary to perform large-scale simulations and effectively process outputs derived from entangled qubits require interdisciplinary collaboration between cosmologists, quantum physicists, and computational scientists. Building effective partnerships across institutions will foster innovation and create a robust framework for exploring this complex domain.

Furthermore, as researchers endeavor to decode dark energy through quantum simulations, they must remain aware of the interpretive nature of their findings. Each simulation must be scrutinized to ensure that the implications drawn from the models align with observational data obtained from telescopes and cosmic surveys. The convergence of theoretical simulations with empirical observations establishes a feedback loop that hones our understanding of dark energy and its role in shaping the universe.

In conclusion, the effort to decode dark energy through quantum simulations marks a critical advancement in our quest to comprehend the empirical mysteries of the cosmos. By embracing the principles of quantum mechanics, researchers can explore complex interactions and phenomena that define our universe's character and destiny. Quantum simulations open new avenues for inquiry, allowing scientists to examine the subtleties of dark energy, its dynamic behavior, and its implications for the fabric of spacetime. This exploration will not only enhance our grasp of the universe but enable humanity to tap into the secrets hidden within, leading us toward a deeper understanding of existence itself. As we push the boundaries of knowledge through the lens of quantum simulations, we prepare to unlock the profound mysteries that dark energy presents, illuminating the magnificent journey ahead in the study of the cosmos.

9.4. Quantum Informed Galactic Mapping

The intricate tapestry of the universe has always challenged human curiosity and scientific inquiry, particularly in the realm of galactic mapping. As we venture further into the cosmos, quantum-informed galactic mapping emerges as a transformative approach that promises to refine our understanding of celestial structures and their dynamic interactions. By integrating quantum mechanics into the methodologies used to analyze and interpret astronomical data, we unlock unprecedented precision and depth in mapping the grand design of galaxies and their constituents.

At the heart of quantum-informed galactic mapping lies the ability to leverage quantum sensors and algorithms that surpass the limitations of classical observational techniques. Traditional methods rely heavily on electromagnetic radiation—capturing light emitted or reflected by celestial objects. However, as we delve deeper into the vastness of space, these methods encounter challenges posed by cosmic dust, limited resolution, and the diminishing signals from remote phenomena. Quantum mechanics offers an alternative framework that enhances our ability to discern subtle signatures from far-flung galaxies and cosmic structures.

Quantum sensors, empowered by entangled states, possess extraordinary sensitivity that allows us to measure gravitational waves and magnetic fields in ways that classical sensors cannot. These sensors can detect the minute shifts in gravitational fields caused by the mass distribution within galaxies, thereby revealing the underlying dark matter that shapes galactic formations. By deploying networks of quantum sensors, we can conduct geophysical surveys of galaxies with a level of detail previously deemed unattainable. This enhanced understanding of mass distributions and gravitational influences leads to more accurate models of galactic evolution and structure.

Moreover, quantum-informed algorithms augment our capabilities for data analysis, enabling scientists to process vast amounts of information concurrently. Unlike classical algorithms, which require sequential processing of data, quantum algorithms harness superposition to analyze multiple paths and scenarios simultaneously. This parallelism means that researchers can explore complex simulations of galactic dynamics at an exponential scale. For instance, modeling the formation of large-scale structures such as galaxy clusters becomes more feasible, as quantum algorithms can rapidly process the interactions of billions of particles over cosmic timescales.

As we apply these quantum techniques to the study of galaxies, we can also investigate their clustering and formation. Understanding how galaxies coalesce and evolve over time depends on accurately mapping their positions, movements, and the gravitational influences acting upon them. By examining the interplay between dark matter and visible matter through quantum-informed methodologies, we can uncover insights into the processes driving galactic mergers, interactions, and the emergence of large-scale cosmic structures.

The mystery of cosmic expansion, particularly the role of dark energy in accelerating this expansion, also benefits from quantum-informed galactic mapping. By modeling the distribution of galaxies across different epochs, researchers can analyze the influence of dark energy on cosmic evolution. Quantum algorithms enable the exploration of various theoretical scenarios for dark energy and how they manifest in the distribution of cosmic structures. This understanding may provide valuable insights into the nature of dark energy itself—a force that still perplexes scientists.

Challenges do exist as we strive toward quantum-informed galactic mapping. The intricate nature of quantum systems necessitates robust engineering solutions to safeguard coherence in quantum sensors amidst the environmental disturbances of space. Furthermore, ensuring that the collected data is transmitted securely and efficiently back to Earth, while maintaining the integrity of quantum information, remains a priority.

Despite these challenges, the prospects of quantum-informed galactic mapping are vast and hold the potential to revolutionize our encounter with the universe. The integration of these quantum techniques exemplifies our relentless pursuit to explore the unknown, refining our comprehension of cosmic phenomena that define the very fabric of existence. Through the synergy of quantum mechanics and astrophysics, we decode the stories written in the stars—unraveling the enigma of galaxies, understanding their evolution, and ultimately charting the grand narrative of our cosmos.

In conclusion, quantum-informed galactic mapping represents a groundbreaking advancement in our quest for cosmic understanding. By embracing the principles of quantum mechanics, we enhance our observational capabilities, broaden our analytical methods, and unlock new opportunities for exploring the universe. As we embark on this exciting journey, we unveil new dimensions of knowledge, revealing the complexities and wonders of the galactic tapestry that shapes our universe. Our exploration not only enriches our scientific endeavors but also fosters a deeper appreciation for the intricate wonders of existence, urging us to continue our pursuit of the infinite mysteries that lie beyond our reach among the stars.

9.5. Hypothetical Universes: Quantum Creation

Hypothetical universes present an enticing and complex framework for understanding the principles of quantum creation. In this context, we explore theoretical constructs that suggest alternate realities and the mechanisms that could give rise to these universes. The concept challenges our traditional notions of existence, offering a lens through which we can examine the multi-faceted nature of reality informed by quantum mechanics.

Central to this exploration is the idea that creation itself might not be a singular event but rather a continuous process characterized by infinite possibilities. In quantum mechanics, the principle of superposition indicates that particles can exist in multiple states simultaneously until observed. This principle could imply that the universe, or universes, may also exist in a state of potential—a vast expanse of possibilities coexisting until confronted by an observer's measurement. Each decision or measurement collapses this superposition into a specific reality, thereby influencing the development of one universe over others.

This interplay of choices and outcomes dives deep into the multiverse theory, suggesting that each potential universe emerges from different quantum decisions made at the fundamental level. Each time a quantum event arises—whether it be a particle decaying, a photon being emitted, or an atom participating in a reaction—it can theoretically branch into various possibilities, giving rise to distinct realities. In such a scenario, we could envision the creation of innumerable universes, each following a unique trajectory based on the quantum events occurring within them.

In contemplating the mechanism of quantum creation, we must also consider the speculative nature of causality within these hypothetical universes. What might seem like chaos at the quantum level could actually give rise to structured realities; thus, exploring how order can emerge from randomness becomes critical. Understanding how these quantum fluctuations can lead to the formation of complex systems within individual universes can guide our understanding of everything from galaxy formation to the very essence of life.

Another vital consideration is that of time itself, particularly how it might be perceived differently across these hypothetical universes. In many interpretations of quantum mechanics, including the many-worlds interpretation, time might not be linear but rather branching. As a result, the evolution of each universe could occur independently, leading to vastly different outcomes and timelines, even following equivalent initial conditions.

Moreover, the study of hypothetical universes opens avenues for contemplating the implications of quantum mechanics on existential questions. Philosophical inquiries regarding consciousness, existence, and the nature of reality itself are invigorated by considering the existence of multiple universes. If every possible scenario exists within a quantum framework, one might ponder the existence of an observer in alternate universes. This reflective inquiry begs the question: does our consciousness influence which reality we inhabit, or is it merely a participant in an extensive tapestry of interconnected possibilities?

For our understanding as seekers of knowledge, the implications extend toward cosmology and the evolution of the universe itself. Could there exist universes where fundamental physical constants differ from our own? If so, what implications does this hold for the laws of nature and the prospects of life in those realities? Exploring these questions can deepen our understanding of our own universe as we place ourselves within a potentially infinite cosmological backdrop.

As we delve further into the frameworks of hypothetical universes and their significance in quantum creation, we encounter considerable challenges. Scientific exploration in this realm often wades into speculative territory, raising the question of how we can derive meaningful experimental predictions from theories that underpin these hypothetical constructs. Developing mathematical models that can be tested and potentially validated remains an ongoing frontier for physicists and mathematicians alike.

In summary, the realm of hypothetical universes shaped by quantum creation invites us to think beyond conventional boundaries of reality. With every quantum measurement, we stand at the cusp of new dimensions, exploring the emergence of multiple realities woven into the fabric of existence. This inquiry not only challenges our comprehension of the universe but also redefines our sense of self as we seek to understand our place within the infinite expanse of possibilities that quantum mechanics presents. As we continue this exploration, we embark on a profound journey that may unveil the intricacies of creation and existence, inviting us to reflect on the very nature of reality itself.

10. Quantum Computing and Astrobiology

10.1. The Quantum Foundations of Life

In a universe permeated by the enigma of existence and the intertwining fabric of time and space, the quest to understand life itself through the lens of quantum mechanics presents a groundbreaking opportunity. The quantum foundations of life rest upon principles that challenge our conventional definitions of biology, evolution, and existence, invoking curiosity and wonder as we explore the pathways through which quantum phenomena shape the very essence of living systems.

As we embark on this exploration, it becomes essential to reconsider the building blocks of life from a quantum perspective. The intricate tapestry of molecular interactions, cellular processes, and biological functions all hinge on quantum mechanics, particularly in the realms of energy transfer, entanglement, and coherence. In organisms, quantum effects could provide an evolutionary advantage, permitting life forms to optimize energy acquisition through mechanisms that classical physics cannot thoroughly explain. This notion invites a deeper inquiry into how life has adapted to utilize these quantum principles to thrive in environments that span from the depths of the ocean to the vastness of space.

Exploring the idea of searching for quantum biomarkers within living systems turns our gaze toward the molecular scale, where quantum phenomena play an integral role in enzymatic reactions, plant photosynthesis, and even consciousness. For instance, in photosynthesis, quantum coherence allows plants to efficiently absorb and convert solar energy, demonstrating how nature harnesses quantum properties to optimize energy transfer processes. These markers of quantum efficiency could serve as indicators of life, guiding us in our search for biosignatures in distant exoplanets where conditions may be drastically different from those on Earth.

Furthermore, modeling evolution in multidimensional spaces offers a powerful lens through which to analyze the trajectory of life's development. Quantum simulations enable researchers to examine evolutionary pathways that encompass varying factors, including environmental pressures, genetic variability, and ecological interactions over time. By employing quantum mechanics, we can create complex models that account for a multitude of interactions simultaneously, revealing how life has adapted or evolved in response to shifting conditions. Such models present opportunities to explore the evolutionary processes that have shaped species across time and space, contextualizing our understanding of life within the grand narrative of the cosmos.

In tandem with evolutionary modeling, the concept of quantum genetics emerges, highlighting the idea that the instructions of life—the genetic code—may bear deeper connections to quantum phenomena. Quantum information theory posits that information is fundamental to the universe, and when applied to genetics, it suggests that the correspondence between DNA sequences and quantum information could unlock new avenues for understanding heredity, mutation, and adaptation. This potentially transformative perspective encourages a re-examination of the genetic mechanisms governing life, positing that they may be influenced by the intricate dance of quantum states at the molecular level.

As we venture further into the realm of the hypothetical, it becomes intriguing to consider the possibility of a cosmic playground of quantum life existing in parallel to our own. This exploration invites us to contemplate the notion of parallel universes and the degrees to which different physical laws may govern them. In these hypothetical realities, life may emerge under entirely novel conditions, leading to forms of existence fundamentally different from what we understand. This realm of speculation raises profound philosophical inquiries regarding the nature of consciousness, existence, and the interconnectedness of all life—a testament to the grandeur of the cosmos and the role that quantum mechanics plays.

To delve into the quantum foundations of life, interdisciplinary collaboration will be essential. Scientists from various fields—quantum physicists, biologists, astrobiologists, and philosophers—must come together to stimulate inquiry, develop innovative technologies, and share insights that cater to this complex landscape. This confluence of knowledge may lead to revolutionary discoveries, reshaping our understanding not only of life here on Earth but also of the potential for life in myriad forms throughout the cosmos.

In conclusion, the quantum foundations of life encapsulate profound possibilities for expanding our understanding of existence. By embracing the principles of quantum mechanics, we can explore the processes that govern life at its most fundamental level, offering insights that may reshape our perceptions of biology, evolution, and consciousness within the cosmic tapestry. As we journey deeper into the mysteries of life, we prepare to unlock the astounding connections between quantum mechanics and the biological phenomena that define our existence, propelling us toward new dimensions of knowledge that await discovery in the vast reaches of the universe.

10.2. Searching for Quantum Biomarkers

Searching for quantum biomarkers opens a fascinating frontier at the intersection of quantum mechanics and the burgeoning field of astrobiology. In essence, these biomarkers represent the unique signatures or indicators that could signal the presence of life—particularly life that harnesses quantum phenomena—in environments beyond our home planet. As scientists endeavor to decode the complexities of potential extraterrestrial life, the sensitivity and intricacy afforded by quantum technologies offer transformative methods of observation and measurement, paving the way for novel discoveries in our quest to understand life in the universe.

At the core of this investigation is the understanding that molecular and quantum processes could influence biological functions in ways that classical physics fails to fully account for. Organisms on Earth exhibit processes that draw upon quantum effects, including photosynthesis, magnetoreception, and enzyme catalysis, suggesting a potential link between quantum mechanics and the mechanisms of life. Quantum biomarkers, therefore, could be defined as the measurable phenomena or patterns arising from these quantum properties, revealing the underlying processes that might govern life in diverse environments, whether on Earth, exoplanets, or other celestial bodies.

For instance, the phenomenon of quantum coherence in photosynthetic organisms has shown that energy transfer processes occur with extraordinary efficiency, leveraging quantum superposition and entanglement to optimize solar energy capture. Such mechanisms represent a potential biomarker, lending insight into the possibilities of life forms that might navigate their environments at the quantum level. Thus, in the realm of astrobiology, the search for life extends beyond merely looking for carbon-based molecules; it encompasses the exploration of quantum processes that could define alternative biochemistries in entirely different contexts.

In the search for quantum biomarkers, researchers can deploy quantum sensors equipped with the ability to detect minute changes in energy states, temperature, or magnetic fields associated with biological processes. For example, utilizing atomic interferometry may allow us to measure fluctuations associated with biochemical reactions in real-time, facilitating the identification of quantum effects influencing metabolic pathways in extremophiles—organisms that thrive in harsh environments—here on Earth and potentially analogous conditions elsewhere.

Moreover, the principles of quantum imaging open new avenues for identifying and cataloging potential biosignatures on distant planets. Conventional methods of direct observation may falter due to distance, atmospheric opacity, or the dimness of signals emerging from exoplanets. By deploying quantum-enhanced telescopes, researchers can capture elusive signals that may indicate the presence of life-supporting environments, such as the detection of specific wavelengths associated with biological activities or the signatures of gases that suggest metabolic processes.

As the search for extraterrestrial life intensifies, experiments aimed at isolating and identifying quantum biomarkers in laboratory settings will help forge connections between theoretical predictions and real-world findings. Testing the efficacy of these biomarkers in varied environments simulating those found on other planets—such as extreme temperatures, pressures, and chemical compositions—allows researchers to determine how quantum processes may manifest in different contexts. Furthermore, rigorous training of machine learning algorithms, informed by quantum datasets, enhances our capacity to recognize the fingerprints of quantum life in fluorescence data, energy spectra, or even magnetic resonance signals.

The challenges in identifying quantum biomarkers stem from not only the inherent complexity of biological systems but also from environmental factors that may obscure the signals we're seeking. Rigorous calibration methods in quantum systems and the necessity for shielding against cosmic radiation are paramount as we expand our observational capabilities into deeper and more remote cosmic terrains. Ensuring that the quantum devices employed maintain coherence and sensitivity in turbulent conditions becomes essential to the success of these initiatives.

Ethical considerations surrounding the search for quantum biomarkers also bear attention. The implications of finding life that operates on fundamentally different principles could prompt philosophical inquiries into the nature of life itself as well as the ethical ramifications of planetary exploration and potential contamination. Responsible stewardship will be necessary as we engage with astrobiological possibilities that may hold profound implications for humanity's understanding of existence.

In conclusion, the search for quantum biomarkers unveils new dimensions of inquiry that intertwine quantum mechanics with the quest for understanding life beyond our planet. By utilizing the unparalleled sensitivity of quantum technologies, researchers are better equipped to uncover the signatures of life that may escape traditional methods of observation. This pioneering investigation not only seeks to locate extraterrestrial biosignatures but also helps redefine our conceptions of life and existence, illuminating our profound connection to the universe and the potential diversity of life that awaits discovery among the stars. As we continue to push the boundaries of exploration, the search for quantum biomarkers serves as both a scientific and philosophical journey, inviting us to reflect on the enduring mysteries of cosmic existence.

10.3. Modeling Evolution in Multidimensional Spaces

In the realm of theoretical physics and cosmology, the pursuit of understanding evolution through multidimensional spaces embodies a profound inquiry into the nature of the universe. Quantum mechanics, with its unique principles, offers a lens through which we can explore the complexity of cosmic evolution across different dimensions of existence. This subchapter delves into the significance of modeling evolution in multidimensional spaces, considering the implications of quantum frameworks and the interplay of various factors that have defined the cosmos.

The concept of multidimensionality is pivotal in both quantum mechanics and the cosmological narratives concerning the universe's structure and evolution. While we are accustomed to perceiving the universe in three spatial dimensions, quantum theories often propose additional dimensions—some even postulate as many as eleven. These higher-dimensional spaces can provide insights into fundamental interactions that govern the universe, including gravity, electromagnetism, and the forces described in the standard model of particle physics.

One of the foremost applications of quantum mechanics in modeling evolution is its capability to address the fundamental question of how particles and forces interact in various dimensional frameworks. The behavior of particles in a multi-dimensional model can lead to conditions and phenomena not observable within our traditional three-dimensional space. For instance, the concept of "string theory" proposes that at the subatomic level, fundamental particles are not point-like but rather one-dimensional strings vibrating in multiple dimensions. The vibrational modes of these strings can determine the characteristics of particles, such as mass and charge, leading to a deeper understanding of the universe's fabric and the forces that shape it.

Quantum mechanics also reshapes our understanding of time—the fourth dimension—within the context of cosmic evolution. As we model evolutionary pathways, the interplay of time and space becomes critical in understanding how galaxies, stars, and planets evolve over cosmic epochs. Quantum theories suggest that for every moment in spacetime, numerous possible futures exist based on the state of particles and their interactions. Harnessing quantum computational techniques opens the door to modeling these possibilities in ways that classical simulations cannot achieve, enabling researchers to simulate the evolution of cosmic structures with resilience to the vast complexities that characterize the universe.

In addition to enhancing our understanding of fundamental interactions and temporal evolution, modeling in multidimensional spaces allows for a more comprehensive approach to investigating chaotic systems such as star formation and galactic dynamics. These processes are inherently nonlinear and influenced by multiple variables, including gravitational interactions, energy flows, and feedback mechanisms regulating the birth and death of stars. Quantum models that employ high-dimensional phase spaces can provide a new context for understanding how these complex systems evolve, ultimately yielding insights into star clustering, supernovae, and the formation of planetary systems.

Furthermore, the implications of modeling evolution in multidimensional spaces extend to dark matter and dark energy—shadows that loom large in cosmic evolution. Quantitative approaches involving multidimensional models can address the distribution and dynamics of dark matter subjected to the influences of the universe's expansion due to dark energy. By examining the interplay between these constituents and their impact on galaxy formation and structure, researchers can develop more nuanced theories that enhance our overarching comprehension of cosmic dynamics.

As we endeavor to model evolution in multidimensional spaces, notable challenges persist. Theoretically and computationally intensive modeling processes require advanced quantum systems capable of capturing the complexities of multi-dimensional phenomena. Developing efficient algorithms to run simulations across these intricate frameworks will necessitate collaboration between physicists, mathematicians, and computer scientists to maximize the power of quantum computing technologies in astrophysical contexts.

Additionally, ethical implications surrounding the exploration of these cosmic dimensions must also be carefully considered. As our understanding of the universe evolves through quantum insights, the ability to manipulate data and constructive inquiry into existence invites broader philosophical dialogues about the nature of our reality.

In summary, modeling evolution in multidimensional spaces offers a transformative perspective on the universe—shaping our understanding of its intricacies and driving inquiries that bridge quantum mechanics and cosmology. Through the innovative application of quantum principles, we seek not only to unravel the mysteries of cosmic evolution but also to find our place within it. This endeavor encourages exploration into the unimaginable depths of existence, paving the way for discoveries that redefine the boundaries of what we consider possible in our journey through the cosmos. As we navigate these multidimensional realms, we equip ourselves with the tools to explore profound questions inherent to our understanding of life, existence, and the very fabric of the universe itself.

10.4. Quantum Genetics: The Cosmic Code of Life

In an age where the mysteries of the cosmos tantalize human curiosity, the quest to decode the cosmic code of life through quantum genetics represents one of the most profound explorations into understanding life's origins and existence beyond Earth. Quantum genetics postulates that the intricate mechanisms governing the code of life may be deeply intertwined with the principles of quantum mechanics, positing that genetic information and biological processes could operate at quantum levels, influencing not only terrestrial life but also the potential for life in the universe.

At the foundation of quantum genetics is the idea that genetic information—encoded within the DNA of organisms—might be subject to quantum phenomena such as superposition and entanglement. These quantum properties afford the possibility that genetic configurations can exist as complex vectors of information in multidimensional spaces, enhancing the adaptability and resilience of life forms. This notion invites us to rethink our understanding of evolution, emphasizing the potential role of quantum mechanics in shaping the very fabric of biological existence.

One of the most crucial areas where we can explore quantum influences is in the mechanisms of hereditary information transfer. Quantum genetics can offer insights into how DNA may function optimally through quantum coherence, potentially enhancing processes such as photosynthesis, enzyme reactions, and metabolic pathways. The efficiency of these biological functions may hinge on the underlying quantum processes allowing organisms to maximize energy usage, survive in extreme environments, and adapt to changing conditions over time.

Moreover, investigations into how quantum states play a role in genetic mutations and evolutionary adaptations could revolutionize our understanding of life's evolutionary pathways. As quantum states could influence molecular bonding configurations or the rates of reaction, exploring these quantum dynamics enables scientists to consider how life may evolve in environments starkly different from those on Earth. In the search for extraterrestrial life, recognizing the role of quantum genetics drives us to consider what forms life might take beyond our planet, potentially adapting to diverse conditions that render traditional biological classifications insufficient.

The potential application of quantum genetic principles also extends to the field of synthetic biology, where scientists seek to engineer life forms that possess desirable traits taught by nature over billions of years. By gleaning insights from quantum genetics, genetic engineers may design organisms that can capture energy more efficiently, synthesize new compounds, or exhibit resilience against environmental stressors—paving the way for future technological advancements in bioengineering and environmental sustainability.

As we hope to uncover the quantum underpinnings of life, we must also strategically consider the technological constraints inherent in probing these questions. Developing methodologies that accurately measure and manipulate quantum states in biological systems presents formidable challenges, particularly as we grapple with quantum coherence, environmental disturbances, and the complexities of biological systems.

Moreover, the ethical dimensions of exploring quantum genetics warrant careful consideration. As we investigate the genetic modifications that quantum principles might enable, questions concerning consent, biodiversity, and the broader implications for ecological systems emerge. A thoughtful balancing of scientific ambition with ethical responsibility will be essential as we journey through this cutting-edge field.

In summary, quantum genetics promises a transformational understanding of life's origins and variations throughout the cosmos, linking the intricacies of quantum mechanics with the complexity of biological systems. By embracing quantum principles, we enhance our comprehension of genetics, evolution, and the potential for life to thrive in dynamic and diverse environments, potentially expanding our grasp of existence itself. As we explore the quantum code of life, we are reminded of the interconnectedness of all beings and the infinite possibilities that await discovery in the uncharted realms of the universe. This endeavor not only fulfills our scientific curiosity but also deepens our collective appreciation for the profound mysteries that lie at the heart of existence itself.

10.5. The Cosmic Playground of Quantum Life

In the grand tapestry of the universe, we find ourselves poised at the intersection of quantum mechanics and the cosmic expanse—an arena where mystery and discovery intertwine. The concept of "The Cosmic Playground of Quantum Life" offers a captivating lens through which we can explore the profound implications of quantum phenomena on the fabric of existence itself. As we journey through this chapter, we will delve into the remarkable potential of quantum mechanics in shaping the origins, development, and interconnectedness of life across the universe.

Imagine a universe in which the very principles of quantum mechanics underpin the fundamental processes of life itself. From the capacity for energy transfer during photosynthesis to the mechanisms of molecular interactions, quantum effects exhibit remarkable potential in enhancing biological efficiency. This emphasis brings forth the intriguing inquiry: could life forms evolve to harness quantum mechanical properties, allowing them to adapt and thrive in environments beyond those on Earth? The answer, as we will explore, may be more than theoretical.

At the heart of this cosmic playground is the delicate balance between the quantum world and biological systems. As living organisms interact at the molecular level, quantum coherence—a phenomenon where particles exist in correlated states—may influence critical processes such as enzymatic reactions and cellular respiration. This quantum influence could confer evolutionary advantages, allowing organisms that process quantum efficiently to excel in energy acquisition and environmental adaptation. The hypothesis invites us to reevaluate the qualifications for what constitutes life, broadening our understanding to encompass the myriad interactions that take place at the quantum level.

Beyond Earth, the search for life among the stars propels us to reconsider how we identify and measure biosignatures across diverse planetary environments. The potential for detecting quantum markers—specific features or patterns arising from the influence of quantum processes—offers a compelling avenue of exploration. Just as our understanding of extremophiles here on Earth underscores the adaptability of life in extreme conditions, we must contemplate how life forms elsewhere might uniquely manifest based on their respective environments. Quantum biomarkers capturing the essence of biological functions could redefine our frameworks for identifying life and unlocking its secrets in extraterrestrial worlds.

As we broaden our inquiry into the possibilities of quantum life, the interplay between consciousness and quantum mechanics also calls for reflection. If consciousness emerges from the complex interactions of particles and fields, how might quantum mechanics shape the nature of awareness across different forms of life? Such philosophical considerations challenge our understanding of existence and highlight the profound connections that bind all living systems—an exploration that may reveal the fabric of reality itself.

Quantum mechanics also compels us to consider the ethical implications of our pursuits. As we advance our understanding of life through quantum inquiry, the potential for manipulating genetic structures and molecular processes prompts both excitement and caution. Responsible engagement with these quantum technologies is vital as we seek to illuminate life thrumming within the cosmos, guarding against unintended consequences that might arise from our explorations.

As we traverse this cosmic playground of quantum life, we must also celebrate the interconnected dimensions of knowledge that unfold before us. Interdisciplinary collaboration emerges as a vital essence in unearthing the mysteries of existence; physicists, biologists, and philosophers must unite to explore the quantum foundations of life holistically. In doing so, we honor the magnificence of the universe— a vast expanse of enigmas awaiting our inquiry.

In conclusion, "The Cosmic Playground of Quantum Life" serves as a nexus for understanding the depths of existence through the principles of quantum mechanics. Our journey into this cosmic playground invites us to explore the pathways through which life emerges, evolves, and interacts with its environment—extending beyond our terrestrial perspectives to embrace the possibility of life among the stars. As we continue to uncover the extraordinary connections between quantum mechanics and the foundations of life, we embark on an exploration that beckons us further into the depths of cosmic understanding—a journey not merely of scientific inquiry but of profound existential reflection amid the infinite wonders that await.

11. Quantum Computing Challenges in Space

11.1. The Influence of Cosmic Radiation

In the context of quantum computing and its applications in space, the influence of cosmic radiation is a vital consideration that evokes both challenges and opportunities. As we venture further into the depths of the universe with advanced quantum technologies, understanding and mitigating the effects of cosmic radiation will be essential for ensuring the reliability and success of missions that rely on quantum systems.

Cosmic radiation, composed of high-energy particles originating from various astrophysical sources—such as supernovae, black holes, and distant galaxies—poses significant threats to electronic systems, particularly those based on delicate quantum states. Quantum bits, or qubits, which serve as the fundamental building blocks of quantum computing, are extremely sensitive to their environment. This sensitivity makes them vulnerable to disruptions caused by cosmic radiation, leading to errors in computation and potentially compromising the integrity of the systems deployed in space.

One of the primary challenges arising from cosmic radiation is decoherence—the process by which quantum coherence is lost due to interactions with the environment. Cosmic radiation can induce unwanted interactions with qubits, pushing them into a classical state and effectively collapsing their superposition. This collapse disrupts the quantum computations being performed, leading to errors that can affect the outcomes of critical tasks, such as data processing, navigation, and communication.

To mitigate the effects of cosmic radiation on quantum systems, engineering solutions must focus on developing advanced shielding techniques. This might include creating robust materials capable of absorbing or deflecting high-energy particles, as well as designing quantum devices with built-in protective mechanisms that minimize exposure to radiation. Implementing redundancy within quantum systems could also serve as a safeguard against errors introduced by cosmic events, helping ensure that the performance of quantum technologies remains reliable even in the dynamic environments of space.

Moreover, as researchers explore quantum error correction algorithms, they must consider the unique challenges presented by cosmic influences. Developments in quantum error correction that detect and address errors caused by radiation interference will be paramount, enabling missions with quantum computing capabilities to function effectively amidst the uncertainties of the cosmos. Designing resilient quantum algorithms that can dynamically adjust to fluctuations in qubit stability will contribute significantly to the robustness required for successful space operations.

The implications of cosmic radiation extend beyond the technical challenges to broader concerns regarding the deployment of quantum systems in long-duration space missions. Flying spacecraft equipped with quantum technology across vast distances may expose them to prolonged exposure to cosmic radiation, raising questions about long-term reliability and maintenance of the quantum devices onboard. Ongoing research into radiation-hardened quantum systems, able to sustain performance and maintain coherence over extended periods, is essential for ensuring the viability of quantum computing in prolonged explorative missions.

Additionally, cosmic radiation is not solely a hindrance but can also offer intriguing opportunities for leveraging quantum properties. As particle interactions with quantum systems occur, the data generated from such exposures can provide insights into the nature of cosmic radiation itself. Researchers are exploring the concept of "radiation sensors" that capitalize on the sensitivity of quantum materials to capture and analyze cosmic events, potentially uncovering useful information about cosmic processes and conditions in the universe.

In conclusion, the influence of cosmic radiation presents a nuanced interplay of challenges and opportunities for quantum computing in space. As we strive to explore the universe with the power of quantum technologies, robust engineering solutions, innovative shielding techniques, and advancements in quantum error correction will be crucial for overcoming the potential disruptions caused by cosmic radiation. Engaging these complexities will not only facilitate the successful deployment of quantum systems in deep space endeavors but will also lead to deeper insights into the underlying cosmic phenomena that shape our universe. By addressing the multifaceted influences of cosmic radiation, we can unlock the full potential of quantum computing, empowering humanity's quest to unravel the mysteries of existence among the stars.

11.2. Dealing with System Calibration at Extreme Distances

Dealing with system calibration at extreme distances involves addressing the intrinsic challenges posed by the unique conditions of space. As quantum computing technologies prepare to unfold across the vast expanse of the cosmos, effective calibration of quantum systems becomes crucial to ensure precision, accuracy, and reliability for missions far beyond Earth's atmosphere.

At its core, calibration entails the process of aligning and adjusting instruments to meet specific standards, establishing reliable performance benchmarks that are critical for gathering data accurately. In the realm of quantum computing, where qubits represent delicate quantum states susceptible to environmental interference, the task of calibration extends beyond traditional methodologies. System calibration must account for a range of factors, including cosmic radiation, temperature fluctuations, and the inherent uncertainties introduced by the quantum mechanics principles themselves.

The first challenge confronting system calibration at extreme distances is the communication delay. Light, the fastest entity in the universe, takes time to traverse the vast distances between spacecraft and Earth-based control systems. For instance, signals transmitted from Mars to Earth can take anywhere from 4 to 24 minutes to arrive, depending on their relative positions in their orbits. This delay introduces challenges in real-time calibration processes—any adjustments made to the quantum system must consider the lag in communication and response time. To address this, autonomous calibration protocols must be devised, allowing quantum systems to self-correct based on pre-set parameters without immediate dependence on ground control.

Moreover, the variability in environmental conditions as a spacecraft travels through space complicates calibration efforts. For instance, temperature extremes ranging from frigid cold in the depths of space to intense heat near celestial bodies impact quantum states. Effective thermal regulation becomes paramount to maintain the stability of qubits during calibration. Advanced materials and insulation techniques must be developed to shield quantum systems from erratic temperature variations, ensuring reliable oscillation frequencies and robustness in measurements.

Another layer of complexity arises from cosmic radiation, which poses a significant threat to the fidelity of quantum systems. High-energy particles from cosmic rays can disrupt qubit operations, compromising measurements and introducing errors into data signals. Calibration processes need to incorporate radiation-hardening techniques, employing shielding materials that minimize exposure, while algorithms capable of detecting radiation-induced errors must be integrated into the quantum systems themselves. This dual-layered approach will enable systems to adaptively recalibrate to their environments, increasing resilience against cosmic interference.

Furthermore, the notion of synchronicity becomes vital when calibrating interconnected quantum systems across multiple nodes in space. Quantum networks may necessitate calibration strategies capable of aligning qubit states among various devices while minimizing signal loss or decoherence during transmission. Utilizing advanced algorithms for entanglement swapping and error correction will enhance coordination between nodes, preserving coherent quantum states essential for accurate navigation and communication across the network.

However, as we confront these complexities, it is essential to remain vigilant regarding the potential ethical implications surrounding calibration in space. The autonomy granted to quantum systems in calibration processes necessitates robust protocols to ensure accountability and transparency in decision-making. This is particularly pertinent as quantum systems increasingly assume roles in critical navigation and communication tasks, where errors could have dire consequences for missions and human safety.

As emerging technologies continue to reshape our understanding of quantum capabilities, expanding the exploration of effective calibration in extreme distances is pivotal. Developing interdisciplinary approaches that join forces across quantum physicists, engineers, and space scientists will be indispensable to address these challenges comprehensively. Collaborative partnerships spanning research institutions, governmental agencies, and commercial enterprises will foster innovation and drive the practical implementation of calibrated quantum technologies in future space missions.

In conclusion, dealing with system calibration at extreme distances encapsulates a multifaceted challenge intrinsic to interstellar exploration. The task requires not only technical innovations to minimize errors and enhance precision but also ethical considerations overarching the autonomous functioning of quantum systems. By addressing these challenges collaboratively, we can pave the way for successful quantum computing applications in space, ultimately unlocking new dimensions of understanding and discovery as we embark on the next frontier of exploration in the cosmos.

11.3. Harnessing Space-Based Quantum Computing Resources

In this transformative chapter of our exploration, we turn to one of the most promising opportunities at the intersection of quantum mechanics and space exploration: the harnessing of space-based quantum computing resources. As humanity extends its reach into the cosmos, we are faced with unprecedented challenges that demand innovative solutions. Quantum computing, with its nuanced capabilities to solve complex problems exponentially faster than classical computation, offers a pathway toward addressing these challenges, paving the way for scientific and technological advancements that could redefine our understanding of the universe.

At the very core of this endeavor lies the concept of quantum computing resources in extraterrestrial environments—utilizing the vastness of space as a platform for developing quantum technologies that can operate beyond the limits imposed by Earth's atmosphere. Space-based quantum computing involves the deployment of quantum devices in satellite configurations, where they can leverage the unique conditions of space to enhance their performance and minimize decoherence—the loss of quantum coherence due to environmental interactions. The development of robust quantum hardware capable of withstanding the harshness of cosmic environments is a crucial aspect of this initiative.

One pivotal aspect of harnessing space-based quantum computing resources is the potential for developing quantum communication networks that can transmit data instantaneously across vast distances. Quantum entanglement, the phenomenon where two particles become linked in such a manner that the state of one affects the other regardless of distance, plays an essential role in this endeavor. Space missions equipped with entangled particles can establish communication systems that are not only faster than classical communication methods but also far more secure, as the act of trying to eavesdrop would disrupt the transmitted information, alerting the communicating parties to interference.

Moreover, the deployment of quantum computers in space can lead to the real-time processing of vast datasets collected from exploratory missions. Traditional data transmission methods often face delays caused by distance and signal attenuation; by utilizing quantum computing and its inherent speed, scientists can analyze data derived from cosmic probes and telescopes instantaneously, enabling timely responses to new discoveries. This advantage could significantly enhance mission capabilities, allowing for the adaptive recalibration of trajectories or the timely implementation of countermeasures in response to unexpected cosmic events.

Quantum computing resources will also play a crucial role in optimizing spacecraft trajectories through advanced algorithms that account for gravitational influences, energy consumption, and even collision avoidance with celestial bodies. As spacecraft travel into increasingly complex environments, leveraging the computational abilities of quantum systems enables us to explore a myriad of possible paths and optimize performance in real time. This multifaceted approach to navigation ensures that spacecraft maintain efficiency while maximizing the scientific yield of their missions.

However, implementing space-based quantum computing resources does not come without its set of challenges. The complexity of developing quantum hardware capable of functionally adapting to varying gravitational and radiation conditions must be addressed. Shielding measures to protect quantum systems from cosmic radiation, along with robust error correction techniques to mitigate decoherence, will be critical components in this technological quest. Ensuring the reliability of quantum devices over extended periods and distances becomes paramount, resulting in the necessity for ongoing research and development to facilitate sustainable quantum technologies capable of operating in the harsh environment of space.

Additionally, there lies a need for extensive collaboration across scientific disciplines. Astrophysicists, quantum physicists, engineers, and computer scientists will need to work synergistically to ensure that quantum technologies are harnessed effectively, aligning their expertise to explore the potential of quantum systems fully. The establishment of interdisciplinary research programs and partnerships among academic institutions, governmental agencies, and private enterprises will foster an environment conducive to innovation and problem-solving.

As we explore the potential of harnessing space-based quantum computing resources, we must also confront the larger ethical implications associated with this frontier technology. As quantum systems become integral to space exploration and data acquisition, considerations around privacy, security, and equitable access arise. Addressing these ethical dimensions early on will support a responsible approach to developing and deploying quantum technologies in outer space, ensuring that humanity's expansion into the cosmos remains thoughtful and principled.

The harnessing of space-based quantum computing resources holds thrilling prospects for windfall advancements in space exploration and understanding the universe. By cultivating the symbiotic relationship between quantum technology and space exploration, we prepare to face the challenges of tomorrow and seize the opportunities they present. As we stand on the precipice of this quantum frontier, the voyage into the boundless cosmos beckons, carrying with it the promise of scientific breakthroughs and transformative insights waiting beyond the stars.

In conclusion, as we venture further into the realms of space through the lens of quantum mechanics, we reaffirm our commitment to exploration through innovation, collaboration, and ethical engagement. The quest for harnessing space-based quantum resources not only opens a new chapter in our cosmic journey but embodies humanity's unyielding spirit of discovery and understanding, inspiring future generations to continue reaching for the stars.

11.4. Temperature and Quantum Stability

In the realm of quantum mechanics, temperature plays a crucial role in determining the stability of quantum states, particularly when it comes to implementing quantum computing technologies in space environments. For quantum systems, the relationship between temperature and quantum stability is pivotal, as temperature fluctuations can significantly influence coherence times and error rates—two crucial factors that dictate the performance of quantum algorithms and the reliability of quantum computations.

As we embark on space exploration, understanding thermal dynamics in the vacuum of space becomes essential. At absolute zero, the thermal motion of atoms and molecules ceases, allowing quantum systems to maintain their coherence. However, reaching and sustaining such conditions in space remains a formidable challenge. The extreme temperature fluctuations found in space, ranging from the stark cold of deep space to the sweltering heat near celestial bodies, can introduce decoherence—the rapid loss of quantum information due to interactions between particles and their environments—compromising the stability of qubits and interfering with computational tasks.

To mitigate the effects of temperature on quantum stability, engineers and scientists must devise innovative thermal control systems that can maintain appropriate operational temperatures within space-based quantum devices. These systems may incorporate advanced materials with exceptional thermal insulating properties, safeguarding quantum states from the environmental stressors that threaten coherence. Furthermore, the potential for utilizing cryogenic cooling techniques, where superconductors are chilled to facilitate quantum operations, represents a powerful strategy for ensuring the reliability of qubits even amidst temperature fluctuations.

The stability of quantum systems is also influenced by the type of quantum computing architecture deployed. For example, solid-state qubits, such as those based on superconducting circuits or trapped ions, exhibit differing sensitivities to thermal dynamics. As we select appropriate qubit technologies for specific missions, we must also evaluate their thermal characteristics to determine which systems will offer the best performance under the variable conditions expected in space.

In addition, the design of error correction protocols becomes vital in optimizing the robustness of quantum computations conducted in the presence of temperature-induced challenges. Quantum error correction codes allow for the detection and correction of errors arising from thermal fluctuations, increasing the effectiveness of quantum devices that may encounter decoherence. Implementing adaptive error-correction algorithms that monitor system performance in real-time can help maintain qubit stability, ensuring that computations remain accurate throughout the duration of a mission.

The complexities of temperature and quantum stability also extend to the interaction of quantum systems with cosmic radiation. Cosmic rays can introduce unwanted fluctuations in qubit states, significantly amplifying the challenges associated with temperature changes. Understanding these interactions not only informs the design of shielding materials for quantum devices but also influences the development of quantum error mitigation strategies that account for the dual threats of thermal dynamics and cosmic radiation.

Furthermore, space-based quantum computing resources encourage experimental approaches to exploring temperature-dependent quantum phenomena. Quantum simulations can model how variations in temperature might influence quantum states and behavior, showcasing the potential for creating systems that harness these properties effectively. Researchers can develop quantum algorithms to investigate the impact of temperature on the properties of quantum systems, leading to deeper insights that enhance our understanding of the relationship between temperature and quantum stability.

As we anticipate the challenges that temperature fluctuations pose to quantum stability in space exploration, fostering interdisciplinary collaboration becomes essential. Astrophysicists, quantum physicists, and aerospace engineers should unite their expertise, creating platforms for innovation that can inform the development of resilient quantum systems designed for operational success in the extreme conditions of the cosmos. Collaborative research initiatives can advance the field, leading to the next generation of quantum technologies that prioritize stability and reliability under temperature extremes.

In summary, the interplay between temperature and quantum stability is critical to the success of quantum computing technologies in space environments. As we harness the power of quantum mechanics for exploring the universe, developing robust thermal control systems, implementing error correction protocols, and understanding the influence of cosmic radiation will be paramount in ensuring the coherence of qubits. By embracing the intricacies of these challenges, we position ourselves to not only navigate the complexities of space but also unlock profound insights into the quantum nature of reality, ultimately deepening our understanding of existence itself among the stars. In so doing, we prepare for a brighter future in cosmic exploration, where quantum mechanics guides us on a path toward discovery and understanding beyond the confines of our terrestrial experiences.

11.5. Securing Quantum Communications in Space

In the context of securing communication in the vastness of space, quantum communication presents a revolutionary approach that safeguards the integrity and confidentiality of interstellar data exchanges. As humanity embarks on ambitious missions beyond Earth, the ability to ensure secure communication channels becomes paramount. Quantum mechanics, with its intricacies and peculiar properties, offers a robust framework for establishing communication systems that are not only extraordinarily fast but inherently secure against interception and disruption.

Central to the security of quantum communications is the phenomenon of quantum entanglement. When particles become entangled, they exhibit instantaneous correlations regardless of the distance separating them. This unique attribute allows for the creation of quantum keys that can be shared securely between parties. Any attempt to eavesdrop on these keys will alter the quantum states, alerting the communicating entities to potential breaches in security. This foundational aspect of quantum key distribution (QKD) positions quantum communication as a formidable defense against traditional threats faced in space transmission.

Implementing quantum communications in space encompasses the development of a vast network of quantum nodes—satellites or relay stations equipped with quantum communication capabilities. These nodes will facilitate the generation, maintenance, and transmission of entangled qubits, creating a resilient tapestry of interconnected systems. As spacecraft venture into the cosmos, these nodes will help secure the flow of information back to mission control, ensuring that critical data from deep space explorations remains protected from potential interception.

However, several significant challenges arise in securing quantum communications in the vast expanse of space. Firstly, maintaining the coherence of entangled states becomes a primary hurdle; cosmic radiation and environmental fluctuations can induce decoherence, leading to the degradation of quantum states. Developing robust shielding mechanisms and advanced materials capable of withstanding cosmic interference is essential for preserving the integrity of quantum communications. Engineering teams must innovate solutions tailored for the unique conditions of space, ensuring that quantum devices can operate reliably over extended durations.

Additionally, the deployment of quantum repeaters will be vital for establishing long-distance quantum communication networks. Quantum repeaters extend entanglement across vast distances, allowing nodes to relay quantum signals while counteracting the degradation that occurs over long pathways. Implementing efficient entanglement swapping methods will amplify the reach of quantum communications, creating a network capable of functioning efficiently across light-years. This system architecture will enable secure and real-time communication among interstellar probes, researchers, and mission control on Earth, transforming how we interact with data from deep within the cosmos.

The influence of time delays also enters the equation, necessitating the development of sophisticated algorithms that can handle communication lags inherent to vast distances. Ground control must design systems that can adjust to incoming data even when faced with transmission delays—a critical consideration as spacecraft may navigate complex cosmic phenomena without real-time input. Incorporating autonomous decision-making capabilities powered by AI will allow quantum communication systems to respond dynamically to new data, ensuring that critical responses remain timely.

The ethical implications surrounding quantum communications in space further deepen the inquiry into this unfolding narrative. As secure data transmission becomes paramount, discussions regarding privacy, data access, and the implications of quantum communication technologies must be brought to the forefront. As we develop quantum systems that facilitate the sharing of sensitive information across the cosmos, ensuring equitable access becomes vital in fostering a global commitment to responsible exploration.

In summary, securing quantum communications in space embodies the potential of quantum mechanics to reshape our understanding of data exchange in the cosmic expanse. By leveraging quantum entanglement and developing innovative technological solutions to overcome related challenges, we can ensure that the data transmitted from deep space remains safe, efficient, and reliable. The journey toward establishing secure quantum communication networks represents not just a technological aspiration, but a pivotal step in advancing humanity's reach within the universe. By diligently addressing the complexities of quantum communication, we illuminate new pathways toward exploration and discovery, ultimately enriching our understanding of existence itself as we navigate the vast unknowns among the stars.

12. The Future of Quantum Space Exploration

12.1. Next-Generation Technologies

In the rapidly evolving landscape of technology, next-generation technologies represent a remarkable turning point in our understanding and exploration of the cosmos. As we stand on the brink of a new era in quantum computing and space exploration, the synthesis of these advanced technologies holds extraordinary potential to reshape our approach to discovering the universe and the phenomenon within it.

At the heart of next-generation technologies is the advent of quantum computing. Unlike classical computing, which processes information in a binary format utilizing bits, quantum computing leverages the unique properties of quantum bits or qubits. These qubits possess the remarkable ability to exist in superpositions of states, allowing them to represent multiple possibilities simultaneously. This exponentially increases the computational power at our disposal, enabling us to tackle complex calculations that would otherwise be infeasible with classical methods. This capability is crucial in the context of space exploration, where scientists frequently encounter vast datasets and intricate models requiring rapid, efficient processing.

Imagine the possibilities that arise from using quantum algorithms to navigate and analyze the data gathered from cosmic phenomena. Quantum algorithms excel at solving problems related to optimization, factorization, and pattern recognition, making them ideal for applications in astrobiology, cosmology, and astrophysics. For example, quantum algorithms can support trajectory optimization for spacecraft navigating gravitational fields from multiple celestial bodies, ultimately facilitating efficient and accurate interstellar travel.

Moreover, the integration of quantum sensors opens as a next-generation technology vital for enhancing our observational capabilities in space. These sensors harness the principles of quantum mechanics, enabling unprecedented levels of sensitivity and precision when detecting faint astrophysical signals. By deploying quantum sensors in space missions, we can gather invaluable data from phenomena such as gravitational waves, cosmic microwave background radiation, and the distribution of dark matter—each providing unique insights into the fundamental workings of the universe.

As we look ahead, the collaborative future of quantum technologies must also be acknowledged regarding partnerships across industries and sectors. The role of public and private sector collaborations is increasingly essential in driving the development and deployment of next-generation technologies. Governmental agencies, academic institutions, and private companies must unite their resources and expertise to foster innovation and accelerate progress in quantum computing and space exploration initiatives. By pooling knowledge and funding, these partnerships can expedite breakthroughs that can transform our understanding of the universe.

However, as we embrace the potential of these technologies, it is crucial to address the ethical implications surrounding their application. The disruption brought about by next-generation technologies prompts important discussions around privacy, data security, and the impact of quantum advancements on societal structures. As quantum computing evolves, we must ensure that the developments are guided by ethical frameworks that respect human rights and acknowledge potential discrimination or inequities that may arise from advanced technologies. The establishment of reflective and proactive policies will be vital to safeguard the interests of all as we embark on this quantum journey.

As we consider the future of quantum space exploration, the challenges posed by cosmic radiation, the calibration of quantum systems at extreme distances, and the reliability of communication must all be confronted. By developing innovative shielding techniques, error correction protocols, and autonomous navigation systems, we can harness the full potential of quantum technologies while ensuring that our exploratory ambitions remain resilient amid the unpredictable cosmic environment.

Incorporating next-generation technologies into our cosmic aspirations will undoubtedly inspire future generations of scientists and explorers. The spirit of innovation and discovery embodied in quantum advancements presents a call to action for young minds to engage with the sciences, fostering curiosity and enthusiasm that transcends boundaries. By investing in education and outreach initiatives, we can nurture the next wave of quantum scientists who will carry forth the torch of exploration as they delve into the infinite expanse of knowledge waiting among the stars.

In summary, next-generation technologies represent a monumental leap in our capabilities for understanding and exploring the universe. As quantum computing, advanced sensors, and collaborative partnerships converge, the potential to unravel the mysteries of cosmic phenomena ignites a spirit of exploration that knows no bounds. As we harness the insights of quantum mechanics, we place ourselves on the precipice of extraordinary discoveries that extend beyond our current understanding of existence. The journey into the cosmos beckons, promising profound revelations about the universe and our place within it—an infinitely exciting venture shaped by the fusion of quantum mechanics and our unending curiosity.

12.2. Ethical Implications of Deep Space Quantum Computing

The exploration of deep space and the integration of quantum computing into this realm presents an uncharted landscape that necessitates a thorough examination of the ethical implications involved. As we embark on this quantum journey, it is crucial to analyze how the development and deployment of quantum technologies in deep space will resonate within the fabric of scientific exploration, societal values, and the moral responsibilities we carry as stewards of both Earth and the cosmos.

At the forefront of these ethical considerations is the nature of informed consent and collaboration in space exploration. Quantum technologies possess the potential to fundamentally alter our understanding of the universe, yet the implications of utilizing these new tools must be addressed through comprehensive ethical discourse. It is essential for scientists, policymakers, and the public to engage in dialogues that examine the potential extraterrestrial impacts of quantum advancements, ensuring that developments are guided by principles of equity and shared benefit.

As quantum computing enables unparalleled capabilities for data analysis and resource extraction, it also raises concerns regarding the potential monopolization of these technologies by wealthy nations, corporations, or individuals. The threat of disparity in access to quantum capabilities could create divisions in societal power and amplify existing inequalities in global exploration efforts. To mitigate this risk, it is imperative for international collaborations to establish inclusive frameworks for developing and deploying quantum technologies, emphasizing cooperation over competition.

Furthermore, as operators of quantum systems in space, ethical considerations extend to the intersection with artificial intelligence. The integration of AI in quantum technologies calls for careful examination regarding decision-making processes, accountability, and transparency. Autonomous systems equipped with quantum capabilities will increasingly be tasked with navigating complex environments, making choices that may have profound implications for mission trajectories and outcomes. Ensuring that these AI systems operate under ethical guidelines and human oversight becomes paramount to safeguarding both scientific integrity and the safety of missions—with transparency in algorithmic decision-making fostering trust among stakeholders.

In addition to considerations regarding equity and autonomy, the ethical implications of quantum advancements must also encompass the potential impact on planetary environments we aim to explore. As we venture deeper into the cosmos, efforts must be made to minimize the ecological footprint of our exploration—a principle often encapsulated within the larger framework of astrobiology and planetary protection. Ethical responsibilities extend to how we approach resource extraction, particularly in the context of quantum technologies, which may enable us to mine celestial bodies for materials needed on Earth. Leveraging these advancements should always respect the integrity of potential extraterrestrial ecosystems, ensuring that our quest for knowledge does not come at the expense of jeopardizing the environments we study.

The moral dimensions of our explorations also extend to the pursuit of life beyond Earth. As we turn our sights toward the search for extraterrestrial intelligence (SETI) and potential biosignatures among distant worlds, the ethical considerations surrounding the discovery of new life forms come to the forefront. The implications of encountering life—whether primitive or complex—necessitate a foundational approach rooted in respect and prudence. These encounters risk challenging our understandings of existence, prompting introspection on how we interact with intelligent beings and the responsibilities we owe to them as potential compatriots in the universe.

In conclusion, as we forge ahead into the depths of space empowered by quantum technologies, a robust ethical framework will guide our endeavors. Navigating the intricacies of informed consent, resource equity, autonomy in decision-making, planetary stewardship, and the search for extraterrestrial life requires deliberate engagement from the scientific community, policymakers, and global citizens. By prioritizing ethical considerations in our pursuit of these transformative technologies, we can cultivate an exploration ethos that resonates with shared human values, fostering a future where our endeavors in the cosmos enrich not only our understanding of the universe but also the collective experience of existence itself. The ethical implications of deep space quantum computing will shape our legacy as explorers and innovators, determining how we engage with the universe and its myriad possibilities.

12.3. Quantum Terraforming Initiatives

In the quest to develop time zones beyond Earth and adapt to various cosmic environments, quantum terraforming initiatives introduce a new dimension to our understanding of space and the potential for life. These initiatives focus on utilizing the principles of quantum mechanics to reshape extraterrestrial landscapes, creating environments conducive to human and other forms of life through advanced technology. As we consider the possibilities of terraforming on other planets and celestial bodies, we must also assess the technological, ethical, and practical implications associated with this ambitious endeavor.

At the heart of quantum terraforming lies the idea that the unique properties of quantum systems can be harnessed to manipulate and transform planetary environments. By employing advanced quantum technologies, including quantum sensors and quantum computing, we can analyze the complex ecosystems of distant planets, understand their atmospheric dynamics, and tailor interventions to optimize conditions necessary for sustaining life. For example, the measurement capabilities afforded by quantum sensors can provide real-time data about the composition, temperature, and pressure of alien atmospheres, enabling scientists to devise effective strategies for introducing life-supporting elements, such as oxygen and water vapor, into the environment.

One potential application of quantum terraforming is the development of self-replicating nanotechnology, which can alter landscapes and atmospheres in ways that promote habitability. Quantum-controlled nanobots—infused with advanced artificial intelligence—could autonomously assess planetary conditions and execute terraforming tasks with incredible precision. Utilizing the power of quantum algorithms, these nanobots could analyze massive datasets while modeling the effects of various interventions, ensuring that the changes made are sustainable and conducive to the emergence of life.

Moreover, quantum terraforming initiatives may encompass innovative approaches to energy management. By harnessing quantum technologies to capture solar energy from distant stars or cosmic radiation, we could create energy-efficient systems that support terraforming efforts and, ultimately, habitation. For instance, quantum batteries—capable of harnessing energy through quantum effects—

could sustain power across the vast distances involved in space travel and terraforming operations. These batteries would provide a lightweight, efficient energy source that aligns perfectly with the ambitions of off-world development.

However, the quest for terraforming presents complex ethical dilemmas that must be navigated with care. The implications of altering extraterrestrial environments raise questions about the protection of potential native ecosystems. Just as proposed initiatives involve the alteration of landscapes to benefit humanity, there may also be legitimate concerns regarding the preservation of alien life forms—be they microbial or otherwise—that could exist in these environments. Thorough assessments of the potential bioethics involved in terraforming endeavors are warranted to strike a balance between innovation and responsible stewardship.

Furthermore, the socio-political implications of quantum terraforming initiatives demand attention. As space exploration efforts escalate, who will control the technology and the processes involved in terraforming? Will there be equitable access to the technology, and how will international partnerships evolve as nations unite around common interests in cosmic exploration? Establishing robust frameworks that promote collaboration and equitable resource sharing will be paramount to fostering positive relationships among various stakeholders in the pursuit of cosmic terraforming and exploration.

Science fiction has long celebrated the possibilities of terraforming, instilling dreams of creating habitable environments on distant planets. As we delve into the world of quantum terraforming, we embrace the spirit of exploration that unveils opportunities for new beginnings among the stars. With groundbreaking advancements in quantum technology and the commitment to ethical consideration, we stand poised to chart a course for reimagining extraterrestrial worlds and extending our reach beyond Earth's boundaries.

In conclusion, quantum terraforming initiatives promise to propel humanity into a new era of cosmic exploration. By integrating quantum mechanics into our strategies for reshaping environments, we can forge paths toward making distant celestial bodies habitable. As we embrace this journey, we must remain vigilant in our ethical considerations, ensuring that the principles guiding our explorations respect the intricate tapestry of existence in the cosmos. Through the fusion of quantum mechanics and the spirit of exploration, we embark on a quest that revels in the infinite possibilities awaiting revelation on the grand stage of the universe.

12.4. The Role of Public and Private Sector Partnerships

In contemporary discussions surrounding space exploration, the role of public and private sector partnerships emerges as a critical component in fueling innovation and ensuring the success of ambitious missions that venture into the unknown. As humanity seeks to expand its presence beyond Earth and unlock the mysteries of the cosmos, collaborative efforts that leverage resources, expertise, and technological advancements from both public organizations and private enterprises hold great promise. This chapter will explore how these partnerships can foster the development of quantum computing technologies, enhance deep space missions, and chart a pathway for the responsible exploration of the universe.

Public sector entities, including government space agencies such as NASA, ESA (European Space Agency), and others, traditionally have been at the forefront of space exploration. Their long-term vision, substantial funding, and established expertise in scientific research form a solid foundation for pioneering endeavors. These agencies possess the political and institutional stability necessary to undertake large-scale projects aimed at exploring the cosmos and addressing complex challenges. By cultivating relationships with private companies that specialize in innovation, engineering, and technology development, public institutions can enhance their capabilities and reduce the timeframes associated with the development and deployment of new technologies.

Private sector companies, on the other hand, introduce a nimble approach to space exploration, characterized by rapid innovation and the ability to quickly pivot in response to emerging challenges and opportunities. The space industry has witnessed a boom in commercial enterprises, ranging from satellite manufacturing to launch services and even in-space operations. Partnerships with these companies allow public agencies to harness cutting-edge technology and foster a culture of innovation. For instance, organizations like SpaceX and Blue Origin have revolutionized the economics of space travel, providing cost-effective solutions for launching payloads while driving technological advancements that propel the industry forward.

In the realm of quantum technologies, this synergy between public and private sectors is particularly significant. Quantum computing is on the cusp of transforming how we model complex systems and process data, a venture that holds immense implications for space exploration. Collaborative efforts can lead to investments in quantum research initiatives, aimed at developing practical applications for quantum computing in mission planning, data analysis, and precision navigation.

As quantum technologies evolve, public-private partnerships can facilitate the development of space-based quantum computing resources. By pooling expertise from both sectors, researchers can explore how to implement quantum computing technologies onboard spacecraft, harnessing their processing power to analyze large datasets generated by scientific observations or missions. This potential for collaboration extends into the design of quantum communication systems capable of transmitting data securely while maintaining coherence despite the challenges posed by cosmic environments.

Moreover, the partnership model fosters an environment conducive to interdisciplinary collaboration. Between physicists, engineers, computer scientists, and space specialists, practitioners from various fields can converge to formulate novel solutions that integrate quantum technologies into existing processes. Creating dynamic teams encourages knowledge sharing and cross-disciplinary innovation, which ultimately drives the success of complex exploration missions.

In addition to technology development, public-private partnerships can play a vital role in promoting the responsible exploration of space. As the quest to acquire resources from celestial bodies intensifies—potentially leading to the emergence of space mining—ethical considerations are paramount. Engaging all stakeholders in the conversation around responsible practices, sustainability, and environmental stewardship will ensure that exploration efforts are conducted with integrity and respect for the cosmos.

Furthermore, as we venture into deeper discussions on governance and regulation in space exploration, collaborative frameworks that unite the public sector's institutional knowledge with private sector's agility can facilitate the establishment of comprehensive policies. These policies can guide exploration efforts while safeguarding the rights of nations and protecting the interests of all humans as we collectively ascend beyond our home planet.

The pursuit of knowledge and understanding drives us toward the stars and beyond, embodying a spirit of exploration that reflects humanity's commitment to discovery. The melding of public and private sector resources, expertise, and vision will undoubtedly propel human endeavors across the cosmic expanse as we seek to unveil the unknown dimensions of the universe.

In conclusion, public and private sector partnerships represent a cornerstone of innovation and progress in our quest for cosmic exploration. By combining the strengths and capabilities of each sector, we will navigate the complexities of deep space exploration more effectively and responsibly while leveraging the transformative potential of quantum technologies. As we stand on the precipice of new discoveries, the collaborative spirit between public institutions and private enterprises will serve as a guiding force, reinforcing our commitment to explore the universe responsibly while unlocking the mysteries of existence that await among the stars.

12.5. Inspiration for Future Generations

In the ever-expanding narrative of scientific inquiry and cosmic exploration, the chapter titled 'Inspiration for Future Generations' serves as a poignant reminder of the resounding impact that quantum computing can have not only in scientific realms but also on the human spirit and the collective aspirations of society. As we stand on the brink of what may seem like an unprecedented era of discovery afforded by quantum technologies, it becomes essential to reflect on how such advancements can inspire the coming generations to dream bigger, think deeper, and aspire to reach beyond the confines of Earth.

The allure of the cosmos has captivated humanity for millennia, igniting passions that have driven exploration, philosophical contemplation, and artistic expression. As quantum computing emerges as a cornerstone for future exploration—promising to unravel the mysteries of dark matter, enhance the speed and security of communication, and elevate our capabilities to analyze celestial phenomena—the potential to nurture this inherent curiosity should galvanize educational initiatives across the globe. By integrating quantum concepts into curricula and emphasizing the accessibility of complex subjects, educators can empower young minds to innovate and contribute to the quest for knowledge unconstrained by traditional boundaries.

Importantly, the inspirational power of quantum advancements transcends educational frameworks. This narrative invites policymakers, industry leaders, and the public at large to embrace a greater responsibility—to foster interdisciplinary collaboration that mirrors the interconnected nature of the universe itself. The fusion of science, technology, arts, and humanities presents a holistic approach where diverse perspectives converge to address the complex challenges faced in the pursuit of cosmic exploration. Encouraging initiatives that promote engagement across disciplines can create supportive ecosystems that nurture future leaders equipped to tackle the unknown.

Moreover, as we consider our emerging relationship with the universe through the lens of quantum computing, we must recognize the ethical implications that underpin these innovations. As each leap into the quantum realm unleashes a wealth of possibilities, the societal values of equity, sustainability, and stewardship must weave seamlessly into the fabric of our exploration. To inspire confidence in future generations, it is imperative to cultivate a culture of responsible innovation that respects the delicate balance between technological advancements and ethical considerations, ensuring that humanity's quest for knowledge does not compromise the integrity of ecosystems —be they terrestrial or extraterrestrial.

The interconnectedness of existence is further amplified by the prospects offered by quantum computing, as we reimagine our understanding of life in the cosmos. The possibility of discovering alternative forms of existence, driven by quantum processes, invites introspection about our cosmic kinship with the universe. This epiphany—a shared existence—can inspire future generations to not merely observe the heavens but to conceive of themselves as active participants within this grand narrative. Inquiring minds may be drawn to the prospects of crafting solutions that bridge science fiction and scientific reality, exploring new realms where life, in its many forms, flourishes amid the stars.

Lastly, it is essential to acknowledge that inspiration is not a singular path; it is a collective journey made richer through collaboration, exploration, and perseverance. As we stand united in our aspirations to uncover the mysteries of the universe through quantum computing, let us foster a spirit of inquiry that transcends individual ambitions or achievements. When each person contributes their insights toward shared goals, the cumulative effect can drive amazing transformations —paving pathways to uncharted territories of understanding and discovery that inspire future generations to continue the legacy of exploration.

In conclusion, the chapter 'Inspiration for Future Generations' not only serves as a testament to the interconnectedness of human experience and cosmic inquiry but also reinforces the critical need to nurture curiosity, creativity, and ethical responsibility in the pursuit of knowledge. As we embark on a journey toward a future illuminated by quantum advancements, we not only honor the pioneering spirits of those before us but also kindle the aspirations of those yet to come —a legacy of exploration that seeks to unveil the infinite dimensions of existence and our place amidst them. The adventure of understanding and discovering the universe continues, and it is the duty of this generation to inspire others to embark on their own journeys into the quantum fabric of reality.

13. Quantum Artificial Intelligence and Space

13.1. Developing Quantum AI for Space Missions

In the quest to explore the cosmos, the development of quantum artificial intelligence (AI) for space missions stands as a transformative frontier. As we prepare to embark on journeys beyond Earth, the integration of quantum computing principles with AI technology promises to enhance our navigation, decision-making, and operational capabilities in ways previously thought unattainable. This subchapter outlines the advancements, challenges, and transformative potential of quantum AI in revolutionizing how we engage with space exploration.

Quantum AI blends the computational power of quantum computing with advanced artificial intelligence techniques. This fusion enables AI systems to process vast datasets and perform complex calculations with astounding speed and efficiency. In the context of space missions, quantum AI can manage the intricacies of data collected from sensors, telescopes, and spacecraft, uncovering patterns and insights that inform mission planning and execution.

One crucial application of quantum AI in space missions is trajectory optimization. When spacecraft navigate the gravitational influences of celestial bodies, quantum AI algorithms can analyze multiple possible paths simultaneously, allowing spacecraft to adjust their routes in real-time for efficiency. By evaluating vast combinations of gravitational interactions and energy expenditures, quantum AI systems enhance the performance of navigational protocols, facilitating responsive adaptations that ensure successful mission outcomes.

Moreover, the differential processing capability of quantum AI can enhance the operational efficiency of autonomous systems deployed in space. As exploratory missions venture into uncharted territories, the ability of quantum AI to analyze incoming data from a variety of sensors in tandem allows spacecraft to make informed decisions without waiting for directives from mission control on Earth—critical in scenarios where communication delays could hinder timely responses. The integration of quantum AI paves the way for self-organizing systems capable of reacting instantaneously to shifting environmental conditions and navigating potential hazards during their journeys.

Nonetheless, the development of quantum AI for space missions does not come without substantial challenges. The technical intricacies of quantum systems must be thoroughly understood to ensure that they can operate reliably in the unique conditions of space. Qubits are inherently delicate and sensitive, and the presence of cosmic radiation can disrupt their quantum states. Engineers and scientists must develop robust methods for shielding quantum devices against environmental disturbances, while simultaneously ensuring the coherence and stability of quantum systems over extended durations.

Additionally, considerations around the ethical implications of integrating AI into space missions take on significant importance. The autonomy granted to AI systems raises questions of accountability and transparency. Establishing ethical guidelines that govern the decision-making processes of autonomous vehicles is crucial to ensure safety, compliance, and responsible use of technology in extraterrestrial environments. It becomes imperative for researchers and mission planners to reflect thoughtfully on the broader implications of deploying such AI capabilities, fostering an environment that prioritizes safety and ethical responsibility within the realm of space exploration.

The collaboration between quantum technology developers and astrobiologists will pave the way for future innovations in space missions. By focusing on the synthesis of ideas from various disciplines, this collaboration will inspire the creation of new quantum AI paradigms that accommodate the complexities associated with space exploration. Engaging in interdisciplinary dialogue allows scientists from diverse backgrounds—physics, computer science, and biology —to address the interwoven challenges of developing effective AI systems for navigation and data management.

As we continue to explore the immense potential of quantum AI in space missions, the inspiration for future generations becomes paramount. Nurturing curiosity and passion within the scientific community is essential for encouraging the next generation of scientists and innovators to participate in the exploration of space through the lens of quantum technology. Educational initiatives that highlight the connections between quantum mechanics, artificial intelligence, and space exploration will empower young minds to think creatively and contribute to the evolution of humanity's cosmic endeavors.

In conclusion, the establishment of quantum AI for space missions signifies an exhilarating opportunity to propel humanity into uncharted territories across the universe. By harnessing the unique capabilities provided by quantum mechanics, we not only enhance our navigation and operational efficiency but also revolutionize our approach to scientific discovery. The voyage into the cosmos beckons us, drawing us toward the possibility of uncovering the intricacies of existence while redefining our understanding of life and intelligence. As we embark upon this journey, we embody the inquisitive spirit of exploration—inviting future generations to join us in unraveling the mysteries of the cosmos through the innovative lens of quantum technology.

13.2. Autonomous Decision Making in Uncharted Territories

In uncharted territories, where the vastness of space challenges our understanding and capabilities, autonomous decision-making takes on heightened significance. As humanity reaches outward toward distant celestial bodies, the need for efficient, reliable, and innovative technologies to navigate and adapt becomes paramount. Here, quantum computing intersects with artificial intelligence to shape a new paradigm in space exploration, enabling autonomous systems that can operate independently while employing a level of sophistication inspired by the principles of quantum mechanics.

The complexity of space environments often precludes real-time communication with mission control on Earth, particularly given the vast distances involved. This elicits a demand for intelligent systems capable of making autonomous decisions during critical phases of exploration. Autonomous decision-making implies the development of systems that can evaluate situations, analyze data, and leverage pre-existing knowledge to respond dynamically to changing conditions. In the context of quantum computing, these systems harness the power of qubits to process vast quantities of information rapidly, offering solutions that classical computers struggle to match.

Quantum algorithms play a crucial role in optimizing the decision-making processes of autonomous systems. For instance, when navigating the gravitational influences of multiple celestial bodies, a spacecraft equipped with quantum AI can simultaneously evaluate numerous potential trajectories, weighing the associated risks and rewards in real-time. This quantum computational capacity empowers missions to react promptly and effectively to unpredictable scenarios, maximizing efficiency and safety.

Moreover, as autonomous systems encounter environmental variables that could affect their operations—such as radiation fluctuations, gravitational anomalies, or sudden changes in atmospheric conditions—quantum decision-making frameworks can process this data and implement immediate adjustments. For example, if a spacecraft approaches an asteroid belt, the onboard quantum AI can evaluate various routes, automatically calculating the safest path while considering potential fuel constraints and mission objectives. This level of adaptability, driven by quantum methods, is integral to the success of deep space missions, as unforeseen challenges will inevitably arise.

As we consider the future of autonomous decision-making in uncharted territories, it is essential to acknowledge the inherent challenges associated with developing these technologies. The calibration of quantum systems, as discussed previously, remains a critical aspect that can influence the reliability of the decisions made by autonomous systems. Furthermore, errors arising from decoherence or cosmic radiation need to be addressed to ensure that quantum devices maintain their operational integrity in extreme space conditions.

Another consideration revolves around the ethical implications of allowing autonomous systems to make decisions without immediate human oversight. As AI assumes greater autonomy in critical processes, societies must engage in discussions about accountability and ethical responsibilities. It raises important questions: How do we ensure that decision-making adhered to ethical standards and aligned with human values? As we explore these ethical dimensions, it becomes paramount to establish frameworks and guidelines that ensure transparency, fairness, and safety in the deployment of autonomous systems.

In transforming the landscape of space exploration, collaborations across various disciplines will propel the development of autonomous systems equipped with quantum capabilities. Engineers, AI researchers, and quantum physicists must work together to create a converging knowledge base, driving innovations that can redefine the possibilities for exploring uncharted territories. It fosters an environment where diverse perspectives can contribute to the creation of intelligent systems capable of addressing the myriad complexities encountered in space.

In conclusion, autonomous decision-making in uncharted territories symbolizes an exciting confluence of quantum computing and artificial intelligence, poised to revolutionize how we explore the cosmos. By embracing these advanced technologies, we can navigate the unknowns of space with heightened knowledge, efficiency, and adaptability. As we venture into this bold new era of exploration, we must remain mindful of the challenges, ethical considerations, and collaborative opportunities that arise in this remarkable journey. The potential for autonomous systems to reshape humanity's understanding of the universe is limited only by our aspirations and creativity, propelling us toward a future where the unknown becomes an invitation to venture even further into the depths of existence among the stars.

13.3. Quantum Robotics: The Future of Space Exploration

In the grand tapestry of space exploration, the integration of quantum robotics embodies the potential to revolutionize how we engage with the cosmos on a fundamental level. As humanity embarks on missions that extend beyond Earth, the fusion of quantum computing and robotics offers unprecedented opportunities for autonomous operations, advanced data processing, and enhanced decision-making capabilities in scenarios that demand precision and responsiveness. This subchapter explores the role of quantum robotics in shaping the future of space exploration, highlighting their applications, benefits, and the technological advancements that underpin this ambitious frontier.

At the core of the concept of quantum robotics lies the utilization of quantum algorithms and quantum-enhanced sensors to optimize robotic functions. Traditional robotic systems rely on classical computing, which, while effective, faces limitations in processing vast amounts of data and making real-time decisions. By harnessing the power of quantum computing, robotics can transcend these constraints, enabling robots to process multidimensional datasets simultaneously and adapt rapidly to changing environmental conditions. This quantum advantage is particularly crucial in space exploration, where autonomous systems must navigate complex gravitational fields, respond to dynamic events, and determine optimal paths without waiting for instructions from ground control.

Consider the potential applications of quantum robots in planetary exploration. Equipped with advanced sensors and quantum AI, these robots could analyze the surfaces of moons or distant planets, gathering data on atmospheric composition, geological activity, and potential hazards. Their ability to process this information in real-time allows for instant adjustments in navigation and functioning, elevating mission efficiency and safety. For example, if a quantum robot detects a significant radiation anomaly or an impending dust storm, it can immediately recalibrate its path to avoid danger, enhancing the overall success rate of missions.

Quantum-enhanced communication systems integrated into these robotic platforms further amplify their utility in space exploration. These systems, utilizing the principles of quantum entanglement, can ensure secure and instantaneous data transmission between robots and mission control. The ability to transmit sensitive or time-critical information without the risk of eavesdropping presents a vital advantage as exploratory missions probe into uncharted territories of the cosmos.

Moreover, the development of quantum robots is intricately tied to advances in materials science, allowing for the creation of lightweight and resilient robotic structures capable of surviving the extreme conditions of space. The construction of robotic systems that incorporate quantum sensors and computing hardware must tackle the challenges posed by cosmic radiation, temperature extremes, and the vacuum of space. Research in radiation-hardening techniques and materials that endure the rigors of space travel will be paramount to enhancing these robots' performance and longevity.

Yet the journey toward realizing fully functional quantum robotics for space exploration involves significant obstacles that must be surmounted. The calibration of quantum sensors, guaranteeing coherence in quantum states, and ensuring seamless integration of quantum algorithms into robotic systems encompass a continuum of challenges. Each of these components must be harmonized to create a cohesive and effective robotic framework capable of carrying out sophisticated tasks in the unpredictable environment of outer space.

Furthermore, the advent of quantum robotics raises important ethical and societal considerations. As autonomous systems take on increasingly complex roles within space missions, transparency regarding their decision-making processes, accountability for actions taken during operations, and the implications for human oversight must be thoroughly addressed. Engaging in ongoing dialogues about responsible innovation will uphold the moral integrity of explorations as technology evolves.

Interdisciplinary collaboration will be essential to advance the development of quantum robotics. Engaging experts across fields —quantum physics, robotics, engineering, and astrobiology—will provide diverse perspectives that inform the challenges and solutions associated with these technologies. As we collectively strive toward harnessing the potential of quantum robotics, it is crucial to cultivate an environment that fosters innovation while ensuring that ethical considerations are embedded within the narrative of exploration.

In conclusion, the emergence of quantum robotics represents a vital leap forward in the pursuit of deep space exploration. By harnessing the unique capabilities of quantum mechanics and combining them with robotics, we unlock a spectrum of opportunities for autonomous operations, precision navigation, and enhanced data collection. As we engage with the cosmos, quantum robotics holds the promise of enabling humanity to navigate the unknowns with unprecedented efficacy, revealing the secrets of existence while pushing the boundaries of exploration into realms previously regarded as unattainable. The future of space exploration is poised to be transformative, illuminating our journey among the stars through the lens of quantum technologies and robotics.

13.4. AI and Human Collaboration: New Paradigms

In the realm of quantum mechanics, the collaboration between artificial intelligence (AI) and human ingenuity is heralding a new paradigm in space exploration. As we stand on the cusp of a technological revolution, the synergy between quantum computing and AI opens vast possibilities for advancing our understanding of the cosmos. This chapter explores the multifaceted implications of AI and human collaboration in the context of quantum technologies, highlighting the transformative potential that lies ahead for deep space missions and beyond.

At the core of this collaboration is the unparalleled processing power of quantum computers, which allows for the rapid analysis of vast datasets and complex simulations that characterize contemporary astrophysics and space exploration. Traditional computational systems often struggle to manage and interpret the overwhelming volumes of data generated by telescopes, spacecraft, and sensor networks. Quantum computing transcends these limitations by utilizing the principles of superposition and entanglement, enabling the simultaneous evaluation of multiple possibilities. Therefore, AI systems integrated with quantum computers can not only enhance navigation and operational capabilities in space missions but also refine the interpretation of celestial phenomena.

One of the most spirited areas of development is the role of AI in optimizing the decision-making processes for autonomous systems deployed in space. As missions venture into uncharted territories, AI systems armed with quantum algorithms can evaluate real-time environmental data, adjusting spacecraft trajectories and calibrating instruments to optimize performance. The ability to process this information rapidly empowers quantum-informed autonomous systems to make informed decisions without waiting for directives from Earth—a strategic advantage in the unpredictable realm of space exploration.

Moreover, the intertwining of AI with quantum technologies heralds the potential for enhancing scientific discovery. By deploying quantum-enhanced AI tools capable of analyzing astronomical datasets, researchers can identify patterns, anomalies, and correlations that would otherwise escape classical analysis. This approach facilitates the discovery of new celestial bodies, enhances our understanding of cosmic phenomena such as dark matter and dark energy, and allows for the identification of possible biosignatures on exoplanets. AI-driven data mining serves as an invaluable catalyst for uncovering the intricacies of the universe, translating cosmic signals into insights that enrich our understanding of existence.

However, as we move forward into this exciting new paradigm, it is critical to acknowledge the challenges and ethical considerations that come with merging AI and quantum technologies. The autonomy granted to AI systems during deep space missions raises questions of accountability, transparency, and responsible decision-making. As these autonomous systems assume greater roles, ensuring proper oversight and ethical governance becomes paramount to maintain public trust and ensure that mission objectives are aligned with human values.

Furthermore, the risk of over-reliance on AI poses significant concerns. As AI systems process vast amounts of information and make complex decisions, proper checks and balances must be instituted to prevent potential bias, errors, or misinterpretations that could have far-reaching implications for missions and scientific integrity. Developing comprehensive protocols that outline the parameters within which AI systems operate is essential to foster a responsible partnership between human operators and autonomous technologies.

Interdisciplinary collaboration will be pivotal in navigating the complexities of AI and quantum technologies. Engaging physicists, computer scientists, ethicists, and engineers will enrich our collective understanding while generating innovative solutions to the multifaceted challenges presented by these advancements. By drawing diverse perspectives, the scientific community can pave the way for the responsible integration of AI into quantum systems used in space exploration.

The role of public engagement and education is equally vital. By inspiring future generations to explore the possibilities of AI and quantum mechanics, we cultivate a culture of inquiry that values exploration and diversity. Educational initiatives that emphasize the significance of these technologies will empower a new generation of innovators capable of contributing to humanity's understanding of the cosmos.

In conclusion, the integration of AI and human collaboration within quantum technologies marks a new paradigm in deep space exploration. By harnessing the extraordinary capabilities afforded by quantum computing, we can transform our navigational strategies, scientific discovery efforts, and operational efficiencies in ways that redefine our engagement with the universe. As we navigate this transformative chapter, it is essential to embrace ethical considerations, foster interdisciplinary collaboration, and involve public engagement. As we look to the stars with quantum-informed AI systems, we prepare to uncover the majestic mysteries that await us amid the cosmos, charging towards a future rich with exploration and discovery.

13.5. Ethical Considerations in Quantum AI

As the excitement around quantum computing in space exploration deepens, it becomes essential to address the ethical considerations surrounding its applications, particularly in the context of Quantum AI. As we journey into this new frontier, we must recognize that with every technological advancement comes a suite of ethical implications that warrant careful analysis and discussion.

At the forefront, there lies the responsibility of ensuring equitable access to quantum AI technologies. As these advanced capabilities unfold across various sectors—from space exploration to healthcare —the risk of exacerbating existing inequalities emerges. We must ensure that advancements in quantum AI are not reserved solely for wealthier nations and organizations. Policymakers and stakeholders need to prioritize initiatives that promote global collaboration, ensuring that developing countries have access to quantum technologies and the opportunities they provide. This focus on equitable access fosters a spirit of shared exploration, inviting diverse perspectives and reducing the risk of technological monopolization.

In conjunction with considerations of access, the question of accountability within quantum AI systems becomes central. As AI increasingly operates autonomously, it is crucial to establish frameworks that delineate the accountability of AI actions. In the context of space missions, where autonomous decision-making is necessary due to communication delays, ensuring responsibility for the behaviors of quantum AI systems will be paramount. Effective governance must articulate clear boundaries for decision-making protocols, ensuring that AI systems operate within ethical parameters and are auditable should issues arise.

Moreover, securing data integrity is critical in the realm of quantum communication, which must also be appropriately addressed. As quantum technologies leverage the principles of entanglement to safeguard communications, it is vital to develop robust standards to protect sensitive data from interception and misuse. This concern amplifies in the vastness of space, where the potential for data breaches could have significant implications not only for scientific integrity but also for national security. Quantum key distribution (QKD) represents a promising avenue for devising secure communication channels, yet ongoing efforts must strengthen these protocols to defend against emerging threats.

The integration of quantum AI in space exploration also raises ethical questions surrounding environmental stewardship. As we advance toward deploying quantum technologies in off-world environments, a commitment to responsible exploration practices must be upheld. Questions emerge pertaining to the potential impact on extraterrestrial ecosystems—be they microbial life on Mars or the pristine surfaces of distant moons. Establishing guidelines for planetary protection becomes essential to prevent contamination and preserve potential biospheres. This involves not only ensuring that we do no harm but also making informed decisions regarding future technologies that could influence extraterrestrial environments.

A key component of these explorations revolves around fostering interdisciplinary collaboration. The convergence of expertise among physicists, computer scientists, ethicists, and engineers will be essential to navigate the ethical landscape effectively. Engaging the public in discussions surrounding the implications of quantum technologies fosters a culture of transparency and dialogue, ensuring that diverse voices contribute to shaping the trajectory of exploration. By creating educational initiatives that emphasize the ethical dimensions of quantum technologies, we can inspire a generation of innovators who are equipped to engage thoughtfully with the evolving challenges of space exploration.

Lastly, as we venture into this quantum era, a reflective approach to embracing our role as explorers is vital. The ethical framework that guides the development and deployment of quantum AI technologies must celebrate our shared humanity and endeavor to promote peace, collaboration, and sustainable practices. As we navigate the complexities of the universe together, the responsibility we carry as stewards of knowledge must echo throughout our engagements, reminding us that exploration is not solely a pursuit of scientific achievement but also an opportunity to deepen our appreciation for existence and the interconnectedness that binds us all.

In conclusion, the ethical implications of quantum AI in space exploration invite us to engage with the complexities of our technological ambitions. By embracing principles of equity, accountability, integrity, environmental stewardship, and interdisciplinary collaboration, we can usher in a future characterized by responsible exploration that enriches our understanding of the cosmos. As we stand at the threshold of this quantum frontier, let us commit to ensuring that our advancements reflect shared human values and contribute positively to the universe we seek to explore. Through this journey, we illuminate not just the expanse among the stars but also our place within the intricate web of existence itself.

14. Multiverses and Quantum Mechanics

14.1. Introduction to the Multiverse Theory

In the context of quantum mechanics, the multiverse theory posits the existence of multiple, perhaps infinite, universes that coexist alongside our own. This theory emerges from the principles of quantum mechanics and challenges our traditional notions of reality by suggesting that each decision, event, or quantum measurement results in a branching of the universe into different pathways. As we explore the multiverse theory, we are invited to contemplate profound questions about existence, reality, and the possible dimensions waiting to be discovered beyond our observable universe.

At the heart of the multiverse theory lies the concept that quantum events do not lead to singular outcomes, but instead give rise to myriad possibilities. The many-worlds interpretation, proposed by physicist Hugh Everett III in the 1950s, suggests that all possible outcomes of a quantum measurement occur, with each outcome manifesting in its branch of the universe. In this framework, every decision made or particle interaction that occurs creates a new universe, leading us to envision a vast web of realities where every possibility plays out. This radical perspective beckons us to ponder the implications for our own decisions, encouraging a deeper understanding of how our choices shape not just our lives, but potentially countless alternate realities.

As we delve into quantum mechanics and the concept of multiverses, one of the exciting avenues of exploration is the idea of branching into new dimensions—the pathways that these alternate realities present. Each branch represents a unique exploration of potential, where variations in events unfold based on existing quantum probabilities. This branching can range from slight variations, such as different career choices, to more monumental events, such as the decisions of civilizations or the paths chosen by entire galaxies. The implications of such interactions invite critical reflection on causality and the interconnectedness of existence across these parallel worlds.

Exploring parallel worlds through quantum computing further enhances our inquiry into the multiverse. Quantum computers, with their capacity to process multiple possibilities simultaneously, offer new methodologies for investigating the nature of existence. Consider the implications of a quantum simulation designed to model the behavior of particles across several branches of the multiverse. By evaluating various outcomes, researchers can assess how even minor changes in quantum states could influence broader cosmic events, enriching our understanding of the multi-dimensional fabric of reality.

The implications for the space-time continuum serve as another fascinating consideration within the multiverse framework. If multiple universes can coexist, how do they interact with one another? Could the fabric of space-time accommodate these dimensions, allowing them to bend, enfold, or connect with one another in ways that challenge our conventional understanding of reality? These questions invite further exploration into the geometric and topological nature of the cosmos, potentially leading to breakthroughs that reshape our understanding of gravity, time, and existence itself.

Theories of teleportation, which often emerge from discussions about quantum mechanics, also contribute to the multiverse dialogue. Quantum teleportation—the technique by which quantum states are transferred from one location to another without physically moving the particles involved—highlights the potential for instantaneous information transfer across vast cosmic distances. This notion generates exciting possibilities surrounding the implications of teleportation for communication and travel between parallel worlds, while also prompting philosophical inquiries regarding the nature of identity and existence when traversing these alternate dimensions.

As we contemplate the multiverse theory within the framework of quantum physics, it is evident that the intersections of quantum mechanics and cosmic existence are poised to redefine our understanding of reality. The implications of branching pathways, parallel worlds, and their connectivity challenge our perceptions and prompt us to consider the broader philosophical ramifications of our exploration efforts. As researchers continue to push the boundaries of scientific inquiry into the realm of multiverses, we are graced with the opportunity to explore the infinite dimensions awaiting discovery, and to unveil the intricate tapestry of existence that we are but one thread within. Through this journey, we invite not just scientific inquiry, but a profound awakening to the mysteries of life and the universe that lie before us.

14.2. Quantum Paths: Branching Into New Dimensions

In exploring the concept of branching into new dimensions, we enter the profound realm of quantum mechanics, where the fabric of reality is intricately woven with possibilities that challenge our conventional understanding. The premise of many-worlds, an interpretation of quantum mechanics, suggests that every quantum event creates a divergence in the universe, spawning a plethora of parallel realities. This concept encourages us to envision a multiverse—an expansive cosmos where every decision, action, or measurement results in distinct branches of existence cohabiting alongside one another.

Delving into this multiverse perspective allows us to speculate on the nature of parallel worlds. Within these alternate realities, different versions of ourselves could inhabit scenarios born of divergent outcomes. The implications of this branching theory extend beyond mere philosophical musings; they challenge the fundamental notions of causality, identity, and existence. Each quantum choice leads to an array of possible outcomes, symbolizing pathways rich with potential, yet tethered to the complexity of quantum mechanics.

Quantum computing serves as a powerful tool to illuminate these multifaceted realities through simulations that evaluate multiple outcomes instantaneously. By leveraging the principles of superposition and entanglement, quantum computers can explore vast spaces of possibilities—facilitating the examination of hypothetical universes through "what-if" scenarios. This capability enhances researchers' abilities to model cosmic phenomena, address complex problems in astrophysics, and predict evolutionary outcomes that contribute to our understanding of existence across multiverses.

Consider the potential of quantum simulations in assessing the implications of various decisions on planetary evolution, cosmic structures, or even the emergence of intelligent life. Through these simulations, scientists could gain insights into phenomena that seem to teeter on the edge of reality, such as the conditions necessary for life to thrive in distant exoplanets or the trajectories galaxies might follow under differing gravitational influences. Quantum computers could also enhance studies in dark matter and dark energy, enabling simulations that explore their interactions across parallel quantum structures. The possibility of modeling the behavior of universes that follow different physical laws invites awe-inspiring inquiries about the nature of reality itself.

As we embrace the idea of branching into new dimensions, we are also compelled to confront the implications for our understanding of space and time. The multiverse theory suggests that our perception of time and the linearity of events may merely be an artifact of our specific quantum reality. If every decision leads to divergence, how do we reconcile our experiences with the infinite pathways laid across the multiverse? This provocation invites contemplation of the interconnectedness of all realities, motivating inquiries into the philosophical realms surrounding existence, consciousness, and the nature of the universe itself.

Teleportation, a tantalizing concept within the scope of quantum mechanics, further stimulates our imagination regarding the branching pathways of new dimensions. The idea of instantly transferring information or even matter from one location to another through quantum processes underscores the transformative possibilities that quantum mechanics presents—not merely for communication or travel, but for our very perceptions of space and reality. It invites us to question the limits of what is achievable as we deepen our exploration into the cosmos.

Ultimately, the notion of branching into new dimensions through quantum mechanics invites profound reflection on existence's intricacies. As we harness the power of quantum computing and engage with the implications of multiverses, we are not merely exploring the cosmos but stepping into realms where the very definitions of reality, identity, and consciousness may be reshaped. Embracing this quantum future unlocks possibilities that could redefine our place within the universe, unearthing insights that linger just beyond our reach among the stars.

In summary, as we embark on this journey through the branches of new dimensions, we deepen our appreciation for the complexities of existence. The interplay between quantum mechanics and the multiverse theory serves as a reminder that reality may be far richer than we can presently conceive. The exploration of the quantum universe invites a sense of wonder, as we delve into the infinite possibilities that lie ahead, challenging us to continue reaching for the stars in a cosmos defined by curiosity, discovery, and the ever-expanding boundaries of human knowledge.

14.3. Exploring Parallel Worlds Through Quantum Computing

As we delve into the profound implications of quantum computing, particularly in the realm of space exploration, we encounter a captivating narrative that redefines how we understand both the cosmos and our place within it. The dance of quantum mechanics, interwoven with the intricacies of the universe, fosters a landscape of exploration where boundaries are blurred, and possibilities are boundless.

Embarking on this journey through parallel worlds as facilitated by quantum computing, we come to appreciate how the very fabric of reality can be shaped by quantum entanglements and superposition states. The ability to harness these principles offers not just theoretical insights but practical applications that can extend humanity's reach far beyond Earth. For instance, considering the existence of multiple branches of reality that emerge from quantum decisions invites a radical reconsideration of our approach to exploration. Could we, one day, navigate between these alternate realities and utilize them to inform our strategies in deep space missions? Each quantum decision could yield invaluable perspectives on potential outcomes, making our exploratory endeavors richer and more informed.

As we contemplate the implications for the space-time continuum, we realize that understanding our universe's structure demands a nuanced approach. Quantum computing opens avenues for simulating cosmic events across various dimensions, modeling phenomena such as black hole mechanics or the dynamics of cosmic inflation. These simulations can unveil secrets that lie hidden beyond the observable universe, deepening our knowledge of fundamental forces and inspiring new theories that guide scientific inquiry.

Teleportation theories, straddling the line between fact and fiction, evoke a sense of wonder as we engage with the potential of instantaneously transmitting information or matter across vast galaxies. Inspired by principles of quantum mechanics, teleportation beckons us to explore the boundaries of possibility—yet, we must remain cognizant of the ethical considerations surrounding such advancements. As we embrace the potential for instantaneous communication with distant worlds, it becomes essential to reflect on the responsibility we bear in ensuring that such technologies promote exploration without jeopardizing the ecosystems and forms of life we encounter.

Turning to the practical applications of quantum technology in galactic mining, we open a chapter rich with opportunity. The ability to wisely map resources in space using quantum technologies equips humanity to venture into new realms of discovery and resource utilization. As we set our sights on the rewards of interstellar mining, we must also cultivate a sensitivity to the environmental consequences and ethical ramifications of such endeavors. Legal frameworks helming space mining must reflect the spirit of cooperation and awareness that resonate with our collective aspirations as explorers of the cosmos.

Navigating the realm of quantum impacts on astronomical discoveries, we unveil the profound connections between quantum mechanics and our understanding of the universe. Employing advanced quantum sensors and quantum-enhanced telescopes, we can uncover cosmic phenomena that elude conventional detection, such as pulsars, quasars, and mysterious signals originating from the vastness of space. These revelations enhance our knowledge of the universe while also nurturing the curiosity that ignited our impetus to explore.

As we consider the broader ethical implications of quantum computing, it is crucial to acknowledge the moral dimensions of our advancements. Ensuring equitable access to quantum technologies is vital, as is contemplating the potential societal ramifications of their deployment. Engaging in discourse surrounding privacy, information security, and the interconnectedness of our planetary systems reinforces the responsibility we hold toward safeguarding the integrity of the ecosystems we explore.

In navigating the challenges and opportunities presented by quantum space initiatives, we must foster a culture of collaboration and integration across disciplines. The journey into the quantum frontier requires synergistic efforts among scientists, engineers, policymakers, and the public, to ensure that we lay the groundwork for a future of exploration defined by responsibility and respect.

As we arrive at our concluding thoughts, we find ourselves on the cusp of an infinite quantum frontier—one that transcends the limits of traditional exploration and invites us to embrace the destiny as cosmic explorers armed with the extraordinary tools of quantum mechanics. The reflections and insights gained from this journey not only encapsulate the advancements made but also signify our commitment to continue pushing boundaries in pursuit of knowledge. As we celebrate the spirit of exploration that drives our endeavors, we recognize that the universe beckons, filled with infinite possibilities waiting to be discovered. Together, let us chart a path forward into the quantum cosmos, where the mysteries of existence await our inquiry, and the spirit of discovery knows no bounds.

14.4. Implications for Space-Time Continuum

The study of the implications for the space-time continuum in the context of quantum mechanics may appear daunting, yet it is pivotal to understanding the nature of our universe as we expand our boundaries. In exploring these implications, we delve into the nuanced interplay between quantum mechanics and the fundamental structure of space-time itself—an endeavor critical to future explorations and our grasp of existence.

To begin, we must appreciate the very essence of the space-time continuum as introduced by Albert Einstein, wherein time and space are inextricably linked, forming a four-dimensional fabric that is shaped by mass and energy. As we apply quantum mechanics to this continuum, particularly through theories such as quantum gravity, we are prompted to examine how quantum phenomena potentially distort or influence the geometric properties of space-time. This interplay raises profound questions about the fabric of reality: how do gravity and quantum effects converge at the scales where each is significant, particularly around singularities and black holes?

The theory of quantum gravity seeks to reconcile general relativity's classical view of gravity with the principles of quantum mechanics. This quest has led physicists to explore concepts such as loop quantum gravity or string theory, theorizing that space-time may have a discrete structure at the scales revealed through quantum interactions. If space-time behaves granularly at such levels, we can speculate that our observable universe evolves from a more complex tapestry that intertwines numerous quantum paths.

One of the significant ramifications of these theories is the idea of information preservation and the holographic principle, suggesting that information about objects within a black hole may be preserved on their event horizons, rather than lost in singularities—as long feared in classical interpretations. Accepting this notion alters our understanding of information flow in the universe, weaving a narrative that recalls the human pursuit of knowledge, understanding, and ultimately, existence itself.

Moreover, the implications for teleportation theories must be considered in this context. Quantum entanglement's ability to link particles enables instantaneous communication across entangled states, which raises intriguing possibilities about whether this capability could extend beyond quantum particles to larger scales. In essence, the capacity to transfer quantum states through entanglement suggests the potential to explore concepts reminiscent of teleportation—an event that challenges our conventional understanding of continuity in time and space.

As we further grapple with these implications, we must also contemplate the philosophical ramifications surrounding the nature of reality and existence itself. If the multiverse theory suggests that, with every decision or measurement, alternate universes branch off, how does this affect our understanding of causality and our place in the cosmos? Every quantum event becomes an intrinsic thread in the larger tapestry of existence, echoing across dimensions and realities that could lead to divergent paths and outcomes.

Addressing the challenges implicit in these explorations forms an ongoing commitment to inquiry and discovery. Continuous innovation in quantum technologies, alongside collaborations across disciplines—quantum physicists, cosmologists, and philosophers—will be fundamental to enhancing our grasp of these implications. As the landscape of quantum mechanics unfolds further, we must employ rigorous methodologies that integrate theoretical advancements with experimental insights, ensuring a comprehensive understanding of potential paradigms linking quantum mechanics and the space-time continuum.

In conclusion, the implications for the space-time continuum offer a rich tapestry of inquiry at the intersection of quantum mechanics and our understanding of the universe. As we advance our knowledge of these principles, we prepare to unlock new dimensions of reality, allowing us to contemplate existence, causality, and knowledge within the vast realms of the cosmos. Embracing these challenges invites ongoing exploration and discovery, where each revelation propels us further into an infinite universe of possibilities waiting to be uncovered. Thus, as we venture forth into this quantum frontier, we not only render ourselves explorers of the cosmos but also participants in the intricate dance of existence itself.

14.5. Teleportation Theories: Fact and Fiction

Teleportation has long captivated the imagination, straddling the line between fact and fiction. In the realm of quantum mechanics, however, what was once relegated to the realms of science fiction now offers the potential for groundbreaking advancements, even influencing our understanding of communication and travel in deep space. This subchapter provides an in-depth examination of teleportation theories, heightened by quantum principles, while discriminating between the speculative and the scientifically grounded.

To begin with, it's essential to delineate the scientific basis for teleportation within the context of quantum mechanics. At its core, quantum teleportation involves the transmission of quantum states rather than physical particles, fundamentally differentiating it from the traditional notion of teleportation portrayed in popular culture. The process hinges on the entanglement of quantum bits, or qubits, which allows two particles to be correlated in such a way that measuring one instantly influences the state of the other, irrespective of distance.

In practical terms, quantum teleportation involves three key components: an entangled pair of qubits, the sender (commonly referred to as "Alice"), and the receiver ("Bob"). To teleport a quantum state from Alice to Bob, Alice performs a joint quantum measurement on the qubit she wishes to teleport and one half of the entangled pair, collapsing the state into a new configuration. Alice then sends the classical information regarding her measurement over conventional means to Bob, who utilizes this information to reconstruct the original quantum state on his side using the other half of the entangled pair. This process demonstrates how quantum information can be transferred across space without the physical movement of particles, a fundamental departure from classical teleportation models.

While the concept of quantum teleportation is grounded in experimentally verifiable theories, there remains a chasm between this scientific understanding and the fantastical depictions typically found in science fiction. For instance, teleportation as usually portrayed—encompassing instantaneous travel of entire human beings from one place to another—renders complex biological systems and the nature of consciousness into mere data packets. The scientific reality differs significantly; quantum teleportation works at the level of information and fundamentally embodies the principles of superposition and entanglement, processes that become increasingly intricate when applied to more complex systems.

Moreover, there are considerable limitations to current understanding and applications of teleportation. While quantum teleportation has been demonstrated and tested with simples states such as photons and small ions, extending this phenomenon to larger systems or complex states still poses significant challenges. The fidelity of such transfers diminishes as systems increase in complexity or size due to environmental decoherence, which disrupts the delicate quantum states upon which teleportation relies. Much research is ongoing in the field of quantum error correction to mitigate these effects and enhance the reliability of quantum teleportation on larger scales.

The potential applications of teleportation in the context of space exploration drive curiosity and optimism within the scientific community. Imagine a future where quantum teleportation can enable secure communication links between spacecraft or facilitate instantaneous data transmission across great distances—transformative advancements that could enhance both our operational protocols in space and potentially our scientific understanding of the universe.

However, these ambitious prospects invite ethical considerations and theoretical inquiries. As we explore applications of quantum teleportation in communication, we must consider the implications of the technology we develop. Questions arise: If quantum teleportation technologies evolve to a point where they can be utilized for data transmission, how might we ensure the integrity of the information exchanged? Will we be ready to grapple with the transformative realities of what data transmission means for our understanding of existence?

Furthermore, the broader implications of teleportation touch upon philosophical inquiries regarding identity and existence. If every quantum state can be teleported, how does this affect our understanding of self—of consciousness and the continuity of experience? This realm of inquiry reflects the intersection of science with metaphysics, urging us to deepen our understanding of what it means to be an observer in the universe.

In summary, teleportation theories span the chasm between fact and fiction within the quantum realm, revealing both the extraordinary potential and considerable limitations inherent in our current understanding. While teleportation may serve as a conduit for immediate applications in quantum communication, we must remain aware of the ethical challenges and philosophical implications that accompany this exploration. As we continue to unlock the secrets of quantum mechanics and its potential applications, we find ourselves at the forefront of scientific inquiry, where the exploration of existence invites us to reconsider our relationship with the universe and the myriad possibilities awaiting discovery among the stars.

15. Quantum Mechanics and Galactic Mining

15.1. Strategic Resource Mapping with Quantum Technology

The chapter on strategic resource mapping with quantum technology serves as a fundamental exploration into how quantum mechanics can revolutionize our approach to resource extraction and management in space. With the expanding ambitions of human exploration beyond Earth, effective resource mapping is essential for sustainable practices and mission success in galactic mining.

As we consider the strategic frameworks employed in resource mapping, we recognize that the vastness of space holds an abundance of untapped resources—minerals, gases, and other materials that may prove crucial for future endeavors. However, the challenge lies in accurately identifying and characterizing these resources amidst the complexities of cosmic environments. This is where quantum technology comes into play, offering advanced methodologies and high levels of precision that can significantly enhance our capabilities in resource mapping.

The principles of quantum mechanics, especially quantum superposition and entanglement, provide novel tools for modeling the characteristics of celestial bodies and their surrounding environments. By utilizing quantum sensors in orbital surveys, researchers can gather data on a plethora of factors, including gravitational anomalies, elemental compositions, and the distribution of crucial resources. For example, quantum gravity measurements—achieved through atomic interferometry—allow scientists to detect variations in gravitational fields, revealing underlying geological structures that may indicate the presence of valuable resources such as metals or hydrocarbons.

Moreover, the adaptive nature of quantum algorithms supports the dynamic analysis of resource data. As spacecraft and landers traverse the surfaces of asteroids, moons, and planets, the quantum algorithms can assimilate real-time data updates, optimizing resource mapping based on the most current information available. This continuous feedback loop enhances decision-making processes in resource extraction efforts, enabling teams to adjust strategies dynamically based on unforeseen conditions or discoveries.

In contemplating the extraction techniques employed, quantum technology also offers innovative solutions that minimize environmental impact. Utilizing quantum-based methods in resource extraction might allow for precise cutting or periodic mining, minimizing waste and preserving the surrounding ecosystems of celestial bodies. Such advancements would encourage responsible practices that align with ethical space exploration—preventing unnecessary disruption and fostering sustainability.

However, the transition to utilizing quantum technologies in resource mapping and extraction comes with its own set of challenges. The realities of cosmic radiation, temperature fluctuations, and the vast distances involved in space operations may impact the performance of quantum systems. Thus, engineers must develop robust shielding solutions and error correction strategies to enhance the reliability of quantum devices in the demanding environments of space.

The legal and ethical dimensions of space mining also play a crucial role in shaping how resource mapping is approached. As we look toward the commercial potential of galactic resources, establishing clear international regulations to govern mining activities becomes essential. The Outer Space Treaty and other existing frameworks must evolve to address the complexities introduced by resource extraction on celestial bodies and establish equitable agreements among nations. Ensuring that practices do not infringe on potential extraterrestrial ecosystems, alongside considerations related to the fair distribution of resources, must guide policy development.

The integration of AI into quantum-driven operations represents another crucial facet of this exploration. AI can enhance quantum technologies by inspecting data gathered from quantum sensors during resource mapping, identifying patterns and anomalies that may indicate untapped reserves. By developing synergies between quantum computing, AI, and robotics, we can create systems capable of operating autonomously in remote environments, analyzing vast datasets, and executing complex extraction strategies informed by real-time feedback.

The chapter then transitions to reflect on how quantum technology reshapes our strategic vision for resource management in space, offering insights into the approaches that will underpin future initiatives. By embracing these innovative frameworks, we are paving the way for sustainable practices that not only advance human exploration of the cosmos but also respect the integrity of the ecosystems we encounter along the way.

In conclusion, strategic resource mapping with quantum technology reshapes our approach to cosmic exploration and mining. By effectively harnessing quantum principles, we unlock new dimensions of possibility, allowing us to navigate the cosmos with enhanced precision and responsibility. As we embark on this transformative journey, it is crucial to remain mindful of the ethical implications and collaborative efforts required to cultivate a harmonious relationship with the universe, ensuring that our explorations yield benefits for humanity while respecting the delicate balance of cosmic environments.

15.2. Quantum Extraction Techniques and Their Benefits

Quantum extraction techniques represent a transformative approach to resource gathering that harnesses the extraordinary properties of quantum mechanics. As humanity extends its reach into the cosmos, the ability to efficiently and sustainably procure resources from celestial bodies becomes increasingly essential. These techniques employ sophisticated quantum technologies that optimize extraction processes, enhance precision, and minimize environmental impacts, thereby offering a multitude of benefits for future space missions.

At the heart of quantum extraction is the application of quantum sensors. These sensors leverage quantum principles, such as super-position and entangled states, to detect minute changes in the physical properties of celestial bodies. When deployed on asteroids, moons, or planets, quantum sensors can identify valuable resources, including water, metals, and rare earth elements, with unprecedented sensitivity. By utilizing quantum-enhanced measurements, explorers can create detailed maps of mineral distributions, facilitating targeted extraction efforts that reduce waste and improve efficiency.

One of the most significant advantages of quantum extraction tech-niques lies in their capacity to enhance the accuracy of resource assessments. Traditional methods often rely on surface sampling and remote sensing technologies, which can yield imprecise predictions of resource availability. In contrast, quantum sensors provide real-time data that accurately reflects the subsurface composition, enabling scientists to make informed decisions about where and how to extract materials. This precision is crucial for optimizing operations and maximizing yield, ensuring the sustainability of extraction endeavors as humanity ventures further into the depths of space.

Additionally, the potential for quantum technologies to facilitate in-situ resource utilization (ISRU) bolsters the viability of long-duration missions. By transforming local resources into usable materials, such as converting lunar or Martian regolith into building materials or ex-tracting oxygen from ice deposits, missions can minimize dependen-cies on Earth for essential supplies. Quantum extraction techniques enhance the efficiency of these processes, allowing space-faring civi-lizations to establish footholds on other planets more sustainably.

Moreover, data collected from quantum extraction processes can be fed into advanced quantum simulations, enabling scientists to model the long-term implications of resource utilization on celestial bodies. Such simulations can reveal how extraction activities may impact planetary environments, guiding responsible resource management practices and ensuring ecological considerations inform decision-making processes.

Despite the numerous benefits, the implementation of quantum extraction techniques in space does present challenges. The harsh conditions of space, including temperature extremes and cosmic radiation, may affect the performance of quantum sensors and systems. Developing resilient materials that protect against these environmental factors is paramount to ensure the reliability of quantum technologies used in resource extraction efforts.

Furthermore, as with any technological advancement involving resource utilization, ethical considerations surrounding space mining must be addressed. Collaborative international frameworks will be essential for establishing guidelines that prevent conflicts over resources, especially as space becomes increasingly populated by various nations and private entities. Ensuring equitable access to resources and safeguarding extraterrestrial environments will require robust dialogue among stakeholders, fostering a spirit of cooperation to guide exploration efforts.

The potential for quantum extraction techniques to revolutionize resource availability and sustainability in space represents a significant advancement in our quest to explore the cosmos. By unlocking the extraordinary capabilities afforded by quantum technologies, we position ourselves to navigate the complexities of extraction in ways that are both efficient and ethically responsible. As we prepare to utilize these techniques in our cosmic endeavors, we set a precedent for how humanity can engage with resources from beyond our home planet—preparing the way for a future where exploration thrives and sustains our aspirations among the stars.

In conclusion, quantum extraction techniques not only pave the way for advanced resource utilization in space but also redefine our relationship with the cosmos. By embracing the principles of quantum mechanics, we can forge a path of sustainable exploration that respects the integrity of celestial bodies while unlocking previously untapped resources. As we tread into the future, we stand at the threshold of opportunities that promise to enrich our understanding of the universe, offering insights that resonate across both scientific and philosophical dimensions. The journey into the cosmic depths beckons, inviting us to uncover the mysteries that lie ahead while embodying the spirit of exploration that fuels our ambitions among the stars.

15.3. Tackling Energy Challenges in Galactic Mining

In the vast reaches of space, tackling energy challenges in galactic mining necessitates an innovative approach that integrates sophisticated technologies with sustainable practices. As humanity sets its sights on extracting valuable resources from asteroids, moons, and other celestial bodies, the intersection of quantum mechanics and resource management emerges as a potentially transformative solution. This subchapter focuses on understanding how quantum technologies can radically improve energy efficiency and resource utilization strategies, all while addressing the myriad challenges encountered in extraterrestrial environments.

At the foundation of energy challenges in galactic mining lies the need for efficient extraction processes that minimize waste and maximize output. Traditional mining methods rely heavily on classical physics principles and well-established resource extraction techniques; however, as we venture into the cosmos, the limitations of these methods become increasingly apparent. Quantum technologies can enhance these processes by optimizing energy consumption and leveraging the unique properties of quantum mechanics to improve the overall efficiency of mining operations.

A significant aspect of utilizing quantum technologies for energy management involves the deployment of quantum sensors capable of assessing the geological characteristics of celestial bodies. These sensors employ principles such as superposition and entanglement to provide real-time data regarding material composition, density, and structural integrity. Equipped with this information, mining operations can fine-tune their energy consumption strategies, targeting areas with higher concentrations of valuable resources while minimizing unnecessary energy expenditure in less productive regions.

Additionally, the application of quantum algorithms in energy optimization introduces opportunities for improving resource extraction techniques. Quantum computing excels at processing large datasets and evaluating multiple variables simultaneously, enabling operators to devise optimal extraction strategies. For instance, quantum algorithms can simulate complex interactions between resources while accounting for varying energy costs, allowing mining teams to refine their approaches and allocate resources judiciously.

Exploring energy sources for in-situ resource utilization (ISRU) further highlights the potential for quantum technology in galactic mining. By harnessing local energy resources—such as solar power—quantum-driven systems can operate sustainably without bringing all energy supplies from Earth. Innovative quantum systems for energy harvesting and conversion can enhance energy sustainability while facilitating autonomous mining processes that capitalize on local resources. Integrating quantum technologies into ISRU initiatives lays the groundwork for more resilient and self-sustaining mining operations, ultimately reducing costs and minimizing our ecological footprint.

Despite the array of benefits presented by quantum technologies, considerable challenges remain to overcome. Cosmic radiation poses significant risks to quantum devices, introducing uncertainties in the stability of qubits and undermining the potential for coherent operations. Engineers must focus on developing advanced shielding mechanisms that protect quantum systems while enhancing their resilience in the hostile space environment. Robust error correction methodologies will be equally crucial to maintain performance and reliability amidst environmental fluctuations.

The ethical dimensions of energy management in galactic mining should also be critically analyzed. As humanity ventures further into space to extract resources, responsible stewardship and environmental protection must guide these initiatives. The potential impacts on extraterrestrial ecosystems—be they microbial life, geological formations, or other unknown entities—must be weighed against the benefits of resource extraction. Developing clear protocols for planetary protection and sustainability will ensure that our exploratory endeavors respect the integrity of the cosmos.

As we navigate these challenges and opportunities, interdisciplinary collaboration emerges as a fundamental component of success. The convergence of expertise across quantum physics, engineering, environmental science, and ethical governance nurtures an environment ripe for innovation. By fostering partnerships among institutions, researchers, and industry stakeholders, we can create a robust framework that addresses the complexities of energy challenges in galactic mining while harnessing the transformative power of quantum technologies.

In conclusion, tackling energy challenges in galactic mining requires a multifaceted approach that leverages the capabilities of quantum mechanics to enhance efficiency, optimize resource extraction, and ensure sustainability. By integrating quantum technologies into our strategies, we stand at the forefront of a transformative era in space exploration—one where the responsible extraction of resources coexists with our commitment to preserving the integrity of the environments we encounter. As we journey toward this future, the challenges we face will inspire us to innovate and navigate the cosmos with greater awareness, ultimately revealing the wonders that lie ahead. The energy challenges in galactic mining exemplify the boundless possibilities within the quantum frontier, driving humanity's spirit of exploration forward into the unknown.

15.4. Legal and Ethical Dimensions of Space Mining

In the rapidly evolving frontier of space exploration, the legal and ethical dimensions of space mining represent critical issues that must be understood and navigated as quantum technologies become integrated into our cosmic endeavors. As we aim to extend humanity's reach beyond Earth and exploit the resources of celestial bodies, it is vital to establish frameworks that protect planetary environments, promote equitable access to resources, support sustainable practices, and uphold ethical standards. This subchapter delves into these complexities, highlighting the interplay between law, ethics, and the responsibilities inherent in space mining initiatives.

To begin, the legal landscape governing space mining is still in a nascent stage, characterized by existing treaties, like the Outer Space Treaty of 1967, which stipulates that space and celestial bodies are the province of all mankind. The interpretation of these treaties regarding resource extraction remains ambiguous, creating uncertainty about the legality of space mining operations. As private enterprises and nations accelerate their plans for extraterrestrial resource utilization, there is an urgent need for comprehensive legislation that clarifies ownership rights, resource accessibility, and the obligations of entities engaged in space mining.

Proposals for establishing frameworks that govern resource extraction activities are already emerging. Legal experts and policymakers are advocating for the need to develop international agreements that delineate property rights and environmental protections, preventing potential conflicts that may arise between competing nations and companies. Such frameworks should prioritize collaborative management of resources to ensure that despite different national interests, the exploration of space remains a shared endeavor that benefits all of humanity. Engaging in dialogue among stakeholders will be vital to crafting policies that respect individual rights while fostering cooperation in the pursuit of knowledge and exploration.

The ethical considerations surrounding space mining also call for serious reflection. As humanity ventures into the cosmos to access resources, we must grapple with the implications of potentially disrupting extraterrestrial environments. Each celestial body presents unique ecosystems, and any extraction processes must account for the preservation of those systems. Ethical frameworks must guide decision-making, ensuring that exploration efforts also respect the integrity of these environments and do not diminish the potential for future discoveries. The lessons learned from environmental management on Earth should inform approaches to maintaining our cosmic ecosystems.

In tandem with environmental concerns, issues of equity and access to resources prominently factor into ethical deliberations. As technologies such as quantum mining enhance our capabilities to extract resources efficiently, the risk of monopolizing opportunities looms large. Ensuring that developing countries have equitable access to the benefits of extraterrestrial resources will require international cooperation and proactive policy measures designed to mitigate disparities. This focus on inclusivity will not only reinforce ethical standards but will also support collaborative efforts that enrich our collective exploration experiences.

The integration of quantum technologies also calls for ethical scrutiny surrounding data management, particularly in relation to security and privacy. As quantum computing enhances our ability to analyze vast datasets for resource mapping and management, safeguarding sensitive information and ensuring the responsible use of data will be paramount. Quantum cryptography emerges as a vital tool for establishing secure communication channels, but researchers and policymakers must delineate protocols that ensure data privacy while promoting transparency and accountability in data utilization.

As we consider the future of space mining efforts intertwined with quantum advancements, interdisciplinary collaboration will be crucial in navigating these legal and ethical dimensions. Scientists, engineers, policymakers, and ethicists must engage in meaningful dialogues to define best practices for resource management while fostering public trust in exploration initiatives. Creating platforms for education and outreach will inspire the next generation to consider the ethical implications of space mining, nurturing a culture of inquiry that respects the complexities of our universe.

In conclusion, the legal and ethical dimensions of space mining, particularly within the context of quantum technologies, necessitate proactive engagement as humanity seeks to expand its presence in the cosmos. By establishing comprehensive legal frameworks, prioritizing environmental stewardship, promoting equitable access and collaborations, and fostering ethical discussions surrounding data privacy, we can lay the groundwork for responsible and sustainable space mining practices. The choices we make today will resonate far into the future, shaping not just our explorations of the universe but the legacy we leave for generations yet to come. As we navigate these emerging challenges, we reaffirm our commitment to the exploration of the cosmos as a shared endeavor—one rooted in ethics, respect, and the inherent value of all forms of existence in the universe.

15.5. The Role of AI in Quantum-Driven Mining Operations

In the domain of quantum-driven mining operations, artificial intelligence (AI) plays a pivotal role by enhancing operational efficiency, decision-making processes, and resource management techniques. As humanity embarks on its quest to extract resources from celestial bodies, the incorporation of AI into quantum mining technologies promises to revolutionize the field. By harnessing the power of quantum computing principles, AI can analyze vast amounts of data, leading to innovative strategies that optimize extraction and ensure sustainable practices on extraterrestrial surfaces.

One of the foremost applications of quantum AI in mining is its ability to process complex geological data in real-time. Traditional mining techniques often depend on extensive geological surveys followed by labor-intensive analysis. However, by employing quantum-enhanced AI algorithms, operators can analyze data gathered from quantum sensors that detect mineral compositions, gravitational anomalies, and structural characteristics of celestial bodies, all while discerning patterns and correlations that may indicate the presence of valuable resources. This acceleration in data analysis translates to improved accuracy in resource identification, allowing mining teams to focus their efforts on the most promising extraction sites.

Furthermore, quantum AI optimizes the logistics of space mining operations. By utilizing machine learning algorithms, these systems can predict equipment failures, streamline supply chains, and facilitate real-time adjustments to resource extraction methods according to changing conditions. In uncharted territories, unpredictable factors such as radiation fluctuations can impact mining activities. Here, AI can rapidly process incoming data from sensors and make autonomous decisions on mitigating risks or recalibrating approaches, leading to safer and more efficient operations.

Another integral aspect of AI within quantum-driven mining is its capability to empower autonomous robotic systems. Quantum robotics, bolstered by AI technology, offer unprecedented potential for exploration and extraction tasks. These autonomous robots, equipped with quantum sensors, can traverse celestial surfaces, conduct in-situ analyses, and carry out extraction processes with minimal human oversight. This reduction of reliance on direct human input is especially crucial in hazardous environments where communication latency with Earth may hinder effective responses to rapidly unfolding scenarios.

Meanwhile, the ethical implications surrounding AI in quantum-driven mining operations warrant careful consideration. As AI assumes greater autonomy, concerns about biases in algorithmic decisions, accountability for potential errors, and the transparent functioning of AI systems must be addressed holistically. It is essential to develop robust governance frameworks that ensure ethical standards guide the design and implementation of AI technologies in mining endeavors, fostering trust among stakeholders and the public.

Moreover, ensuring the sustainability of extraterrestrial mining practices will hinge on utilizing AI in conjunction with quantum technologies to develop strategies that minimize environmental impact. AI can analyze the footprints left by extraction activities to assess and mitigate ecological consequences, creating feedback loops that inform ongoing operations about best practices in resource management. Emphasizing sustainability within the quantum mining narrative will ensure that future generations inherit a rich and diverse cosmic landscape, unimpeded by our hunger for resources.

Collaborative partnerships between the public and private sectors will be essential in advancing the development of quantum AI technologies for mining. By pooling resources, expertise, and funding, partnerships can facilitate research and development that brings cutting-edge quantum solutions to bear on field operations, ensuring we navigate the complexities of deep space mining responsibly. This collaboration must be informed by interdisciplinary engagement that blends insights from astrophysics, engineering, and ethical governance, yielding innovative solutions that address challenges head-on.

In conclusion, the role of AI in quantum-driven mining operations is vital; it enhances our capabilities for exploring and extracting resources from celestial bodies while ensuring that our practices remain ethical and sustainable. As we push the boundaries of technology and exploration, the symbiotic integration of quantum computing and AI will pave the way for a new era in space resource management. By clarifying our understanding of the future implications of quantum-driven mining, we position ourselves to embark on cosmic journeys that enrich our understanding of the universe and secure a future that resonates with our shared aspiration for exploration and discovery.

16. Quantum Impacts on Astronomical Discoveries

16.1. New Cosmic Phenomena Observed through Quantum Lenses

In a universe teeming with intrigue and unsolved mysteries, the observation of new cosmic phenomena through quantum lenses emerges as a groundbreaking frontier of research. Quantum mechanics, with its foundational principles of uncertainty, entanglement, and superposition, offers unprecedented tools for detecting and analyzing cosmic events that have long eluded our comprehension. As we embark on this exploratory journey, we will delve into its implications for our understanding of the vast cosmos and the innovative techniques that leverage quantum technologies to reveal the intricacies of the universe.

At the core of this journey lies the power of quantum sensors, which harness the unique properties of quantum states to achieve sensitivity levels beyond the capabilities of classical instruments. These sensors can exploit phenomena such as quantum entanglement to detect minute changes in energy, gravitation, and electromagnetic fields. By equipping space missions with quantum sensors, researchers are positioned to observe cosmic phenomena with enhanced resolution, yielding invaluable insights into the workings of the universe.

One of the most intriguing cosmic events witnessed through quantum lenses is gravitational waves—ripples in spacetime caused by the collision of massive objects like black holes or neutron stars. Quantum-enhanced gravitational wave detectors bring a frontier of sensitivity that allows for the observation of these elusive signals, ultimately confirming predictions made by general relativity. By capturing these waves with sophisticated quantum technology, scientists can begin to characterize the dynamics of such events, unveiling hidden details about how celestial bodies interact and shape the fabric of the universe.

Similarly, the study of dark matter—the mysterious substance that constitutes a significant part of the universe—has benefited immeasurably from quantum advancements. Traditional approaches to detecting dark matter have faced considerable challenges, primarily due to its non-interactive nature. However, using quantum sensors designed to measure gravitational effects induced by dark matter can offer unprecedented insight into its distribution and composition. Through finely-tuned quantum instruments, researchers can explore the gravitational lensing of galaxies—a phenomenon indicative of dark matter's presence—revealing its structural influence in the cosmos.

Another thrilling area that quantum sensors illuminate is the observation of pulsars and quasars. These celestial objects emit streams of radiation that can be difficult to parse amidst the cosmic noise. Quantum-enhanced imaging techniques allow astronomers to chart the nuanced behaviors of pulsars—rapidly rotating neutron stars that emit beams of radiation—and quasars, the brilliant cores of distant active galaxies. Through advanced quantum-driven algorithms, researchers can analyze these signals, gaining deeper insight into their compositions, behaviors, and the fundamental processes governing their existence.

Quantum measurements are also set to uncover subtleties in cosmic radiation—the omnipresent background radiation that permeates the universe. The cosmic microwave background (CMB), an afterglow from the Big Bang, offers a wealth of information about the universe's early moments. Quantum sensors can detect minute temperature fluctuations in the CMB, allowing researchers to probe the structure and evolution of the early universe with remarkable precision. By ultimately decoding these temperature variations using quantum analytics, we stand to deepen our understanding of cosmic inflation, the formation of large-scale structures, and the overall dynamics of the universe.

While the potential for observing new cosmic phenomena through quantum lenses is vast, it does not come without challenges. Cosmic environments typified by extreme conditions—radiation exposure, temperature fluctuation, and dust—constitute adversities that can compromise instrument reliability and data integrity. As further research unfolds, developing shielding mechanisms and error-correction protocols becomes essential to ensure that quantum sensors operate effectively within the harsh contexts of deep space.

Moreover, the ethical implications associated with these observational advancements must be addressed. As our understanding of the universe expands, so too do our responsibilities regarding stewardship of possible planetary ecosystems or the preservation of fundamental cosmic entities. Engaging in thoughtfully structured public dialogues about the ramifications of these advancements will help pave the way for responsible exploration.

In conclusion, the observation of new cosmic phenomena through quantum lenses represents a transformative hallmark in our exploration of the universe. By harnessing the principles of quantum mechanics through advanced sensors and technologies, researchers can uncover insights that redefine our understanding of cosmic dynamics and existence. As we embrace these opportunities, we must remain vigilant in addressing the challenges and ethical implications that arise, ensuring that our quest for knowledge resonates with a commitment to responsible stewardship of the cosmos. While the journey is fraught with complexities, the potential for discovery amidst the stars is boundless—inviting humanity to venture further into the endless realms of understanding that await us in the quantum frontier.

16.2. Unraveling the Mysteries of Pulsars and Quasars

In the vast expanse of the cosmos, where time and space dance intricately around phenomena that boggle the human mind, two enigmatic entities—pulsars and quasars—stand as beacons of curiosity for astronomers and physicists alike. As we delve into the depths of these celestial wonders, quantum mechanics emerges as a crucial lens through which we can unravel their mysteries. Pulsars, rapidly spinning neutron stars emitting beams of radiation, and quasars, the luminous cores of distant galaxies, both carry stories of the universe's evolution that quantum principles help elucidate.

Understanding pulsars begins with their formation, typically resulting from the supernova explosion of massive stars. The remnants of these explosions collapse under gravity's relentless pull, resulting in neutron stars that can rotate rapidly due to the conservation of angular momentum. Pulsars are thus born, emitting beams of electromagnetic radiation that sweep across space like lighthouse beacons. As these beams reach Earth, we detect regular pulses—a cosmic rhythm that offers insights into the fundamental physics governing these compact objects.

The application of quantum measurements to pulsars enhances our capability to study them. Quantum sensors, equipped to detect precise changes in gravitational fields and electromagnetic radiation, can provide highly accurate data, enabling astronomers to monitor pulsar behavior with extraordinary precision. This accuracy allows researchers to examine how the immense gravitational forces around pulsars influence nearby objects, test the predictions stemming from general relativity, and probe into quantum gravitation theories. Furthermore, the ability to detect gravitational waves generated by neutron star mergers provides unique opportunities to explore these systems' characteristics and their contributions to cosmic events.

Quasars, on the other hand, present an entirely different tapestry of cosmic mystique. These distant, brightly shining entities arise from supermassive black holes at the centers of galaxies, where material accretes at such high rates that it emits powerful jets of electromagnetic radiation, often outshining the host galaxy. The unique properties of quasars make them invaluable tools for studying the distant universe's evolution, providing insight into the formation of galaxies and black holes.

Quantum simulations stand as an essential technique when analyzing quasars. By modeling the interactions between matter and radiation as they spiral into a supermassive black hole, quantum algorithms can enhance precision in understanding the dynamics of the accretion disk and the resultant emissions. The use of high-fidelity quantum computing methods enables researchers to simulate various conditions under which quasars emit their luminosity, casting light on the historical evolution and activity of these enigmatic structures.

Furthermore, the study of cosmic radiation, particularly in detecting faint signals associated with quasars, benefits significantly from advancements in quantum technologies. Quantum sensors can achieve remarkable sensitivity, allowing astronomers to observe how quasars influence their surrounding environments across vast distances. This ability to capture subtle signals enhances our understanding of how quasars affect galactic evolution and their role in shaping large-scale structures in the universe.

In navigating the chasm between their profound complexity and our growing understanding, both pulsars and quasars showcase the immense transformative potential of quantum mechanics in unraveling cosmic mysteries. As we transition to advanced observational techniques leveraging quantum principles, innovative research initiatives will uncover the intricate threads of connections between these celestial entities and the underlying physics that governs them.

However, challenges remain, and as we deepen our inquiry into pulsars, quasars, and the quantum underpinnings of their existence, we should also acknowledge the technological hurdles that require our attention. The sensitivity of quantum sensors must be safeguarded against cosmic radiation and environmental noise. Developing error correction protocols and robust shielding methodologies will be essential to their success in providing the high-fidelity measurements necessary to study pulsars and quasars effectively.

Ultimately, exploring the mysteries of pulsars and quasars through a quantum lens not only propels our astronomical understanding but also invites broader philosophical reflections on existence and the universe's nature. Each discovery may act as a stepping stone toward deeper knowledge, inspiring future generations of scientists, researchers, and explorers to continue probing the cosmos and seek understanding amid the infinite realms of possibility that await understanding.

In conclusion, as we delve deeper into pulsars and quasars—two of the universe's most captivating phenomena—we harness the power of quantum mechanics to extend our reach beyond current frontiers. The intersection of quantum principles with observational astronomy ensures that our pursuit of knowledge continues with vigor and inquisitiveness. As we uncover these cosmic mysteries, we invite subsequent generations to embrace the adventure—charting a course toward unveiling the intricate patterns of existence that define the universe we share.

16.3. Quantum Measurements of Cosmic Radiation

In the grand narrative of our exploration of the cosmos, the measurement of cosmic radiation through quantum-based technologies has emerged as a crucial chapter, underpinning our quest for knowledge and discovery. Cosmic radiation is the persistent backdrop of the universe, composed of high-energy particles that impact every aspect of our space environment, from the tiniest quantum systems to the largest structures of the cosmos. Understanding and accurately measuring this radiation through a quantum lens invites profound insights into the nature of the universe while simultaneously bridging mysteries that have long perplexed humanity.

At its core, measuring cosmic radiation involves the utilization of advanced quantum sensors that leverage the unique properties of quantum mechanics—particularly superposition and entanglement. These sensors are capable of detecting even the faintest radiation signals, significantly enhancing our observational capabilities beyond traditional methods. The sensitivity afforded by quantum detectors makes them indispensable in astrophysical research, especially as we seek to explore the origins and evolution of cosmic phenomena, such as the cosmic microwave background radiation (CMB) and high-energy cosmic rays.

One of the paramount challenges in cosmic measurement lies in deciphering the signals emitted by distant astrophysical events. Cosmic radiation is not uniform; it carries rich information about the processes that occur throughout the universe. Quantum measurements facilitate this decoding process by providing real-time analyses of radiation spectra, revealing the signatures of gravitational waves, dark matter interactions, and potential signals from extraterrestrial sources. Consequently, by situating quantum sensors in cosmic observatories, researchers can harness the power of quantum mechanics to unveil new cosmic phenomena with unprecedented clarity.

Moreover, the potential for quantum measurements to address the mysteries of dark energy and dark matter—the very bedrock of cosmic evolution—cannot be overstated. Quantum sensors can detect the subtle gravitational effects associated with dark matter as it interacts with surrounding matter, advancing our attempts to map its elusive properties across the universe. This intricate interplay between quantum measurement techniques and our understanding of cosmic structures fosters a new generation of inquiries into the fundamental forces that govern our universe.

As we consider the implications of measuring cosmic radiation, ethical considerations emerge. Quantum technologies designed for cosmic exploration raise questions about data privacy, accountability, and access. For instance, the data transmitted from quantum sensors may contain sensitive information about the conditions and environments of extraterrestrial bodies, necessitating robust protocols to ensure that such data is safeguarded. Establishing clear ethical guidelines will be paramount to ensuring that advancements in quantum measurements do not compromise integrity or equitable access to valuable scientific knowledge.

Navigating the influence of cosmic radiation on quantum systems also highlights the necessity for ongoing research focused on enhancing resilience and adaptability. Quantum devices deployed in space face threats from cosmic rays and other radiation, which can interfere with the coherence of quantum states, leading to errors in data acquisition. As engineers and scientists continue to design shielding mechanisms and error correction protocols that are capable of withstanding the challenges posed by cosmic environments, the reliability of quantum measurements will improve.

The role of interdisciplinary collaboration becomes crucial in advancing the field of quantum measurements in space exploration. Experts from physics, engineering, computer science, and ethics must come together to tackle the complexities associated with cosmic radiation, ensuring a comprehensive approach that fosters innovation while addressing the moral responsibilities entwined with exploration.

In summary, measuring cosmic radiation through quantum technologies represents a transformative approach in our exploration of the universe. By exploiting the principles of quantum mechanics, we enhance our ability to decode the signals emitted by cosmic events, ultimately pushing the boundaries of our understanding of existence and the universe as a whole. As we strive to expand our quantum measurements of cosmic radiation, we stand poised to unlock new dimensions of knowledge, illuminating the mysteries that continue to beckon us from the vast reaches of space. In this grand adventure, the fusion of quantum inquiry and cosmic exploration serves as a testament to humanity's enduring curiosity, inviting us to explore, learn, and ultimately celebrate our collective journey through the cosmos.

16.4. Decoding Cosmic Background Radiation

Decoding Cosmic Background Radiation represents a monumental step in our understanding of the universe's origins and its intricate evolution. The Cosmic Microwave Background (CMB) radiation serves as a relic of the early universe—an echo of the Big Bang that has filled space since the universe cooled sufficiently to allow photons to travel freely. By harnessing the principles of quantum mechanics and advanced observational technologies, scientists can parse this background radiation to unravel the mysteries of cosmic formation, structure, and the composition of the universe itself.

The CMB is fundamentally a snapshot of the universe approximately 380,000 years after the Big Bang, revealing an isotropic glow that permeates all directions in the cosmos. Each anomaly or fluctuation within this radiant backdrop carries vital information about the universe's initial conditions, its expansion, and the clumps of matter that would later evolve into galaxies and larger structures. The intricacies of decoding these subtleties from the CMB reside in the ability of quantum sensors—especially those integrating quantum-enhanced imaging techniques—to capture minute variations in temperature across the background radiation.

Introducing quantum technologies enhances the sensitivity and resolution of measurements made on the CMB, allowing researchers to observe fluctuations on incredibly small scales. By employing advanced quantum algorithms for data analysis, scientists can effectively translate the temperature variations within the CMB into maps that represent matter density and spatial distribution throughout the early universe. This quantum-level resolution holds the potential to refine our models of cosmic inflation, the rapid expansion that occurred shortly after the Big Bang, and elucidates how these processes shaped the universe we observe today.

Furthermore, the application of quantum computing in processing the massive datasets generated by CMB observations facilitates a deeper exploration of cosmological parameters. Quantum algorithms exhibit the ability to handle complex calculations that determine aspects such as the curvature of space-time and the rate of expansion of the universe with extraordinary efficiency. This computational power allows researchers to refine the parameters of cosmological models that govern our understanding of dark energy, dark matter, and the fundamental forces that drive cosmic evolution.

One of the groundbreaking implications of decoding CMB radiation lies in exploring its relation to the multiverse theory—the idea that multiple universes may coexist and emanate from quantum events that shape reality. By analyzing the fluctuations in the CMB, researchers can garner insights into whether evidence exists for these parallel universes and how their interactions may influence the observable universe.

Yet the inquiry into cosmic background radiation and its implications does not come without challenges. The fidelity of measurements can be impacted by factors such as cosmic noise, atmospheric influences, and the thermal properties of observational instruments. Developing advanced quantum hardened sensors that are resilient to these disturbances will be essential for ensuring the integrity of data collected.

Moreover, as scientists decode the information embedded within the CMB, they must also grapple with the broader ethical implications associated with this profound understanding. Knowledge of the universe's origins, development, and intricate structure may lead to philosophical inquiries surrounding existence itself, consciousness, and humanity's role within a dramaturgically expanding cosmos. Engaging in thoughtful discourse surrounding the implications of these revelations will enrich our understanding while reinforcing our ethical commitments as explorers of the universe.

In conclusion, decoding cosmic background radiation through quantum technologies represents a pivotal advancement in cosmology and our understanding of the universe. As researchers utilize quantum sensors and algorithms to unravel the mysteries encoded in the CMB, they illuminate pathways for further inquiry that extends beyond the observable universe, addressing fundamental questions about existence, reality, and the nature of the cosmos. As we embark on this exciting journey into the heart of the universe, the revelations awaiting us hold the promise of transformative discoveries that may resonate through the ages, shaping our understanding of the infinite dimensions that define the reality we inhabit.

16.5. Quantum Inquiry into Dark Sky Mysteries

In the vast tapestry of the cosmos, the dark skies hold mysteries that have captivated scientists and astronomers for eons. As we delve deeper into understanding the universe, quantum inquiry emerges as a transformative tool, promising to illuminate hidden realms within the vast darkness. This chapter explores the intersection of quantum mechanics and the celestial phenomena that lie beyond the reach of conventional observation, particularly focusing on dark matter, dark energy, and the cosmic events that shape our reality.

The quantum world is characterized by uncertainty, entanglement, and superposition, offering a radically different perspective from classical physics. In the search for answers to the deep cosmic mysteries, quantum principles enable us to formulate new hypotheses and mechanisms for unraveling complexities that have long eluded detection. For instance, the nature of dark matter—an enigmatic substance that makes up approximately 27% of the universe—remains an area of intense investigation. Using quantum techniques, researchers can explore the gravitational effects of dark matter on visible galaxies, improving our understanding of its distribution and influence within the cosmos. Quantum algorithms can simulate interactions and behaviors of dark matter particles, facilitating insights into their potential roles in galactic formation and evolution.

Similarly, the enigmatic presence of dark energy—a force believed to drive the accelerated expansion of the universe—invites quantum inquiry. By employing quantum simulations, scientists can model its effects on cosmic structures and the dynamics of cosmic inflation. Quantum computers have the potential to analyze the vast datasets collected by telescopes and other observational methods, revealing correlations and revealing the impact dark energy has on the universe's fate in ways that classical techniques struggle to decipher.

As we turn our gaze toward cosmic events such as pulsars, quasars, and gamma-ray bursts, quantum tools facilitate unprecedented observations. Quantum sensors, with their enhanced sensitivity, can detect minute fluctuations in radiation from these phenomena, offering valuable data regarding their origins and interactions. Pulsars emit beams of electromagnetic radiation that can be detected as regular pulses on Earth, and with quantum sensors, we can analyze the interactions occurring around pulsars to probe the limits of gravitational theories and explore the fundamental principles of physics.

In the realm of cosmic background radiation—the afterglow of the Big Bang—quantum mechanics equips us with methods to decode the information embedded in this cosmic relic. Fluctuations in this radiation correspond to the density variations that occurred in the early universe. Advanced quantum techniques allow researchers to assess these variations with extraordinary precision, providing insight into the universe's structure and the forces that guide its expansion.

However, the journey into dark sky mysteries is fraught with challenges. The complexities of quantum systems require precision in experimental design and careful management of environmental influences. Cosmic radiation and other perturbative forces can disrupt delicate quantum states, undermining the accuracy of measurements. It is essential to develop robust shielding materials and instrument designs that maintain coherence while enduring the extreme conditions of space.

Furthermore, the ethical implications surrounding quantum inquiry in deep space must be thoughtfully considered. As we enhance our capabilities in cosmic exploration through quantum technologies, we must navigate the implications regarding planetary protection, the preservation of potential extraterrestrial ecosystems, and the responsible use of knowledge gained through these endeavors. The scientific community carries a moral obligation to ensure that quantum advancements reflect our commitment to the shared future of humanity and respect the integrity of the broader cosmos.

As we venture into the realm of quantum inquiry into the dark sky mysteries, the future of space exploration blends science with philosophy, raising essential questions about our existence and our role in the universe. Embracing this intersection encourages an enduring spirit of curiosity and exploration, reminding us that each breakthrough has the potential to deepen our understanding of the cosmos and reveal new dimensions of existence.

In conclusion, quantum inquiry into dark sky mysteries embodies a revolutionary approach to exploring the universe. By harnessing the principles of quantum mechanics, we illuminate the pathways to unraveling the nuances of dark matter, dark energy, cosmic phenomena, and the fabric of spacetime itself. As we delve into these questions, we prepare not only to uncover the mysteries that await but also to reflect on humanity's place within the grand narrative of the cosmos —revealing the interconnectedness that lies at the heart of existence itself. In this journey, we embrace curiosity as the guiding light, propelling us through the expansive realms of the universe, forever seeking the truth that awaits in the vast, dark skies above.

17. Quantum Computing Ethics and Space

17.1. Moral Considerations of Quantum Advancements

Moral considerations surrounding quantum advancements in the context of deep space exploration represent a vital area of inquiry that invites a profound examination of our responsibilities as we ascend to new heights of technological capability. As quantum computing unfolds, promising remarkable transformations in the way we explore the cosmos, deepen our understanding of existence, and interact as a global society, we must remain vigilant in evaluating the ethical dimensions linked to these advancements.

The advancement of quantum technologies brings forth a host of moral dilemmas connected to social equity, privacy, and the long-term implications of our actions in space. As nations and corporations vie for leadership in quantum computing and its applications, we face the very real risk of exacerbating inequalities both on Earth and in outer space. The promise of quantum computing may amplify existing disparities if access to these transformative technologies remains confined to wealthy nations or privileged organizations. Therefore, fostering inclusivity in research, development, and deployment is essential to ensure that the benefits of quantum technologies are equitably distributed and accessible to all—especially to underrepresented communities that may not have the resources to participate in these advancements.

Furthermore, as quantum computing becomes integral to space exploration, it raises critical questions about privacy and the security of data collected from space missions. Quantum technologies offer unprecedented levels of protection against eavesdropping, thanks to principles like quantum entanglement. However, the reality of operations in space demands that we remain cognizant of the boundaries we cross regarding what data is collected, how it is shared, and the implications of such information for individuals, communities, and nations. Ensuring that the quantum systems used for communication and data collection maintain robust security protocols to protect sensitive information is crucial, particularly as the scope of missions expands and the volume of data transmitted rises.

The impact of quantum advancements on global sustainability is another important consideration. As we enhance our abilities to extract resources from celestial bodies, either for supporting space missions or for utilization on Earth, we must navigate the moral obligations to protect extraterrestrial environments and ecosystems. The ethics of planetary protection must guide our extraction activities, ensuring that our pursuits do not compromise potential life forms or disrupt fragile cosmic ecosystems. The lessons gleaned from environmental ethics on Earth can serve as guides for responsible extraction practices and sustainable space exploration.

Moreover, as we develop quantum capabilities, it is paramount to consider the long-term consequences for society at large. As quantum advancements redefine our approach to exploration, we must assess their implications on employment, societal structures, and the socio-political landscape. Preparing society for a future intertwined with quantum technologies involves dialogue about potential advantages and disruptions, ensuring that the transition to a quantum-enabled world occurs equitably and purposefully.

On the forefront of these considerations is the need for continuous dialogue involving diverse stakeholders—from scientists, ethicists, and policymakers, to the broader public. Collaborative discourse fosters transparency and trust, laying the groundwork for responsible governance as quantum technologies advance. Establishing guidelines that prioritize ethics, inclusivity, and sustainability as foundational principles of quantum advancements ensures that the legacy of our explorations resonates positively for future generations.

In summary, the moral considerations surrounding quantum advancements in deep space exploration embody a delicate balancing act, requiring a holistic consideration of equity, privacy, sustainability, and the broader impacts on society. As we navigate this transformative journey, embracing our responsibilities as explorers and innovators will guide us toward a future where quantum technologies enrich our understanding of the universe while reinforcing ethical commitments to humanity and the cosmos. By taking deliberate strides to ensure that advancements are developed responsibly, we prepare to unveil the mysteries that lie ahead, fostering a spirit of inquiry and discovery that echoes across the infinity of space.

17.2. Space Law and Quantum Technologies

In an era where space exploration intersects with groundbreaking technological advancements, the domain of quantum technologies presents unique legal and ethical challenges that merit extensive scrutiny. As we navigate a path through the cosmos, particularly involving quantum computing, it becomes critical to ensure that the governance frameworks in place are robust, equitable, and forward-thinking. Space law itself is an evolving field, and as quantum technologies rapidly develop, it is imperative to consider how they will influence legal structures, ethical standards, and international cooperation in our endeavors beyond Earth.

Quantum technologies open new avenues for exploration, but they also challenge existing legal frameworks that govern the use and ownership of extraterrestrial resources. The Outer Space Treaty of 1967 serves as the cornerstone of international space law, stating that space is the province of all mankind and that celestial bodies cannot be claimed by any nation. However, as we increasingly pursue resource extraction on celestial bodies—such as the mining of asteroids or the utilization of lunar materials—questions arise surrounding ownership rights, commercial interests, and equitable access to these resources. Ensuring that these advancements do not lead to conflicts of interest or disputes among nations must be a goal of future space law.

Moreover, the ethical dimensions of quantum technologies extend to the environmental impact of space exploration. Quantum advancements may enhance our capabilities to access and manipulate resources, but we must be mindful of the responsibility that comes with such power. The potential for disruption to extraterrestrial environments and ecosystems beckons attention, necessitating that space agencies and commercial enterprises adhere to principles of sustainability. Establishing ethical guidelines that prioritize planetary protection will prevent contamination and promote stewardship of celestial bodies as we extract their resources.

Another critical aspect of quantum technology's impact lies in the privacy concerns it raises. With quantum encryption and advanced communication systems capable of transmitting secure information across vast distances, the safeguard of sensitive data becomes paramount. As we employ quantum key distribution (QKD) to secure communications in space, we must also ensure that privacy rights are respected throughout the data collection and transmission processes. Developing robust ethical standards concerning data management in quantum systems is essential to build trust and accountability among stakeholders.

Incorporating these considerations into the development of quantum technologies will require interdisciplinary collaboration across multiple sectors. Scientists, engineers, legal experts, ethicists, and policymakers must work together to create frameworks that guide the deployment of quantum advancements in a responsible and sustainable manner. Such collaboration will foster innovation and enable the development of technologies that respect both human and extraterrestrial ecosystems.

The role of education in shaping the future of quantum technologies cannot be overstated. As the field of quantum mechanics evolves alongside our exploration of space, it will be vital to equip future generations with the knowledge and skills necessary to navigate the complexities of quantum ethics and law. By fostering a culture of inquiry and inspiring curiosity about the cosmos, we empower young scientists and leaders to contribute meaningfully to the discussions surrounding these transformative technologies.

As we reflect on the significant implications of quantum technologies in space law and ethics, it is clear that we stand at a threshold filled with both promise and responsibility. The excitement of exploration invites us to unravel the mysteries of the universe, yet we must proceed with mindfulness toward the legal and ethical complexities that surface along the way. As our understanding of the cosmos grows and our capabilities expand, let us ensure that the frameworks we construct resonate with fundamental values—a commitment to equity, sustainability, and responsible exploration that will serve future generations as they continue to push the boundaries of human knowledge in the infinite expanse of space.

In conclusion, the intersection of quantum technologies and space law demands proactive engagement and thoughtful deliberation. As we embrace the advancements that quantum computing offers, we must ensure that ethical principles guide our exploration, highlighting our responsibilities as global citizens and stewards of the universe. By fostering collaboration, emphasizing education, and addressing ethical concerns, we chart a course for a future where humanity's quest for knowledge advances in tandem with a deep respect for existence and the cosmic environments we seek to explore. The journey into the unknown beckons us with the promise of discovery, and it is our duty to approach this endeavor with integrity and foresight.

17.3. The Impact on Global Sustainability and Society

The impact of quantum computing on global sustainability and society resonates as a crucial subject in the pursuit of knowledge and exploration among the stars. As we harness the power of quantum technologies in deep space exploration, we must not only consider the technical advantages these innovations afford us but also their broader implications for the world we inhabit and the future we strive to build.

Global sustainability, at its core, encompasses the balance between our resource use and the health of the planet. It calls for innovative solutions that allow us to meet current needs without compromising the ability of future generations to meet theirs. Quantum computing offers transformative potential in this regard, enabling us to address complex, data-intensive problems across various sectors. From optimizing resource allocation in energy sectors to enhancing agricultural efficiencies through predictive modeling, the computational power of quantum systems can foster more sustainable practices on Earth. In deep space, the applications are no less significant. The integration of quantum computing into space exploration can lead to the responsible extraction of resources, reducing the ecological footprint of exploratory missions.

For instance, in the context of galactic mining, quantum algorithms can model and simulate the environmental impacts associated with resource extraction on planetary bodies, guiding operations toward sustainable practices that align with planetary protection protocols. By understanding the consequences of our actions, we reinforce our commitment to ethical stewardship of celestial environments while securing vital resources needed for future human endeavors.

The societal implications of quantum advancements also provoke thoughtful consideration. The potential for economic growth as a result of deploying quantum technologies is remarkable, paving the way for the establishment of a new economic sector focused on quantum applications. However, we must reflect on the implications of creating a quantum economy. The risk of deepening socio-economic divides must be addressed, ensuring that the benefits of quantum innovations are equitably distributed. Education and training programs designed to empower individuals across demographics with knowledge about quantum technologies and their applications will help promote a fairer transition into the quantum era, ultimately fostering a workforce that is diversified and resilient.

As we introduce quantum networks for secure communication across interstellar distances, we also confront the privacy challenges inherent in an interconnected universe. Quantum cryptography offers unprecedented security features; yet, we must remain vigilant against the potential misuse of these powerful technologies. Establishing protocols that prioritize individual privacy rights and protect sensitive information from becoming the targets of automated quantum attacks must be an integral part of our exploration initiatives. Striking a balance between harnessing quantum powers for technological advancement and ensuring that societal values are respected will be critical as we navigate this digital frontier.

The implications of quantum computing transcend national borders, inviting collaborative efforts on a global scale. As countries, agencies, and industries invest in quantum technologies, creating alliances that promote mutual advancement can foster innovation while addressing common challenges. Global partnerships that harness collective expertise will enhance progress in quantum computing applications for sustainable exploration, data sharing, and ethical governance.

As we delve into the impact of quantum computing on society, we must also acknowledge the importance of public engagement. Encouraging dialogues about the ethical implications, societal responsibilities, and the transformative potential of quantum technologies can empower citizens to participate actively in the evolving narrative of exploration. Fostering a culture of inquiry and curiosity, where diverse perspectives are welcomed, not only enriches our understanding but also strengthens our commitment to a future shaped by shared values.

In conclusion, the impact of quantum computing on global sustainability and society presents an extraordinary opportunity accompanied by profound responsibilities. As we embrace the power of quantum technologies, we must navigate the complexities associated with their implementation thoughtfully. Ensuring equity, promoting collaboration, safeguarding privacy, and validating ethical practices will be vital in creating a future where technological advancements serve to uplift humanity and preserve our shared environments. As we explore the quantum realms and venture further into the cosmos, let us remain steadfast in our commitment to responsible stewardship, forging pathways toward a future that resonates with hope and potential for generations to come. The journey into the unknown is not solely about discovery; it is a momentous chance to define who we are in alignment with the world we wish to create.

17.4. Privacy Concerns in an Interconnected Universe

In an interconnected universe where data flows instantaneously and the vastness of space beckons exploration, privacy concerns emerge as a fundamental aspect of quantum computing applications in space. As humanity pushes the boundaries of its reach into the cosmos, the integration of quantum technologies in communication, navigation, and resource extraction offers not only immense benefits but also intricate challenges related to data security and privacy. This subchapter delves into the implications of these concerns, examining how quantum advancements can reshape our understanding of privacy while emphasizing the ethical considerations that must guide us through this transformative landscape.

At the foundation of quantum privacy lies the unique properties of quantum mechanics, particularly entanglement and superposition. Quantum communication systems, built on these principles, provide unprecedented levels of security compared to classical methods. For example, quantum key distribution (QKD) enables the creation of secure cryptographic keys that can be shared between parties. In the context of deep-space communication, any attempt to intercept or eavesdrop on quantum signals alters the quantum state, instantly alerting the communicators to potential security breaches. This inherent property elevates the security standards of space communications, but it also brings forth new questions concerning data ownership and control.

As scientific organizations and space agencies gather and transmit a wealth of data across vast distances, concerns arise regarding who owns this information and how it is protected. The potential for data breaches must be addressed rigorously, as sensitive information pertaining to missions, scientific discoveries, and technological innovations becomes increasingly valuable—both for scientific advancement and potential malicious use. Ensuring robust data protection measures is imperative, and quantum cryptography may serve as a cornerstone in defending against unauthorized access.

The dynamic nature of quantum communication systems must also be examined through an ethical lens. As we transition to space-based quantum communication infrastructure, there is a risk that disparities in access could arise, potentially creating gaps in data security and availability. The ownership and control of these quantum infrastructures might become concentrated among a small number of private entities or governments, leading to monopolistic practices detrimental to the collaborative spirit essential for space exploration. As such, establishing equitable frameworks that promote the responsible development and management of quantum communication systems is crucial.

Moreover, as we develop quantum communication systems capable of securely transmitting information between deep-space probes and mission control, the privacy of individuals and organizations must remain paramount. Space missions often involve multinational partnerships and collaborative research efforts, meaning that the data shared may carry significant implications for governments, corporations, and scientific institutions. Striking a balance between transparency and confidentiality becomes pivotal, ensuring that information shared among parties remains secure while fostering a culture of collaboration and trust.

As we grapple with these privacy concerns, fostering public discourse surrounding the ethics of quantum technologies and privacy will be essential. Engaging with the broader community, including policymakers, scientists, and the public, can help set the groundwork for establishing ethical standards that govern data collection, dissemination, and security in quantum communication systems. Initiatives aimed at educating the public about quantum technologies' implications will also democratize knowledge and empower individuals to participate in discussions surrounding privacy, fostering a collective commitment to responsible exploration.

Looking ahead, we must also acknowledge the challenges posed by emerging quantum threats. As quantum technologies evolve, classical encryption methods may become vulnerable to breaches by advanced quantum algorithms capable of solving problems faster than any human could. The development of quantum resistance algorithms, designed to withstand potential quantum attacks, will play a critical role in securing sensitive information both on Earth and in deep space.

In summary, as we explore the implications of privacy concerns in an interconnected universe, we come to understand that quantum computing offers both transformative potentials and significant challenges. By leveraging the principles of quantum mechanics, we can usher in a new era of secure communication systems that respond to the needs of deep-space missions while acknowledging the ethical dimensions surrounding data ownership, control, and access. Establishing robust frameworks that prioritize security, transparency, and equity will enable us to tap into the benefits of quantum technologies while fostering an exploration ethos grounded in respect and responsibility. As we venture into the cosmos, let us remain vigilant stewards of information, ensuring that our advances honor the spirit of collaboration and exploration that unites us all amidst the stars.

17.5. Developing Responsible Quantum Capabilities

The evolution of responsible quantum capabilities in the context of space exploration offers a nuanced inquiry into the fundamental and ethical dimensions of integrating quantum technologies into our cosmic endeavors. Quantum computing promises to transform how we understand and interact with the universe by providing unprecedented computational power and efficiency. However, with such transformative potential comes the responsibility of ensuring that its applications are aligned with ethical standards, sustainability, and equitable access.

To begin, understanding the intricacies of quantum capabilities requires a digest of their fundamental principles. Unlike classical computing, which operates on binary bits, quantum computing harnesses quantum bits—qubits—that can exist in multiple states simultaneously. This unique feature allows quantum computers to process vast information concurrently, making them particularly suited for complex calculations related to space exploration. However, as quantum technologies advance, attention must be directed toward implementing responsible approaches that ensure these capabilities are developed and used ethically.

The operationalization of quantum capabilities must begin with robust frameworks emphasizing transparency, inclusivity, and accountability. Establishing clear governance structures will be paramount in addressing the ownership and access issues associated with quantum technologies. The insights generated from quantum computing should benefit all of humanity' and ensure that equitable access to advancements is prioritized. Engaging with international agreements can facilitate collaborative approaches that promote shared ownership of quantum technologies, minimizing the disparities that could arise from their deployment.

Moreover, the environmental implications of deploying quantum capabilities in space must be carefully considered. As humanity begins to extract resources from celestial bodies, we must promote sustainable practices that minimize ecological footprints and respect the integrity of potential extraterrestrial ecosystems. Quantum technologies can play a role in optimizing extraction processes, but they must be matched with ethical considerations that ensure responsible stewardship of the cosmos.

Quantum capabilities in space also prompt important discussions about privacy and data security. As quantum communication systems are deployed to transmit sensitive information across great distances, robust security measures must be implemented to protect against unauthorized access. The use of quantum key distribution (QKD) can provide a secure framework for communication among spacecraft and ground stations, protecting sensitive data throughout deep space missions. Establishing clear protocols and ensuring transparency in data management is vital for maintaining public trust in these technologies.

Additionally, as the potential of quantum capabilities unfolds, ensuring the workforce equipped to engage with these technologies becomes increasingly critical. Building educational initiatives centered on quantum science will inspire the next generation of researchers and innovators, empowering them with the knowledge needed to navigate this rapidly evolving field. Interdisciplinary approaches, combining physics, engineering, ethics, and computer science, will cultivate well-rounded professionals who can contribute effectively to responsible quantum exploration.

Navigating these dimensions also requires continuous engagement with ethical considerations. As we embrace the advancements afforded by quantum capabilities, we must remain cognizant of their implications for societal structures and human interactions. Ethical governance must guide decision-making processes and address potential biases that may arise within quantum AI systems, ensuring equitable outcomes that reflect societal values.

Moreover, the potential of quantum capabilities as an empowerment tool for societal progress must be embraced. By harnessing quantum technologies, we can tackle pressing global challenges—such as climate change, resource management, and transformative scientific breakthroughs—through the lens of responsible innovation. The collaborative spirit embodied within the realm of quantum exploration can mobilize communities to engage with the cosmos, transforming perceptions about our capabilities and our responsibilities toward preserving the cosmic environment.

In summary, the development of responsible quantum capabilities in space exploration requires us to embrace a multifaceted approach that integrates ethical governance, sustainability, and inclusivity. As we harness the extraordinary potential of quantum technologies to explore and understand the universe, we must align our ambitions with our collective responsibilities, ensuring that our endeavors serve the greater good of humanity as we journey into the unknown. Through these efforts, we not only redefine our relationship with the cosmos but also ensure that the legacy of exploration echoes values that promote harmony, stewardship, and empowerment for generations to come. As we venture into the realms of quantum exploration, let us remain steadfast in our commitment to responsible practices, celebrating the limitless potential of discovery while nurturing a profound respect for the universe that surrounds us.

18. Quantum Cryptography in the Cosmic Realm

18.1. Cryptography Basics: A New Cosmos of Security

In an age of relentless discovery, the advent of cryptography presents an essential aspect of ensuring secure communication within the vast expanse of space. As humanity ventures further into the cosmos and embarks on a multitude of complex missions, the need for robust security protocols becomes paramount. The intersection of quantum computing and cryptography lays the groundwork for a new cosmos of security—one that leverages the principles of quantum mechanics to safeguard sensitive information exchanged across deep space missions.

Quantum cryptography harnesses the unique properties of quantum mechanics, particularly the principles of superposition and entanglement, to develop secure communication protocols that are fundamentally unbreakable by classical means. At the core of quantum cryptography lies the concept of quantum key distribution (QKD). Unlike traditional cryptographic systems that rely on the mathematical complexity of certain problems, QKD ensures security through the physical principles of quantum mechanics. In practical terms, if an eavesdropper attempts to intercept the quantum keys being exchanged, the very act of measurement alters the state of the quantum system, thereby alerting the communicating parties to possible breaches in security.

This fundamental advantage heralds a transformative shift in how we perceive secure communication in space. For instance, as spacecraft traverse vast interstellar distances, QKD can be employed to establish secure links between mission control on Earth and exploratory probes on distant planets or within asteroid belts. By leveraging entangled particles, quantum sensors equipped with QKD capabilities can ensure that sensitive data—including navigational information, scientific findings, and operational protocols—remains protected from potential interception or interference, maintaining the integrity of interstellar communication.

The development of secure protocols tailored for space missions is integral to the success of future explorations. Establishing a quantum communication infrastructure will necessitate collaboration between space agencies and quantum technology developers to design systems that can bridge the vast distances involved in cosmic communications while ensuring robust encryption measures are in place. The role of international cooperation will be critical, as the complexity of managing quantum systems—and the secrets they safeguard—will require shared knowledge and resources to ensure collective success.

Moreover, the application of quantum cryptography in the cosmos extends beyond mere data transmission. As humanity considers mining celestial bodies and extracting resources essential for future endeavors, the importance of protecting sensitive information about these activities becomes paramount. Quantum cryptography provides a secure means to communicate operational details, safeguarding against unauthorized access and ensuring transparency in resource management.

Yet, while quantum cryptography presents transformative opportunities, it also introduces challenges that must be addressed. Implementing quantum communication systems capable of functioning effectively over vast distances involves complexities related to maintaining the coherence of quantum states amidst cosmic radiation and other environmental disturbances. Advances in error-correction algorithms and the development of robust quantum repeaters will play crucial roles in ensuring that entangled states remain intact over extensive distances without degradation.

Additionally, exploring real-world applications of quantum resistance necessitates the integration of forward-looking algorithms capable of withstanding future cryptographic attacks. As quantum technologies progress, adversaries may develop techniques that leverage quantum capabilities to breach traditional security measures. Policymakers and industry leaders must proactively foster dialogue around evolving cryptographic standards that emphasize the need for resilience against potential threats, ensuring that our quantum security measures remain robust and effective.

Ultimately, the evolution of quantum cryptography calls for interdisciplinary collaboration that extends beyond the confines of physics and computer science. Engaging experts in ethics, law, and policy will be essential to address the multifaceted dimensions associated with quantum security technologies. By fostering a holistic dialogue that includes diverse stakeholders, we can build networks of collective expertise that work toward responsible and equitable practices in managing quantum cryptography across space.

In conclusion, the emergence of quantum cryptography marks a significant leap forward in securing communication in the cosmic realm. By harnessing quantum mechanics and developing robust protocols for space missions, we can ensure that the information shared across vast distances remains confidential and protected. The integration of quantum cryptography not only facilitates the success of future explorations but also strengthens our ethical commitment to responsible stewardship of the cosmos. As we navigate the complexities of quantum security, we position ourselves to embrace the infinite possibilities that await us in the uncharted territories of the universe. The continued advancement of quantum cryptography will ultimately pave the way for a future where exploration and discovery work in harmony, empowering humanity to unlock the mysteries of existence amidst the stars.

18.2. Developing Secure Protocols for Space Missions

In the realm of space missions, the development of secure protocols is paramount to safeguarding sensitive information and ensuring the integrity of quantum computing technologies. As humanity anticipates a future driven by quantum advancements, the responsibility to implement robust security measures becomes increasingly critical, particularly in light of the vast challenges and potential vulnerabilities introduced by deep space exploration.

At the core of establishing secure protocols for space missions lies the integration of quantum cryptography—a revolutionary approach that harnesses the principles of quantum mechanics to create unbreakable communication channels. The very essence of quantum cryptography is rooted in quantum key distribution (QKD), a method that guarantees secure information exchange through the fundamental properties of quantum states. In a quantum key distribution system, any attempt to eavesdrop on the key generation process alters the quantum states involved, thereby alerting the communicating parties. This level of intrinsic security is uniquely suited for the complex and often perilous nature of space communication, where the stakes of sensitive data transmission are extraordinarily high.

To build secure protocols tailored for space missions, it is essential first to establish an infrastructure capable of supporting QKD across interstellar distances. The deployment of quantum communication nodes—satellites equipped with advanced quantum technologies and entangled qubits—forms the backbone of this initiative. Such nodes would serve as relay points for secure communications between spacecraft and mission control on Earth, effectively creating a network of interconnected quantum communication channels that significantly enhance security.

Implementing efficient quantum repeaters within the communication network will also be crucial for maintaining the integrity of entangled states over long distances. These repeaters will utilize entanglement swapping techniques to extend the reach of quantum signals, ensuring that secure communications remain uninterrupted despite the challenges posed by cosmic environments. With a reliable network of quantum communication infrastructure in place, we can facilitate seamless data transmission from deep space missions, where the safeguarding of proprietary or mission-critical information is paramount.

Moreover, addressing cosmic radiation's potential impacts on quantum systems is another crucial aspect of developing secure protocols. The harsh conditions of deep space, including exposure to high-energy cosmic rays, can induce decoherence and disrupt the performance of quantum communication devices. Engineers and scientists must develop advanced shielding methods and error correction protocols that safeguard quantum systems against these environmental influences, ensuring that they remain operationally effective throughout the duration of missions.

In addition, securing information within quantum communication systems necessitates a cohesive strategy for managing potential vulnerabilities and risks. Quantum algorithms must be continuously updated and tested against emerging threats, particularly as our understanding of quantum capabilities evolves. Building quantum-resistant algorithms capable of withstanding both classical and quantum attacks ensures that protocols remain secure against malicious entities intent on interception or disruption.

As we forge ahead into the future, the ethical implications surrounding the deployment of secure quantum protocols in space exploration require thoughtful consideration. Not only must we ensure that our technologies protect sensitive information, but we must also engage in discussions about privacy, accountability, and the impacts of these advancements on society. Establishing transparent governance frameworks that guide the ethical development and use of quantum technologies will reinforce trust in these systems and underscore our commitment to responsible exploration.

Furthermore, interdisciplinary collaboration can amplify the successes of secure protocols in space missions. By engaging experts from various domains—including physics, computer science, engineering, and ethics—we can foster a holistic approach that addresses the complex issues inherent in space communication. Public and private sector partnerships will also play a vital role in promoting innovation and advancing secure protocols that safeguard interactions across the cosmos.

In conclusion, developing secure protocols for space missions represents a crucial endeavor that intertwines the advancements of quantum mechanics with the responsibilities of exploration. By harnessing quantum cryptography, implementing quantum communication infrastructure, and addressing cosmic challenges, we create pathways for secure and efficient communication in the vastness of space. As we embrace these innovative advances, we set the stage for successful interstellar missions that prioritize the integrity of information exchange and shine a light on our commitment to ethical practices in the very fabric of our exploration endeavors. The evolution of secure quantum communication protocols will undoubtedly play a vital role as we navigate the future, ensuring that our explorations of the cosmos unfold responsibly and with respect for the mysteries awaiting discovery.

18.3. Quantum Key Distribution: Space Applications

In the current era of exploration, where quantum mechanics intertwines with space technology, Quantum Key Distribution (QKD) emerges as a pivotal advancement essential for secure communications in the vastness of space. The applications of QKD in this context are vast, addressing the pressing need for secure information exchange among space missions, research outposts, and communication networks. This section delves into the theoretical foundations of QKD, its implementation in space systems, and its role in ensuring that humanity's forays into the cosmos remain both effective and protected.

Central to quantum key distribution is the principle of quantum entanglement and the application of quantum states to facilitate secure communication channels. Unlike classical encryption methods dependent on mathematical complexity and fixed algorithms, QKD relies on the fundamental properties of quantum mechanics. When two particles become entangled, any attempt to measure or intercept information exchanged between them alters their state, alerting the communicating parties to potential eavesdropping. This intrinsic feature of quantum systems enables QKD to provide a layer of security that is fundamentally unique and unassailable.

In space applications, implementing QKD signals a transformative breakthrough in securing interstellar communications. Space missions generate and transmit vast amounts of sensitive data, including navigational information, scientific findings, and mission-critical operational protocols. Should this information fall into the wrong hands, the repercussions can be profound—not only undermining mission integrity but also posing risks to national security and international collaborations in space. By deploying QKD systems aboard spacecraft and interplanetary satellites, we can ensure a secure communication infrastructure that safeguards the integrity of data transmissions, essential in an environment fraught with challenges.

The realization of QKD in space requires robust engineering beyond the traditional bounds of terrestrial implementations. Space environments introduce unique challenges that necessitate engineering solutions tailored for the cosmic context. These challenges include the high-energy cosmic radiation that could affect the quantum states and the long distances involved in communication that might lead to decoherence or loss of entanglement. Developing advanced quantum repeaters capable of maintaining entangled states across vast distances while compensating for potential signal degradation becomes critical for operational success.

Furthermore, designing space-based QKD systems that efficiently process entangled particles while ensuring compliance with international regulations on space activities will require ongoing collaboration across governmental and private sectors. As nations and organizations compete within the emerging landscape of quantum technology, establishing cooperative principles will be vital. This dialogue must focus on shared benefits and collective responsibilities, allowing quantum advancements to serve as a tool for peaceful exploration and collaboration among nations.

In considering the economic implications of QKD in space applications, we must acknowledge that these technologies hold significant promise for creating new industries and opportunities. The demand for secure communication systems can drive investments, leading to the launch of startups and initiatives focused on proprietary space-based quantum solutions. As the commercial sector increasingly invests in space exploration, quantum technologies capable of providing secure communications will enhance the capacity of private companies to operate efficiently while adhering to security standards necessary for interplanetary ventures.

Societal engagement is another critical factor shaping the development of quantum key distribution and quantum technologies in space. Creating awareness and education around QKD empowers society to understand the value of robust security measures in deep space exploration. Educational initiatives that emphasize quantum mechanics and its implications for security and resilience equip the next generation with the knowledge and skills required to navigate the complexities of this field, fostering enthusiasm for careers in quantum technology and space exploration.

Ultimately, the integration of quantum key distribution in space applications reaffirms humanity's commitment to exploration, ensuring that our endeavors across the cosmos are grounded in principles of security, transparency, and cooperation. As we harness the power of quantum mechanics to protect information in the darkest reaches of space, we forge a path forward that honors the inherent curiosity of humankind while taking seriously our responsibilities as guardians of knowledge and the future of exploration.

In conclusion, quantum key distribution presents an invaluable avenue for ensuring the security of communications across space systems. By embracing the principles of quantum mechanics, we can protect sensitive information and navigate the complex landscape of space exploration with confidence. The adoption of QKD, backed by robust engineering, collaborative efforts, and societal engagement, will not only fortify our operations in the cosmos but also exemplify the spirit of progress that characterizes humanity's relentless pursuit of discovery among the stars. Through these advancements, we pave the way for a future where the integrity of exploration aligns harmoniously with our quest for knowledge and understanding of the universe.

18.4. Protecting Information in Space Systems

In the realm of space exploration, the safeguarding of information stands as a critical pillar underpinning the success of missions traversing the cosmos. As quantum technologies emerge as vital components of our exploratory toolkit, protecting data transmitted across vast distances becomes an essential focus. Quantum computing, with its unique capabilities, provides unprecedented methods for securing information in the depths of space, ensuring both confidentiality and integrity amidst the challenges posed by the universe.

The rapidly evolving landscape of quantum communication systems enables the establishment of secure channels that leverage the principles of quantum mechanics. Central to this endeavor is quantum key distribution (QKD), which allows for the secure exchange of cryptographic keys between parties. The beauty of QKD lies in its reliance on the fundamental nature of quantum states: any attempt to eavesdrop on the communication process alters the state of the qubits involved, alerting the communicating parties to potential breaches. This natural safeguard against intrusion establishes QKD as an invaluable tool for protecting data transmitted from spacecraft to mission control, ensuring that sensitive information remains confidential in an environment fraught with uncertainties.

Space missions generate vast amounts of data that require secure transmission—from navigational coordinates to scientific observations about distant celestial bodies. Implementing quantum cryptography can significantly fortify this data, mitigating risks associated with interception or manipulation by adversaries. As humanity increases its presence in the cosmos, ensuring that quantum communication systems are deployed effectively becomes paramount to maintaining the integrity of mission-critical information.

Yet, the complexities of protecting information in space systems extend beyond the realm of quantum key distribution. The operational realities of space introduce challenges such as cosmic radiation, thermal variations, and potential signal degradation over vast distances —all of which can impact the performance and reliability of quantum systems. Addressing these challenges requires developing advanced shielding mechanisms to protect quantum devices from radiation and environmental factors that could compromise their integrity. Engineers must innovate solutions to ensure that quantum states remain coherent, safeguarding against the influences inherent in deep space environments.

Moreover, the implementation of comprehensive error correction techniques is essential in maintaining the reliability of quantum algorithms deployed in protecting information. As quantum systems face the dual threats of environmental influences and operational errors, fostering robust error correction methodologies ensures the precision of the data transmitted across quantum systems. The development of adaptive algorithms that respond to operational challenges will enhance the reliability of quantum communications, ensuring that security measures remain intact in the face of potential disruptions.

In the pursuit of effective communication protocols, collaboration among diverse stakeholders becomes crucial. The intersection of quantum technologies, aerospace engineering, and cybersecurity necessitates a multidimensional approach that fosters innovation and addresses the unique challenges posed by space environments. Researchers, engineers, legal experts, and ethicists must engage in meaningful dialogue to ensure that the deployment of quantum communication systems is guided by principles of equity, responsibility, and sustainability.

As we consider the implications of protecting information in space systems, it is vital to reflect on the broader societal consequences of these advancements. The security afforded by quantum communication systems has far-reaching implications not only for space exploration but for countless applications on Earth—from securing financial transactions to safeguarding personal information in a digital world. The lessons learned in the cosmos may offer insights into responsible practices and innovations that resonate within our global community.

In summary, protecting information in space systems encapsulates the promise inherent in quantum technologies. By leveraging quantum key distribution and advancing quantum communication infrastructures, we position ourselves to ensure that data transmitted from deep space missions remains secure and reliable. Moreover, addressing the challenges posed by cosmic conditions calls for interdisciplinary collaboration and innovation, reinforcing our commitment to responsible exploration while safeguarding the integrity of cosmic communication. As we stand at the forefront of this quantum age in space exploration, we encapsulate the dual spirit of inquiry and stewardship—ensuring that our quest for knowledge is harmonious with the principles that define our shared existence among the stars.

18.5. Quantum Resistance: Future-Proof Algorithms

As the realm of quantum computing and its implications for space exploration continues to unfold, 'Quantum Resistance: Future-Proof Algorithms' emerges as a pivotal chapter examining how we can safeguard quantum technology against potential threats posed by rapid advancements in quantum capabilities. With the rise of quantum computers capable of executing tasks that far exceed classical machines, the need for algorithms that withstand the scrutiny of quantum attacks becomes paramount. This chapter explores the intricate landscape of quantum resistance, the challenges we face, the opportunities that arise, and the methods we can utilize to ensure the longevity and security of our quantum infrastructure.

At the heart of this discussion lies the recognition that traditional cryptographic algorithms—like RSA or ECC (Elliptic Curve Cryptography)—rely on mathematical problems that quantum computers can solve relatively quickly using algorithms such as Shor's algorithm.

This poses a significant risk to the security of communications, data integrity, and our information systems. Quantum resistance is directly tied to developing new cryptographic techniques that remain secure even in the presence of quantum-capable adversaries.

One of the primary avenues for creating future-proof algorithms is the exploration of post-quantum cryptography (PQC). PQC refers to cryptographic systems that have been deliberately constructed to be secure against quantum attacks. Researchers are actively investigating various mathematical structures, such as lattice-based cryptography, code-based cryptography, multivariate polynomial cryptography, and hash-based signatures, to establish secure foundations. Each of these avenues presents potential advantages, but they also come with a unique set of challenges related to implementation, efficiency, and practicality.

For instance, lattice-based cryptography offers resilience against quantum attacks, and potentially serves as a pathway for various applications, yet its complexity in terms of computational overhead may hinder real-world implementation initially. Here, balance is essential—identifying algorithms that provide security while remaining operationally efficient for both current classical systems and future quantum environments is critical.

Another facet of quantum resistance revolves around the concept of quantum key distribution (QKD), which fundamentally redefines how we secure data transmissions. While QKD offers remarkable security by leveraging quantum entanglement properties, its effectiveness is contingent on practical implementations that function over long distances and in diverse environments. Ensuring that QKD systems are integrated into communication protocols while being robust against the realities of space—where delays, decoherence, and cosmic radiation may present hurdles—is crucial for optimizing their role in future quantum communication ecosystems.

The race toward developing quantum-resistant algorithms inevitably invites considerations related to global collaboration. Nations, academic institutions, and private sector entities must recognize the necessity of sharing knowledge and resources to fortify quantum infrastructure. International partnerships can facilitate research initiatives that pool efforts toward advancing post-quantum cryptographic standards or refining QKD systems, ensuring that advancements are equitable across the global stage.

In educating the next generation of scientists and quantum experts, the development of quantum-resistant algorithms becomes a focal point. By incorporating coursework that emphasizes both the fundamentals of quantum mechanics and the emerging field of post-quantum cryptography, educational initiatives can prepare a skilled workforce capable of tackling the challenges posed by quantum advancements. Engaging young minds in quantum-resistance discussions fosters not only innovation but also a culture of ethical responsibility—an acknowledgment that with great power comes the obligation to safeguard our digital future.

As we venture deeper into the cosmos, the implications of quantum resistance extend beyond technical challenges. It invites reflections on the broader societal consequences of our quantum ambitions. With the potential to impact data security, privacy rights, and communications on a global scale, the discourse surrounding quantum resistance must encompass ethical considerations that resonate with our collective values. Preparing for the evolution of quantum technologies prompts us to consider how these capabilities will shape our interactions with one another, the information we share, and the responsibilities we hold toward future generations.

In conclusion, the chapter on 'Quantum Resistance: Future-Proof Algorithms' underscores a foundational imperative as we advance into the quantum era in space exploration and technology. By prioritizing the development of secure quantum-resistant algorithms alongside robust collaborative efforts, we can mitigate potential threats while ensuring the integrity and longevity of quantum systems. This commitment to secrecy and security resonates across our exploration initiatives and serves as a promise to ourselves and future explorers that innovation and ethics can unite as we journey into the unknown. As we navigate the complexities of quantum resistance, we prepare for a future defined not only by scientific advancement but by our collective responsibility to ensure a safe and equitable digital landscape for all.

19. Challenges and Opportunities in Quantum Space

19.1. Identifying and Overcoming Quantum Complexities

In the context of quantum computing, the breadth of complexities inherent to this field poses both challenges and opportunities as we navigate the uncharted territories of deep space exploration. Identifying and overcoming these quantum complexities is vital for harnessing the full potential of quantum technologies in mission-critical applications across the cosmos.

One of the forefront challenges lies in the very nature of quantum systems, which are inherently sensitive to external environments. Decoherence—where quantum states lose their coherence due to interaction with surrounding noise—is a significant barrier to effective quantum computing in space. Cosmic radiation, temperature fluctuations, and gravitational anomalies can disrupt qubits, potentially leading to errors in calculations or data transmission. Thus, engineers and researchers must prioritize innovative shielding techniques to protect quantum systems, along with designing robust error correction protocols capable of maintaining performance under these adverse conditions. On the one hand, this necessitates ongoing research, innovation, and collaboration among multiple disciplines, intertwining physics, engineering, and materials science to engineer resilient solutions.

Moreover, the challenge of interconnectivity among quantum devices deployed in space space emerges as an area needing attention. Quantum networks—much like classical internet infrastructure—require efficient frameworks for ensuring that qubits can communicate securely across vast distances. As researchers develop quantum repeaters to extend entanglement links, they must also evaluate the functionality of these systems in the harsh environments of deep space. This highlights the need for global collaborations between research institutions and space agencies, fostering partnerships that can accelerate technological advancements needed to overcome inter-connectivity challenges.

Opportunities abound within quantum computing that can fundamentally enhance our understanding and exploration of the universe. The power of quantum computers to process vast datasets enables us to tackle complex problems related to astrophysics and cosmology. For instance, simulating the behavior of black holes and dark matter interactions can yield new insights that redefine our understanding of the universe's structure and formation. Similarly, quantum algorithms designed for optimization problems can aid in trajectory planning, permitting spacecraft to navigate through complex gravitational fields efficiently. Harnessing these opportunities requires a careful balance between advancing technology and generating ethical frameworks that guide their implementations.

The economic and industrial aspects of quantum space exploration represent another critical facet of this discussion. As quantum technologies advance, investing in the quantum economy promises to usher in new industries focusing on quantum computing, quantum communications, and quantum-enhanced sensors. This development enhances our capabilities in space while driving innovation and workforce development—a symbiotic relationship that can redefine the landscape of scientific exploration. Engaging stakeholders from academia, industry, and governmental sectors will be crucial for promoting responsible growth while ensuring equitable access to the benefits of these technologies.

In light of these developments, collaborations with global quantum initiatives present an invaluable avenue for fostering innovation. International partnerships create a platform where expertise converges, driving forward research and development efforts geared toward overcoming quantum complexities. Moreover, these collaborations can serve as a framework for establishing collective policies and regulations that govern the deployment of quantum technologies in space, reinforcing principles of cooperation and shared commitment in our exploration endeavors.

Education forms the bedrock of future advances in quantum space initiatives. As we identify the challenges and opportunities inherent within quantum technologies, it is essential to develop educational programs that inspire the next generation of quantum scientists and engineers. Engaging young students in understanding quantum principles propels curiosity and nurtures a workforce ready to tackle the intricacies of quantum mechanics. Interdisciplinary education programs that connect physics, computer science, and engineering can create a holistic approach, inspiring innovation in quantum technologies as they relate to space exploration.

Additionally, as we delve further into the realm of quantum empowerment across disciplines, we discover the potential for bridging gaps between scientific inquiry and public engagement. Encouraging discourse and debate surrounding quantum technologies empowers citizens to participate meaningfully in conversations about our responsibilities as explorers of the universe. This engagement fosters a culture of transparency, allowing society to hold scientists and policymakers accountable as we navigate the complexities of quantum exploration.

In conclusion, while the challenges of identifying and overcoming quantum complexities within the realm of space exploration are substantial, they present exciting opportunities that can redefine our understanding of the cosmos. By focusing on interdisciplinary collaboration, navigating technological constraints, and developing educational initiatives, we position ourselves to harness the insights offered by quantum mechanics effectively. As we embark on this journey into the quantum frontier, let us embrace the complexities as avenues for growth and understanding, allowing us to chart a path that resonates with our shared aspirations for exploration, knowledge, and discovery across the infinite dimensions of existence.

19.2. Economic and Industrial Considerations

In an increasingly interconnected world and the vast, uncharted territories of deep space, understanding the economic and industrial considerations surrounding the development and deployment of quantum computing technologies becomes paramount. As we venture beyond our home planet into the cosmos, the interplay between advanced quantum systems and industry dynamics presents challenges and opportunities that can significantly influence the future of space exploration and human endeavors.

The burgeoning field of quantum computing possesses the potential to unlock vast economic prospects. Industries are recognizing the transformative power of quantum technologies in sectors such as telecommunications, pharmaceuticals, materials science, and cybersecurity. This recognition of value is fostering an environment where public and private investments in quantum research are intensifying, fueling innovations that can drive exploration and industrial applications. As competitive entities strive to harness the advantages of quantum computing, the race toward dominance in this space generates new research initiatives, spurring economic growth and creating jobs.

Startups and established companies are actively exploring quantum technologies for applications in space: from optimizing satellite communications to enhancing navigation systems and developing advanced data analytics methodologies for vast datasets generated during space missions. The capabilities that quantum computing introduces could redefine how these industries operate and engage with opportunities beyond our planet. For example, improved optimization algorithms realized through quantum systems may facilitate more efficient uses of satellite constellations, reducing operational costs and enhancing the clarity of global communications networks.

However, with these opportunities come vulnerabilities. The rapid pace of quantum technology development necessitates that regulatory frameworks keep pace to foster innovation while addressing concerns surrounding ethical use, security, and equitable access. The potential for monopolization in quantum technology markets poses risks to fair competition, particularly if only wealthier nations or corporations have access to the most advanced quantum technologies. Establishing fair access protocols and fostering collaborative research across borders are essential for equitable benefits from these advancements.

Furthermore, workforce development emerges as a crucial consideration in shaping the economic landscape surrounding quantum computing. The transition to quantum systems will require a skilled labor force trained in quantum mechanics, quantum information science, and AI methodologies. Educational initiatives that emphasize these fields will nurture the next generation of scientists and engineers equipped to lead in this emergent domain. Through universities and research institutions, fostering quantum literacy within the education system creates pathways for young individuals to engage with this technology, ultimately shaping a workforce prepared to meet the demands of an evolving industry.

Additionally, the global nature of economic considerations in quantum technologies leads to the importance of international collaboration. As nations recognize the implications of quantum advancements on both competitive advantage and cooperative exploration, collaborative initiatives become vital in fostering a global ecosystem conducive to innovation. Sharing research, resources, and insights among nations can accelerate progress, widen the talent pool, and create a framework for collective missions that reflect a shared commitment to understanding the cosmos.

As we examine the impact of economic and industrial considerations, we must remain cognizant of the ethical dimensions associated with these advancements. Responsible exploration necessitates a commitment to preserving the integrity of both terrestrial and extraterrestrial environments. As humanity embarks on the journey of utilizing quantum technologies in space mining or resource extraction, ensuring that we respect the natural balance of cosmic systems becomes of utmost importance. Ethically sound decision-making must guide our use of quantum technologies while encouraging sustainable practices for engaging with celestial environments.

In conclusion, the economic and industrial considerations surrounding quantum computing technologies in space exploration encompasses a continually evolving landscape rich with potential. The promise of economic growth, technological advancement, and the cultivation of a skilled workforce meshes with the complexity of ethical responsibilities and the need for collaborative frameworks. As we advance into this new frontier, the careful balance between exploration and stewardship, innovation and equity, will shape the trajectory of humanity's quest to uncover the mysteries of the universe. By forging connections and understanding that our actions echo through time, we can craft a future where quantum advancements serve to elevate our shared exploration of the cosmos while fostering respect for existence itself across all dimensions.

19.3. Collaborations with Global Quantum Initiatives

In the context of global advancements in quantum technologies, collaborations among various entities have become crucial in pushing the boundaries of what we can achieve in both quantum computing and space exploration. Quantum computing, with its transformative potential, has necessitated a concerted effort from public institutions, private enterprises, and academic research communities. This subchapter delves into the dynamics of such collaborations, their significance, and the immense impact they have on unlocking new opportunities as humanity ventures further into space.

The need for collaborative efforts arises from the multifaceted challenges associated with quantum computing and its applications in space exploration. Quantum computers represent an entirely new paradigm in information processing that diverges from classical computing methods, making it imperative that stakeholders work together to share expertise, resources, and innovative ideas. These collaborations serve as a bridge between theoretical development and practical implementation, allowing faster advancements that are essential for tackling the complexities of interstellar missions.

Public sector space agencies, such as NASA, ESA, and others, have historically been at the forefront of exploration. Their extensive experience and institutional frameworks provide stability and structure for ambitious projects. By aligning with private enterprises specializing in emerging quantum technologies, public agencies can quickly harness cutting-edge innovations that enhance mission capabilities. For instance, partnerships with startups focused on quantum algorithms can lead to rapidly developed solutions for optimizing spacecraft navigation or resource management in deep space.

Private companies, on the other hand, inject a spirit of agility and creativity into the research landscape. They often operate with fewer bureaucratic constraints, enabling them to innovate rapidly and adapt to emerging challenges. The dynamic interplay between public institutions and private enterprises fosters a symbiotic relationship, allowing for the integration of innovative solutions into long-standing exploration initiatives. Such partnerships not only accelerate the development of quantum technologies but also draw on diverse skill sets, ultimately enriching the collective knowledge in the field.

Creating joint research initiatives that emphasize interdisciplinary approaches further enhances collaboration. Engaging scientists, engineers, and ethical experts from various fields will deepen the understanding of quantum technologies and their cosmic applications. Cross-disciplinary teams can tackle multifaceted issues that arise during space missions—such as data security in quantum communications, sustainability in resource extraction, and the ethical dimensions of exploration—leading to more comprehensive solutions that account for the complexities of the universe.

Moreover, global quantum initiatives can pave the way for international collaboration in space exploration. As nations increasingly recognize the significance of quantum technologies, establishing shared goals inspires a cooperative approach to understanding and harnessing these advancements. By pooling resources and expertise, international partnerships foster innovation while promoting responsible use of quantum technologies, emphasizing transparency and equitable access to the benefits derived from space exploration.

In the essence of collaborative efforts, education plays a pivotal role in inspiring the next generation of scientists and researchers. By promoting interdisciplinary education in quantum technologies and space exploration, we can cultivate a skilled workforce capable of navigating the complexities of these emerging fields. Encouraging engagement among students across physics, computer science, and engineering can ignite passions for innovation, ultimately contributing to a robust labor pool equipped to tackle the challenges of the future.

Furthermore, the success of collaborative initiatives hinges on public engagement. As quantum technologies evolve, fostering a culture of understanding around their implications is essential. By educating the public about the significance of quantum advancements and their potential to transform exploration, we can nurture curiosity and enthusiasm that resonate across societal landscapes. Promoting outreach initiatives, public lectures, and interactive demonstrations will enable communities to participate actively in the dialogue surrounding quantum technologies and their role in shaping our future.

In summary, collaborations with global quantum initiatives represent a cornerstone of progress in space exploration. By fostering partnerships between public institutions, private enterprises, and international organizations, we can accelerate advancements in quantum technologies while addressing the overarching challenges associated with these endeavors. As we work together to unravel the mysteries of the universe, we empower the next generation of quantum scientists and explorers, ensuring that humanity's journey among the stars remains characterized by cooperation and shared understanding. The road ahead is illuminated by the spirit of collaboration, guiding us toward new horizons in our quest to unlock the secrets of existence in the vastness of the cosmos.

19.4. Educating the Next Generation of Quantum Scientists

In the rapidly evolving landscape of quantum computing and space exploration, educating the next generation of quantum scientists is a crucial step towards ensuring that we are well-equipped to tackle the myriad challenges and opportunities that lie ahead. As humanity stands on the precipice of unprecedented technological advancements, the importance of fostering a knowledgeable and skilled workforce cannot be overstated. This involves not only imparting a deep understanding of quantum mechanics but also nurturing the creativity and problem-solving skills essential for innovation in an increasingly complex field.

The foundation of education in quantum science should begin early, integrating quantum principles into curricula at various educational levels. Science, technology, engineering, and mathematics (STEM) programs can incorporate quantum mechanics and quantum computing fundamentals into their core teachings. Engaging students with hands-on experiments and simulations can reinforce theoretical concepts, making them more accessible and comprehensible. By introducing quantum principles in an engaging manner, we can cultivate curiosity and inspire future generations to explore the versatility and potential of quantum technologies.

Higher education institutions must play a pivotal role in training the next generation of quantum scientists. Establishing dedicated programs in quantum computing and quantum information science will create an academic environment that fosters specialized expertise. Interdisciplinary initiatives that bridge physics, computer science, engineering, and ethics will be beneficial, allowing students to approach complex challenges from various angles. Collaborations with the private sector can ensure that students have access to cutting-edge research and real-world applications of quantum technologies, preparing them for careers that directly contribute to advancements in the field.

Exposure to current research activities in quantum science is vital in nurturing the scientific minds of tomorrow. Summer internships, research assistant positions, and mentorship programs can provide students with firsthand experience in contributing to groundbreaking projects. Facilitating opportunities for collaboration among students, researchers, and industry professionals encourages the exchange of ideas and cultivates a spirit of inquiry that transcends traditional academic boundaries.

Furthermore, as we educate future generations, we must also be mindful of the ethical dimensions associated with quantum technologies. Instilling a sense of social responsibility in aspiring quantum scientists will empower them to consider the broader implications of their work. Discussions about data privacy, the ethical use of quantum technologies, and the societal impacts of their advancements will create a generation of scientists who approach their research with conscientious awareness.

Global collaboration in quantum education is another essential aspect of preparing the next generation. International partnerships among universities, research institutions, and industries can facilitate knowledge sharing and create a sense of camaraderie among quantum scientists worldwide. By fostering joint educational programs, collaborative research initiatives, and exchange opportunities, we can cultivate a diverse community enriched by a shared vision of exploring the mysteries of the universe.

Simultaneously, as we guide students in their quantum education, engaging the public through outreach and community involvement becomes instrumental. Educational initiatives that emphasize quantum mechanics in popular science programs, public talks, and interactive workshops can demystify complex concepts and inspire curiosity among broader audiences. When society at large is engaged in the conversations surrounding quantum technologies, public support for scientific endeavors can flourish, ultimately enriching the field and generating interest among future scientists.

In conclusion, educating the next generation of quantum scientists is not merely an academic pursuit but a profound investment in the future of humanity, exploration, and knowledge. By integrating quantum principles into educational frameworks, fostering inter-disciplinary collaborations, and promoting ethical awareness, we empower young minds to confront and navigate the challenges and opportunities presented by quantum technologies. As we stand at the threshold of this transformative era, let us cultivate a spirit of curios-ity, innovation, and responsibility, ensuring that the advances made in quantum science are reflected in a brighter future, where the quest for understanding the universe continues to inspire and unite us all. The future of quantum science—shaped by the inquisitive minds we nurture today—holds infinite potential, beckoning us toward deeper revelations within the cosmic expanse.

As we prepare for the quantum revolution, let us celebrate the spirit of inquiry that propels us forward, fostering a legacy of exploration that transcends boundaries as we unveil the mysteries of existence together. Quantum technologies offer us the opportunity to extend our reach into the universe and redefine our understanding of reality itself. Through the foundation of education we lay today, we invite the next generation to join us on this incredible journey, exploring the vast quantum frontier with wonder and anticipation.

19.5. Quantum Empowerment Across Disciplines

The concept of 'Quantum Empowerment Across Disciplines' under-scores the transformative power of quantum technologies as they increasingly infiltrate various fields of science, engineering, and even social sciences. As quantum computing matures and potential appli-cations expand, we witness a compelling synthesis of disciplines that not only pushes the boundaries of what was once thought possible but also redefines collaborative paradigms in research and explo-ration. This multifaceted approach reveals profound implications for humanity's understanding of the universe and our role within it.

One of the most significant areas where quantum empowerment is evident is in the intersection of astrophysics and quantum mechanics.

Quantum technologies are shedding light on complexities related to cosmic phenomena, including the nature of dark matter and dark energy, the evolution of galaxies, and the intricacies of black holes. As multidimensional quantum simulations enable scientists to model these phenomena with a level of precision unattainable by classical methods, they facilitate new insights into the fundamental framework of the universe. This integration of disciplines fosters a holistic understanding of cosmic evolution that is critical as we deepen our exploration of the universe.

Moreover, the applications of quantum technology extend well beyond astrophysics. In fields such as materials science, pharmaceuticals, and environmental science, quantum sensors and algorithms are revolutionizing data analysis. Quantum computing unlocks new potentials in drug discovery by enabling simulations of molecular interactions at unprecedented scales, while quantum sensors enhance our capabilities for environmental monitoring and management. As these advancements converge across disciplines, they yield multifaceted solutions that resonate with the global commitment to improve quality of life and sustainability on Earth.

Yet the promise of quantum empowerment across disciplines does not come without challenges. As we navigate this new landscape, ensuring equitable access to these revolutionary technologies is essential, prompting discussions about the implications of exclusive resources and the need for inclusive collaboration. The complex legal and ethical dimensions that arise from quantum advancements necessitate thoughtful planning and strategic frameworks to foster responsible practices and equitable benefits for society.

Interdisciplinary collaboration has never been more critical. By bringing experts across various fields together—quantum physicists, engineers, computer scientists, ethicists, and social scientists—we can cultivate a comprehensive framework that addresses the complexities of implementing quantum technologies responsibly. This effort will inform research initiatives and optimize outcomes for space exploration and related disciplines, driving the development of innovative solutions that enhance humanity's understanding of existence.

As we reflect on these challenges and opportunities, it is imperative to acknowledge the role of education in preparing future generations to engage with the quantum frontier. Education should inspire curiosity and foster critical thinking about the implications of quantum technologies, thereby empowering young scientists to contribute meaningfully to exploring the depths of the cosmos.

In conclusion, the concept of 'Quantum Empowerment Across Disciplines' encapsulates the far-reaching potential of quantum technologies to drive transformative advancements across various fields of study. As we learn to harness these capabilities, we engage not only with complex scientific inquiries but also acknowledge our collective responsibilities to ensure that the integration of quantum technologies serves to benefit humanity as a whole. The spirit of exploration that propels us toward uncovering the mysteries of the universe invites us to navigate the infinite quantum frontier, illuminating paths that reveal the intricate connections between life, existence, and the cosmos itself.

As we chart our course into this new era—where quantum technologies shape our understanding of the universe—we embrace the call to illuminate the mysteries, extend our reach, and forge a future grounded in inquiry, creativity, and collaboration. The journey into the depths of the unknown is rife with potential, waiting for those who dare to reach out and explore the uncharted dimensions that await us among the stars.

20. Concluding Thoughts: The Infinite Quantum Frontier

20.1. Summarizing Key Scientific Advances

In the multifaceted exploration of quantum computing and its myriad applications, it is imperative to pause and summarize the key scientific advances that encapsulate our journey thus far. From the foundational principles of quantum mechanics to the intricate technologies being developed for space exploration, we have witnessed remarkable innovations that challenge conventional understanding.

The essence of quantum mechanics lies in its ability to capture the intricate behaviors of particles at the quantum level—phenomena such as superposition and entanglement have been harnessed to usher in groundbreaking advancements across various disciplines. Quantum computing stands apart as a pivotal development, presenting capabilities that far exceed classical computing for specific tasks, including optimization, cryptography, and simulations of complex systems. The evolution from classical bits to qubits represents a foundational shift that fundamentally changes how we process and understand information.

In the context of space exploration, quantum technologies have established themselves as vital tools for enhancing our observational abilities and navigational precision. Quantum sensors have revolutionized the detection of cosmic phenomena—from gravitational waves to dark matter signatures—with sensitivity and accuracy that allows researchers to unravel the mysteries of the universe with unprecedented clarity. As we deploy these sensors alongside advanced quantum algorithms, we improve our ability to simulate cosmic events and explore the interstellar landscape.

Moreover, the collaborations between public and private sectors have catalyzed the rapid growth of quantum technologies and their applications in space. Partnerships foster innovation, enabling the translation of theoretical advancements into practical technologies designed for exploration. The potential benefits of quantum capabilities extend beyond traditional frameworks to encompass areas such as environmental stewardship, sustainable resource management, and ethical considerations surrounding space exploration.

Reflecting on the infinite possibilities that quantum mechanics offers, we find ourselves navigating a landscape rich with opportunity. The multiverse theory invites profound philosophical inquiry, challenging our understanding of existence and reality itself. It prompts us to reconsider the nature of life and its potential manifestations through-out the cosmos, expanding the boundaries of what we deem possible. As our understanding deepens, we open pathways for exploration that transcend our current limits, inviting new narratives shaped by quantum discoveries.

As we chart a path forward in quantum exploration, it is crucial to establish a framework that prioritizes ethical decision-making, sustainability, and equitable access to technologies. The pursuit of knowledge and innovation must be tempered by a commitment to responsible practices—preserving the integrity of celestial environ-ments and ensuring that advancements benefit all of humanity. By fostering interdisciplinary collaboration, we can address complex challenges facing space exploration, cultivating a holistic approach anchored in shared values.

Importantly, society plays a pivotal role in shaping the future of quantum technologies and space exploration. Engaging the public through education and outreach initiatives will nurture curiosity and connection to the vast cosmos, encouraging a culture of inquiry and collaboration. As we inspire future generations, we cultivate a workforce capable of navigating the complexities of the quantum frontier, empowering them to make meaningful contributions to our understanding of existence.

In conclusion, our journey through the infinite quantum frontier has illuminated remarkable scientific advancements while inviting reflection on the possibilities that lie beyond our current grasp. The convergence of quantum mechanics with space exploration fosters a spirit of exploration that resonates across cultures and disciplines, uniting us in our shared commitment to unlocking the secrets of the universe. Let us honor this legacy of inquiry and discovery as we embark on new adventures, forever celebrating the human spirit's desire to explore the mysteries that await us among the stars.

20.2. Reflections on Infinite Possibilities

In an age marked by unparalleled advancements in technology and a renewed enthusiasm for space exploration, the chapters of this journey converge into a pivotal moment of reflection and anticipation. As we stand on the threshold of quantum exploration, the possibilities that lie ahead are both infinite and profound. The integration of quantum mechanics into the framework of space science not only promises to redefine our understanding of the universe but also challenges us to reconsider our role within it.

Through rigorous exploration of key scientific advances, we have witnessed the remarkable transformation that quantum technologies bring to space exploration. The principles of superposition and entanglement have sparked innovations capable of handling the complexities of cosmic phenomena, providing insights that were once relegated to the realm of speculation. Quantum sensors are reshaping how we observe the universe, enhancing our ability to measure, analyze, and understand cosmic events that govern the dynamism of existence. As we decode the intricate signals and patterns that define the fabric of space, we step closer to unraveling the mysteries surrounding dark matter, dark energy, and the fundamental forces that shape our reality.

As we chart a path forward in quantum exploration, it is imperative to acknowledge the challenges and responsibilities that accompany this undertaking. The integration of quantum technologies into space missions necessitates careful consideration of ethical implications, environmental stewardship, and equitable access to resources. We must ensure that as we harness the extraordinary capabilities of quantum mechanics, our advancements are guided by core principles rooted in respect for life and the ecosystems within which we navigate. Collaborative frameworks that span disciplines will be essential in addressing these complexities, fostering innovation while promoting responsible practices.

Moreover, the role of society in shaping the trajectory of quantum evolution cannot be overstated. Engaging communities in the discussions surrounding quantum technologies fosters public understanding and appreciation for scientific pursuits. Education will remain a powerful tool to ignite curiosity and inspire future generations, empowering them to become pioneers in the urgent quest to explore the cosmos. By weaving the threads of education, awareness, and engagement into the fabric of quantum exploration, we strengthen the foundation upon which future discoveries will unfold.

As we celebrate the spirit of exploration, we are reminded of the shared human desire to seek knowledge, to push boundaries, and to embrace the unknown. The cosmic frontier invites us to look beyond, to dream bigger, and to imagine possibilities that surpass our current understanding. The journey into the infinite quantum frontier represents not just technological advancements, but a revitalized commitment to inquiry, collaboration, and ethical responsibility.

In conclusion, as we embrace the myriad opportunities and challenges that quantum technologies present, we embark on an exhilarating journey that holds the promise of transforming our understanding of existence itself. May we continue to foster this spirit of exploration, driven by curiosity and guided by ethical considerations, as we venture into the expanses of the cosmos, unlocking the secrets that await us among the stars. In doing so, we shall nurture not only a deeper understanding of the universe but also a profound appreciation for the interconnectedness of all life, enabling us to chart a path that resonates with care and inspiration. The infinite awaits, and we, as explorers of the unknown, are tasked with unveiling its mysteries.

20.3. Charting a Path Forward in Quantum Exploration

Charting a Path Forward in Quantum Exploration signifies an essential juncture in humanity's quest for knowledge, as we seek to bridge the exciting possibilities presented by quantum mechanics with our aspirations to explore the cosmos. Through profound advancements in quantum technologies, we stand on the precipice of unprecedented discoveries that could redefine our understanding of the universe and our place within it. The challenges faced during this journey—ranging from technological hurdles to ethical considerations—invite us to approach exploration with a spirit of curiosity and responsibility, ensuring that our advancements reflect shared human values.

As we move forward into this new era, interdisciplinary collaboration must become a cornerstone of our initiatives. The complexities inherent in quantum exploration demand diverse expertise, drawing from fields such as quantum physics, computational sciences, ethics, engineering, and astronomy. By fostering collaboration among scientists, researchers, and industry leaders, we can cultivate a unified approach that addresses the multifaceted challenges presented by advanced technologies while maximizing the potential for innovation and discovery.

While the technological challenges associated with quantum exploration are substantial, they also present exciting opportunities for addressing critical issues we face on Earth. Quantum technologies can enhance our capabilities in data analytics, environmental monitoring, and resource management, offering sustainable solutions that benefit both space exploration and life on Earth. By embracing these opportunities, we lay the foundation for a future where exploration serves as a catalyst for positive change.

The ethical dimensions of quantum technologies and their implications for society must not be overlooked as we chart this path forward. Quantum advancements introduce critical questions regarding equity, data privacy, and responsible stewardship of both terrestrial and extraterrestrial environments. Ensuring that the deployment of quantum technologies aligns with ethical values—focusing on inclusivity, transparency, and sustainability—will strengthen public trust and foster a supportive atmosphere for scientific inquiry.

As we embark on this quantum exploration journey, the role of society in shaping the narrative becomes increasingly important. Engaging the public in discussions surrounding quantum technologies fuels curiosity and inspires the next generation of scientists, engineers, and explorers. Educational programs that emphasize quantum principles, space exploration, and ethical considerations will empower young minds to pursue careers in these domains, ultimately driving innovation and growth in the field.

Celebrating the spirit of exploration is essential as we embrace our journey into the depths of the cosmos. Quantum exploration embodies humanity's enduring quest for understanding, pushing the limits of our knowledge and fostering a culture of inquiry that reverberates across generations. As we navigate the challenges and seize the opportunities that lie ahead, let us remain committed to exploration that is not only driven by knowledge but also by our responsibility to safeguard our existence and that of future generations.

In conclusion, the path forward in quantum exploration presents an exhilarating prospect that invites us to unify our collective aspirations and embrace the challenges that lie ahead. By fostering interdisciplinary collaboration, prioritizing ethical engagement, and inspiring societal participation, we can navigate the infinite possibilities embedded within quantum mechanics. As we take our next steps into the cosmos, let us do so with a sense of purpose and wonder, celebrating the art of exploration and the profound connections that bind us to the universe and each other. The journey awaits us, and together, we can chart a bright future that resonates with discovery, understanding, and unity among the stars.

20.4. The Role of Society in Quantum Evolution

In an era defined by rapid advancements in technology, the role of society in the quantum evolution narrative is both crucial and multifaceted. As we stand on the brink of transformative breakthroughs facilitated by quantum computing and its applications in space exploration, the engagement of society—comprising individuals, communities, and institutions—becomes paramount.

At the heart of this evolution lies the recognition that the potential benefits of quantum technologies extend far beyond the scientific community. Society, as a collective entity, has a stake in how these advancements are developed, implemented, and integrated into daily life. This interaction not only drives innovation but also fosters a collective sense of responsibility that shapes the future trajectory of quantum evolution.

One of the most significant aspects of societal involvement in quantum evolution is ensuring equitable access to the technologies being developed. Quantum computing and related advancements promise to redefine numerous fields—from healthcare and communications to energy management and environmental sustainability. However, the risk of technological disparities must be addressed. It is imperative to promote inclusive educational initiatives that demystify quantum principles and engage diverse segments of society, ensuring that the benefits of these innovations are shared broadly. This can be achieved through outreach programs, community workshops, and school curricula that prioritize accessibility and foster interest in science and technology among younger generations.

Moreover, the ethical implications arising from the deployment of quantum technologies must be a focal point of societal discourse. Engaging the public in conversations about privacy, security, and the responsible use of advanced technologies is essential for cultivating a sense of shared responsibility. As quantum communications become integral to interstellar exploration or terrestrial data management, society must grapple with the potential pitfalls and challenges that accompany these advancements. Open forums for dialogue, participatory research approaches, and transparent policymaking can empower individuals to voice their concerns and contribute to the ethical frameworks that guide the responsible use of quantum technologies.

The spirit of exploration intrinsically tied to quantum evolution further emphasizes our interconnectedness with the cosmos. As humanity embarks on cosmic journeys to probe the mysteries of deep space, it's crucial to recognize the cultural narratives that interlace with these endeavors. The quest for knowledge, driven by curiosity, is a fundamental aspect of our shared existence—it nourishes the human spirit and inspires generations to dream bigger and think deeper. Artistic expression, literature, and philosophical discourse can all contribute to a cultural framework that celebrates the art of exploration and invites societal engagement with the wonders of the universe.

Institutional support plays a pivotal role in fostering innovation, as governments, research institutions, and private enterprises engage collaboratively to advance the field. By prioritizing investments in quantum research, fostering public-private partnerships, and creating multidisciplinary collaborations, we can chart a course that amplifies the impact of quantum technologies in society. Such collaborations can drive not only technological advancement but also contribute to sustainable practices that honor our shared commitment to preserving the ecological and cosmic environments we encounter.

As we trace the path forward in quantum evolution, the engagement of society must be seen as a dynamic, ongoing process—one that evolves alongside advancements in quantum technologies. The journey into the quantum realm is not solely about acquiring knowledge; it is about nurturing responsible exploration that acknowledges the ethical, societal, and cultural implications of our pursuits.

In conclusion, the role of society in quantum evolution is paramount in shaping how we understand and engage with the world of quantum computing and its applications in space exploration. By fostering equitable access to technologies, encouraging ethical discourse, and nurturing the spirit of exploration, society can contribute meaningfully to the quantum narrative—one that binds scientific inquiry with the hopes and aspirations of humanity. As we venture into the realms of the unknown, let us celebrate the richness of our shared journey and remain committed to guiding our quantum evolution with integrity, responsibility, and a sense of wonder as we reach for the stars. The cosmos await us, inviting collaboration, discovery, and the exploration of infinite possibilities.

20.5. Celebrating the Spirit of Exploration

In the uncharted expanse of the cosmos, where the silences of space resonate with the echoes of scientific inquiry, the spirit of exploration flourishes as an embodiment of humanity's deepest aspirations. It is a call to venture beyond familiar realms, to question, to discover, and ultimately to connect with the universe. The convergence of quantum mechanics and space exploration paints a vivid tapestry of possibilities, where the pursuit of knowledge intertwines with the quest for understanding our very existence. As we embark on this profound journey, we celebrate not only the scientific advances that propel us into the unknown but also the indomitable spirit that fuels our collective desire to explore.

The foundation of exploration is rooted in curiosity—a fundamental aspect of the human experience that beckons individuals to look toward the stars and ponder the mysteries that lie beyond. Quantum science offers tools that allow us to approach these mysteries from new angles, expanding our perceptions of what is possible and igniting a broader understanding of the universe. Amidst the vast unknowns, quantum mechanics reveals intricate workings that govern the fabric of reality, offering insights that ripple across various domains—from astrophysics to life sciences. Through research and discovery, we unlock new dimensions of understanding, affirming our position as engaged participants in the cosmic narrative.

Exploration is not merely a scientific endeavor; it is a rich journey characterized by the interplay between discovery and imagination. As we develop quantum technologies, we find ourselves at the intersection of science and creativity—a crossroads where storytelling, art, and philosophy merge with empirical inquiry. The vastness of space inspires artistic expressions that capture the wonder of the universe, resonating with individuals who may not be scientists, yet find beauty and meaning in the quest for knowledge. This cultural tapestry enriches our collective understanding, reminding us that exploration transcends disciplines and resonates deeply with the essence of what it means to be human.

As we chart our pathways to distant worlds and remote stars, the ethical dimensions of exploration become paramount. The commitment to responsible exploration is essential as we navigate the complexities of quantum technologies and their applications in space. Environmental stewardship, equitable access to resources, and respect for potential extraterrestrial ecosystems are guiding tenets that must shape our actions. By celebrating the spirit of exploration, we embrace the moral responsibilities that come with our advancements, ensuring that we proceed with care and consideration as we venture into the vast unknown.

The role of collaboration in exploration cannot be overstated. The pursuit of knowledge thrives on diverse perspectives, drawing from the strengths of scientists, engineers, policymakers, and the public alike. Interdisciplinary partnerships foster innovation and create an environment where ideas can flourish, leading to breakthroughs that elevate our understanding of the universe. As we engage in shared explorations, we build bridges that unite us in our aspiration to uncover the secrets cloaked in cosmic darkness—a testament to humanity's ability to work together across cultures and disciplines.

In celebrating the spirit of exploration, we must recognize our place within the broader cosmic narrative. As we advance our inquiry and probe the mysteries of the universe, we engage with something larger than ourselves, contributing to an ongoing saga that transcends time and space. Each discovery, each leap into the unknown, adds to the collective tale of humanity—an enduring legacy that propels future generations to look up at the stars and dream of what lies beyond.

In conclusion, as we embrace the spirit of exploration anchored in quantum science, we invite everyone to participate in this grand adventure. Whether through rigorous inquiry, creative expression, or ethical stewardship, each individual can contribute to the unfolding narrative of our journey through the cosmos. The possibility of unlocking the universe's mysteries resides not only in technologies but also in the hearts and minds of those who dream and dare to reach for the unknown. As we celebrate the spirit of exploration, we reaffirm our commitment to knowledge, discovery, and the exquisite complexities of existence awaiting us among the stars. Together, we embark on a journey where curiosity knows no bounds, and the quest for understanding illuminates the infinite pathways of our cosmic odyssey.